Modern Language Association of America

Options for Teaching

Joseph Gibaldi, Series Editor

Teaching Environmental Literature

Materials, Methods, Resources

Edited by

Frederick O. Waage

The Modern Language Association of America
New York   1985

Copyright © 1985 by The Modern Language Association of America

Library of Congress Cataloging in Publication Data

Main entry under title:

Teaching environmental literature.

(Options for teaching; 7)
Bibliography: p.
1. American prose literature—Study and teaching (Higher)—Addresses, essays,
lectures. 2. Environmental literature—Study and teaching (Higher)—Addresses,
essays, lectures. 3. Ecology in literature—Study and teaching (Higher)—Addresses,
essays, lectures. 4. Nature in literature—Study and teaching (Higher)—Addresses,
essays, lectures. 5. Natural history literature—Study and teaching (Higher)—Addresses, essays, lectures. 6. English prose literature—Study and teaching (Higher)—
Addresses, essays, lectures.
I. Waage, Frederick O., 1943–   . II. Series.
PS366.E58T42   1985   818'.08   84-27179
ISBN 0-87352-308-3
ISBN 0-87352-309-1 (pbk.)

Published by The Modern Language Association of America
New York, New York

For
David Brower
and
Friends of the Earth

Contents

Introduction

1. *Teaching Environmental Literature*: The Book Itself

The purpose of *Teaching Environmental Literature* is to introduce college teachers to, and provide them models and ideas for, courses in environmental literature and, more broadly, courses that combine humanities and environmental studies disciplines, with literature and writing as major components.

More specifically, the book seeks to encourage the introduction of courses akin to the ones described in college English and other humanities curricula. One outgrowth of such diversification of curricula would be greater enrollment in English and other humanities courses and in non-humanities courses with a humanities component. Another would be increased recognition among teachers and students alike that the humanities are, in the provocative word of the Commission on the Humanities report of 1980, "practical." Another desired effect of this volume would be increased support for the sort of integrative courses that have been recently, and often wrongly, discredited by financial and ideological enthusiasm for "basic" education. A final goal, which I particularly desire, is increased awareness among my colleagues in language and literature of "environmental literature" as a distinctive and vital genre and tradition and a greater presence of environmental concern and awareness in literary disciplines.

Although anyone interested in contemporary pedagogy in higher education should find interesting possibilities in this text, English language and literature teachers in particular (especially those concerned with expanding curricular possibilities in their departments at a time of fiscal constraint) should find significant material here. This book also explores possibilities of interest to a more general academic public for interdisciplinary courses and programs involving many liberal arts and science disciplines that bear a relation to literature and environmental studies—such as history, art, biology, and civil engineering.

There are two major sections in this volume. The first consists of essays presenting and describing courses in environmental literature and humanities–environmental studies integrative courses. In addition, there are several essays defining and proposing a canon of "environmental literature." The second section contains listings of resources useful in such courses, including texts, bibliographies, information centers, periodicals, and organizations and agencies.

The first section consists of five parts, each part preceded by an introduction that surveys its contents. Part 1, "Contexts," gives an overview of the material used in many of the courses described in the subsequent four parts. Its first essay, "What Teaching Environmental Literature Might Be," defines "environment" and "environmental literature" in a pedagogical context. The following three essays, "American Literary Environmentalism before Darwin," "American Literary Environmentalism, 1864–1920," and "The Nature Book in Action," discuss major writings, themes, and historical situations of environmental literature since the early nineteenth century.

The subsequent four parts consist of essays describing different approaches to teaching the above and related material. These essays are arranged in a sequence that (in general) moves (a) from courses taught primarily in a traditional classroom setting toward those with a primary focus on extramural field experiences, and (b) from courses mainly employing the canon of environmental literature (explored in part 1) as subject matter to those integrating this literature with diverse other materials and experiences. None of the courses described is purely classroom-bound or purely field-bound, and all of them have *some* interdisciplinary component. All of them primarily emphasize the experiences of writing and reading.

Part 2, "Environmental Literature in the Classroom," contains five essays describing environmental literature pedagogy primarily in a traditional classroom setting and employing traditional "literary" reading material. The three essays in part 3, "Nature Writing," describe courses whose primary goal is the *creation* of environmental literature and that present nature writing as taught in radically different learning environments. Part 4, "Environmental Literature in the Field," elaborates on course plans that use classroom and field experience on an equal footing. Its four essays provide different models for integrating field experience and classroom instruction in learning environments both far from and close to the classroom itself. Finally, part 5, "Regional Studies," is devoted to courses that, while varying in their use of experiential education, take as their subject matter and teaching environments the diverse natural and cultural manifestations of a particular United States geographical region. The three regions represented here are the Colorado River, the Mississippi River, and New England.

The reader should note that the introductions to these parts provide expanded and more detailed summaries of their contents.

The second section of the book provides information that could be useful to anyone interested in developing familiarity with environmental literature. The list of works cited includes many works—primary and secondary—generally used in environmental literature courses and referred to in writing on the subject. There are as well lists of additional significant works, of bibliographies of material on environmental writing and environmentalism, of the major periodicals currently publishing material of significance to interdisciplinary environmental studies, and of organizations active in the environmental area. Representative syllabi of courses described herein and other similar ones, while they cannot be included in this volume because of lack of space, are available from the editor at Box 24,292, ETSU, Johnson City, TN 37614.

2. *Teaching Environmental Literature*: The Educational Context

Unquestionably at this writing there is much turmoil and uncertainty in American higher education. To many educators, particularly those in language and literature, the extended treatment of an area of interdisciplinarity in this book may initially appear hard to justify. We usually have a hard time simply maintaining enrollment in our traditional upper-class offerings.

I can match anyone's experience in this regard, having participated for three years in a grant-supported interdisciplinary preprofessional humanities curriculum that has not yet been able to garner enough support from any segment of the university, including students, to be self-sustaining. Another point of personal reference is the "issues" poll I take at the beginning of "Freshman Composition," when my students are asked to agree or disagree with (among others) the statement that "the main purpose of a college education is preparation for a job." Last time, forty agreed and four disagreed.

Such accepted despair and personal testimony are easy to come by. Nonetheless, I feel that integrative courses, intelligently presented, *are* a means of redirecting such currents of student interest and that they *can* be created without impossible demands in sensitive areas. I think that programs relating literature and environmental concerns, such as the ones described here, have a particularly strong potential for interesting even job-oriented first-year students. It might be noted that in the poll described above the same students were in favor of wilderness preservation by a lopsided margin. Environmental concerns seem to engage even those students whose academic specialization leaves the least room for traditional humanities.

In the following pages, I will try to give some substance to these contentions by placing them in the environment of current thoughts on higher education in the humanities.

As Leon Botstein (along with many others) has recently noted, undergraduate college curricula today are in the trough of a "third wave" following the stress on "individual options" of the 1960s and the return to general education that has been the "active and dominant theme" in undergraduate curricular reform since the mid-seventies. Botstein emphasizes that a "serious and sustained neoclassic effort" like the current general education movement must not be merely a reaction to the "excessive changes" of the 1960s, whose memory will fade, but must involve "the task of creative adaptation of past models of curriculum and standards of education" (28).

Botstein defines three priorities for a new integrational phase in curricular planning. "Pragmatic anxieties will not fuel a desire for learning. Therefore we must shed the past even as we invoke it." Particularly we must "incorporate the crucial area of science and technology into the liberal-arts experience that every student ought to have," "fight the inappropriate fragmentation of the curriculum by disciplines," and make the arts "part of any broad-based effort toward general education" (28).

The institutionalization of Botstein's priorities might be considered increasingly necessary to make an individual college graduate "well-educated" in accord with traditional humanistic criteria, such as those of Joseph Kockelmans:

Today we call a person well-educated if he understands the tradition or the cultural heritage to which he belongs, has some knowledge of other cultures, can express himself clearly and engage in a meaningful dialogue with others, can understand the works of his tradition and respond to them meaningfully, is familiar with science and technology, has learned to think critically, and has some field in which he is really well prepared for either teaching, research, a vocation, or a profession. (40–41; see also Bouwisma)

The integrative curricular option presented in this volume—environmental literature, humanities and environmental studies—has the potential of responding to Botstein's curricular priorities and of contributing to the making of a "well-educated" person, under a dispensation that can both shed and invoke elements of the past.

Undergraduate courses in environmental literature or more wide-ranging ones involving several humanities and scientific disciplines integrated around an environmental studies framework also respond directly to the priorities articulated in the influential report of the Commission on the Humanities, *The Humanities in American Life*. This report acknowledges the financial and ideological constraints on open-ended curricular experimentation and the professional needs of students today, while insisting that vocationalism, basic education, or other movements responding to these constraints should not be allowed to compromise the meaning of "well-educated." In the words of *The Humanities in American Life*, "The need to interrelate the humanities, social sciences, science, and technology, has probably never been greater than [sic] today" in such areas as medicine, computer technology, natural resources management. The report goes on to deplore the "fundamental kind of illiteracy" involved in the continuing failure of collaboration between academic humanists and scientists.

So long as it prevails, humanists will hesitate to use new technologies, including television, to the advantage of learning. Scientists and technicians will not appreciate the relevance of the humanities. As the physical and social conditions of life change, few people will understand the real areas of interaction or divergence among science, technology, and human values. (6–7)

Similar congruence can be found between the value of environment-humanities courses and the recommendations of *A Nation at Risk*, the 1983 report of the National Commission on Excellence in Education. Specifically, the report's suggestions for implementing its first recommendation, the institution of "New Basics" in high school curricula, include: (1) "The teaching of English in high school should equip graduates (among others) to know our literary heritage and how it enhances imagination and ethical understanding, and how it relates to the customs, ideas and values of today's life and culture"; and (2) "The teaching of science in high school should provide graduates with an introduction to (among others) the social and environmental implications of scientific and technological development" (*New York Times* 27 Apr. 1983, B6).

A premise for the usefulness of this volume is acceptance of the three issues in humanistic education defined above as important and as needing to be addressed directly. New undergraduate curricula that combine tradition and innovation must be designed. The traditional ideal of a "well-educated" person must be maintained and, in many cases, resuscitated; it must be enhanced by the inclusion in higher education of new general competencies made necessary by new life circumstances, without the elimination of persisting necessary ones. Sciences and humanities, still "two cultures" in much of academia, must be made more responsive to each other, as in the "real world" they are implicated together in more and more life-determining choices. Jeremy Bernstein says, "There are at least two cultures: that of the scientifically literate and that of the scientifically illiterate, and the question that concerns me is how to take from the former and add to the latter" (8). We could add the *humanistically* literate and illiterate to Bernstein's ironic formulation and come up with four cultures that, in the view of the commission's report and this volume, should be reduced to two: the humanistically literate and the scientifically literate. And of course the "well-educated" person should be able to participate in both.

Most of the courses described in this volume's essays are centered on literature, in the humanities, and on environmental studies, in the sciences. Both of these are "synthetic" disciplines, which require for their understanding the interrelating of insights derived from several disciplines. Thus, their interweaving can be more effective than the interdisciplinary treatment of more discipline-limited materials in furthering the goals of new curricula, well-educated individuals, and science-humanities responsiveness. Also, most environmental literature courses or environment-humanities courses with a strong literary component directly address what *The Humanities in American Life* calls "acts of the imagination," which "give public expression to private experience" (69). If anything in recent years has primarily drawn students away from literature in particular and humanities disciplines in general, it has been their perceived irrelevance to a prioritized "public" realm of vocation, action, and decision making. The actual and necessary connection between imaginative, private aesthetic experience and public action and choice can be more clearly made in terms of a holistic vision of the world provided by ecological science and writing than in terms of individual career choice alone or the content of individual disciplines considered separately. Environmental values and conclusions drawn from environmental perspectives are often criticized for their "subjectivity"—particularly for involving the condition of the observer in that which is observed. But for this very subjectivity the environmental approach is more compatible than are other scientific discipline areas taken separately with the affectively biased humanistic disciplines. The truth value, the foundation in experimental method, of any insight of biology, chemistry, or physics is not lost but rather enhanced, especially for the potential nonspecialist (i.e., most everybody), when placed in an environmental context with insights derived from many disciplines. Almost every action has an environmental impact, and if this impact is not anticipated it can be destructive or self-destructive.

In effect, environment-humanities courses, however structured, embody a vital dialogue between imaginative and active, practical and contemplative, experience. The absence of this dialogue may be a root cause of the decline both of humanities in education and of the ideal of the well-educated person. As Charles Altieri says, describing his experience conducting a seminar in literature for social scientists:

> The aesthetic tradition has at its root a vision of the social value of literature based on the importance of distinguishing between the practical and the contemplative approaches to concrete cases. We cheat ourselves even more than we do others if we fail to see how the contemplative approach need not be an end in itself but can in fact deepen our capacity to project imaginative hypotheses about the world. (29–30)

To embody this observation in example, John Muir's lyrical and definitely contemplative vision of Yosemite Valley or the glaciers of Alaska cannot and should not be isolated from his valid observations of species interaction or glacial movement or from the issues of land-use policy that his writings brought to public consciousness—resulting in significant public action—and that are more urgent than ever in 1985. Muir's writing can be discussed as much in terms of transcendentalism and nineteenth-century prose style as in terms of forestry practices, geology, and political history and can be related to more discipline-defined work in these areas to enhance understanding of him and them. Similarly, a college course relating writers such as Muir to both literary tradition and the scientific disciplines on which their work impinges can do much to enhance the meaningfulness of knowledge gained from these disciplines. Such a course can increase a student's ability to deal with the actual problems of his or her own future private and public living, problems that will not divide themselves neatly into discipline areas or into realms of subjectivity and objectivity.

This plea for the validity and importance of environment-humanities courses should also mention difficulties readers may have with the premises of these courses, as well as some other ways in which they fulfill the recommendations of the Committee on the Humanities report.

First, I would like to make several assertions in regard to these difficulties, with the understanding that these assertions can hardly be proved in the few paragraphs of an introduction.

1. "Environmental" literature and "environmental" studies of any kind do not imply a particular ideological or political bias, even though materials used in courses based on them may well be strongly political or ideological.

As Leon Botstein says, the view of "environmental" as "radical" is colored by "the memory of the excessive changes of the early 1960's and early 1970's" (28). Or, as James E. Swan characterizes the environmental movement of that time, "the initial position . . .was that of social criticism," and "Many people in the environmental movement seem to equate 'returning to nature' with giving up all the gains of Western scientific society"(45, 47). The reader of these essays will certainly be able to discern the subjective biases of the authors, but what teacher in the humanities can involve students in feeling- and value-related material without possessing and expressing feelings and values of his or her own? On the contrary, all effective environmental literature courses, such as those presented here, provide a context of dialogue, investigation, and self-discovery for students of relations with the nonhuman world, through experience and the written views of others on this relationship. Content and methods in these courses are in no way a function of antiestablishment syndicalism, which is one extreme on a spectrum of viewpoints they may suggest. "Environmental" in the context of this book refers to "our relationship to all the environment, not the least of which is the rest of mankind" (Pursell 5), or, as George Perkins Marsh put it in the first American environmental study, *Man and Nature* (1864), to the "influence of man" on the "mutual relations and adaptations" of the "organic and inorganic world" (36).

2. Integrated courses are not "luxuries," nor are they "elitist" (as environmentalists themselves are often naively described). They are not within the financial and logistic means only of well-supported educational systems, and they do not ignore the needs of people who have limited resources and require every minute of their educational experience to contribute to mastering job skills.

On the contrary, as the diversity of institutions, students, and levels of instruction in the courses described will testify, a striking quality is their adaptability to different pedagogical situations and different levels of achievement. Courses taught in a community college in Miami, a state university in Memphis, an experimental college in the Appalachians, and a private denominational university in Washington state are included here. It is rather the "indiscriminate use of new program ideas without systematic reflection on the implications and probable outcomes of program changes" that has "undermined intellectual credibility" (Bergquist et al. xvi) of such programs as these. The reader will find that these courses owe their diversity to their successful adaptation to specific constituencies, from first-term students to honors seniors and from little-endowed to greatly endowed institutions. Many of these courses demonstrate methods of employing a regional approach, often involving little expense and few resources, to involve the world outside the classroom in the study of environmental literature (see the chapter "Space: Maximizing the Use of Instructional Settings On- and Off-Campus" in Bergquist et al. 43–74).

3. Integrated courses such as these need not "dilute" the knowledge contained in the disciplines that contribute to them unless they are poorly set up, as any course may be.

Any course, no matter how content-specific it is, may appear superficial in respect to some deeper level of understanding. A good multidisciplinary integrated course is the enemy of the sort of educational elitism that makes deep-versus-superficial distinctions, because it does not assume that one has to have some certifiable expertise in a discipline before relating it to other disciplines or the world as a whole. In science-humanities integrative courses, the burden of proof unfortunately is usually placed on the humanist, whose ignorance of science is often seen as paradigmatic. The difficulty with this assumption is the "objectivistic" and reductive view of interdisciplinary education as being "an assimilation, however integrated, of a *subject matter*" rather than an "integrative process" (Kavaloski

234). But even as subject matter, interdisciplinary knowledge can exist in different degrees of objectivity without being something its subjective holder need be ashamed of. In my own experience teaching medicine and literature, I found that dialogue between people with different degrees of ignorance and knowledge about both disciplines, with an integrative text as a common point of reference, was more enlightening to me, a literary nonpractitioner, than introductory pathology and introductory literature taken separately could have been (although a member of this particular class might have been inspired to take either of these disciplinary courses subsequently, because of exposure to the disciplines in an integrative context) (Waage). Again, the diversity of courses, content, and personnel described in these essays belies the stereotypical formulation of superficiality.

4. Integrative courses are not inherently difficult to establish and are not impossible to implement because of departmental rivalries, teaching-load constraints, etc.

The informal, personal approach of many of the essays in this volume permits the authors to describe how they established and conducted their courses. Some are imaginative variations of conventional catalog courses; some benefited from released-time arrangements, credit sharing, grants. Depending on whether their content is environmental literature per se, containable within the bounds of one department, or whether it is elaborately multidisciplinary or something in-between, there are possibilities here for innovation within many different types of constraints. What are most important, it seems from these writings, are the interest and commitment of the individual faculty member(s) and the ingenuity for which college teachers are well-known.

The reader of *The Humanities in American Life* will find many harmonies between the recommendations of the commission and the goals, if not achievements, of the environmental literature and humanities–environmental studies courses offered as models in this volume. In particular, the commission's recommendation 12 deserves to be quoted in full:

> . . . we recommend the following general strategies for strengthening education in the humanities at various kinds of institutions:
> —instruction in writing that is spread across the course of study;
> —courses integrating themes and subjects from the humanistic disciplines with each other and with other fields of study;
> —clear sequences of courses in each of the disciplines of the humanities;
> —use of resources from local cultural institutions;
> —the development of new materials for teaching the humanities. (71–72)

Most of the courses described emphasize writing as a major component. Usually, the writing covers subjects beyond the scope of traditional composition courses, and some courses, like the one conducted by Paul Bryant (part 3), emphasize the issue of popular versus specialized rhetoric emphasized in the commission's report: "Good writing in any field becomes more difficult as knowledge of the field leads to a specialized vocabulary and special modes of thought" (72). Many courses, particularly those described in "Regional Studies" (part 5), use the resources of local nature and cultural institutions extensively. This volume itself represents the sort of "new material" for teaching the humanities whose development the report encourages. Finally, the integrative nature of all the courses described here is harmonious with the major emphasis of the recommendation: "At all levels, integrative courses allow students to explore the interrelationships among various kinds of knowledge and to gain perspective on a major field or chosen career. . . ." As the report points out, "the terms *interdisciplinary* and *team-taught* have acquired a mystique that may be misleading; they can disguise shoddy, ill-conceived courses that merely dilute a variety of subjects rather than unite them in any coherent or imaginative synthesis" (76). However, well-conceived integrative courses, as I believe all those represented here are, can play a vital and versatile role in humantistic education. They "can introduce students to the disciplines of the humanities while connecting these with students' vocational or intellectual interests." And they can also "encourage students to explore the regular curriculum of the humanities" (76).

PART 1:

Contexts

Introduction

The initial essays in this book seek a preliminary definition for the genre environmental literature. Walter Clark, Jr.'s "What Teaching Environmental Literature Might Be" discusses the relation of different concepts of "environment" to teaching. Clark distinguishes between "teaching environment" and "educating environmentally." The former takes "environment" as subject matter, and the latter uses "environment" as a tool for teaching any subject matter. He discusses how "environment" and "literature" can be taught in relation to each other and considers the goals of liberal education in light of this relationship.

The subsequent three essays survey the literary history and canon of "environmental literature" and literary environmentalism in the United States in the nineteenth and twentieth centuries. Bruce Piasecki's "American Literary Environmentalism before Darwin" is concerned with pre-Darwinian environmental thinking and its literary expression, particularly in Whitman's vision of nature. My "American Literary Environmentalism, 1864–1920" covers major environmental writers between the Civil War and World War I, such as John Muir, John Burroughs, and Mary Austin, and major forces in creating such writing—for example, the geological and geographical surveys and the city-planning movement of Frederick Law Olmsted. Finally, Richard Lillard, in "The Nature Book in Action," discusses directions and major writers in the last several decades.

What Teaching Environmental Literature Might Be

Walter H. Clark, Jr.

I follow two threads in this discussion. One is definitional. What might it mean to talk about environmental literature? Implicit in the attempt to deal with the question of meaning is the belief that "environment" has certain implications that all who teach environmental literature must reckon with. The other thread is programmatic. What might be made of environmental literature? Here I allow myself some scope, since decisions about what to do with environmental literature require that one say some things about environmental education in general, as well as about liberal education.

I offer my own views on these subjects less to persuade the reader of their validity than to exemplify what seems to me a necessary approach to curricular innovation. At some point one has to turn from statements such as "You could do it this way" or "This is what we did" to statements having some imperative force: "Do it this way." What follow are the views of a person who believes that the best liberal education tries to meld cognitive, affective, physical, and social aspects and that one way it can do so is by shaping the educational environment. This is not the place for extended philosophical justification of such views, but I hope the reader will find supporting illustrations in some of the accounts of teaching environmental literature contained in this book.

Environment

"Environment" is a relational concept. Wherever there is environment there is necessarily something surrounded and something that surrounds. "Environment" points to that which surrounds.

It is natural to ask how far our environment extends. Logically, it is all that surrounds us, whether near or far, whether of great or small importance in our lives, whether we are aware of it or not. In this sense, environment is to be distinguished from visual periphery, which is sharply defined. But in actual usage, the concept is more circumscribed. We talk about environment when we wish to direct someone's attention to elements of his or her surroundings hitherto ignored or discounted. Usually when we talk of environment we have in mind things whose immediate origins are near to us and that we feel affect us. Because of the premise that environment affects the individual, remarks about environment are often oblique commentaries on human action, carrying explanatory or normative overtones. Talk about environment often occurs in connection with attempts to get others to see themselves and/or the world in certain ways that may have moral or political implications, ways that may expand their spheres of responsibility.

Usually when we talk about environment we have in mind only a small portion of the totality that surrounds us. The language of environment frequently employs the image of a sphere. We live in the midst of an atmosphere, a biosphere, a sociosphere. When our sense of environment is less physically conceived we are less apt to use the image of the sphere: we also live in environments of ideas, feelings, spiritual influences, but perhaps we do not think of them as forming rule-governed networks about us in the way that physical and social phenomena do.

Discussions of environment shape themselves around plants, animals, and, above all, human things. In talking about environmental education, we must heed this practice, bearing in mind the central core of human concerns, in terms of which environmental education achieves its significance.

Environmental Education

All education takes place in an environment. The lecture takes place in the surroundings of the classroom; the college education takes place on a campus. When we realize how much classroom and campus can influence learning, we understand that decisions about educational environment are as significant as decisions about curriculum.

Although the conditions under which education takes place must surely count as environmental education, the question as to whether there may not be a more strictly curricular sense of the term is at first somewhat puzzling. Is "environment" to be treated like one of the traditional academic disciplines? Might there be a department of environment as there are departments of English, biology, and sociology? This proposal founders, I believe, on the observation that environment is a relational concept. Such concepts, taken by themselves, are not the stuff of which disciplines or departments are made. The concept of environment, furthermore, is one that easily travels across disciplinary boundaries. Biology departments offer courses in environmental biology; environment is relevant to the concerns of psychology, sociology, geography; the purpose of this book, indeed, is to consider environmental literature. Although environmental education has a place in many disciplines, it is not itself a discipline, because the distinction it rests on is not strong enough to carry the weight of a scholarly subdivision.

If not a discipline, perhaps "environmental education" belongs at the opposite extreme. Might it be more like a slogan or label, a rallying cry around which people with a variety of roughly similar interests join in common allegiance, possibly without having too clear an idea of what it is that unites them? If "environmental education" is the name of a movement, we should ask what its ideology is or how it looks at the world. If we regard it as an educational program, we might ask what it wants to do in education.

The distinction between subject matter and method may prove useful. We can approach the question of what "environmental education" might be by asking what is being taught or we can ask if there is a characteristic way of teaching that might be characterized as "environmental." The difficulty in viewing environmental education as a subject matter, as we have suggested, is that the concept crosses so many disciplinary boundaries. What is more, its role within any discipline tends to be ancillary rather than central. If we treat environmental education as subject matter, we find either that it reduces to a fairly abstract concept or that it spreads out in such a way that the same concept is deployed in a variety of fields otherwise unrelated.

The justification for environmental subject matter at the present time, aside from the needs of various disciplines, would seem to lie in our need for increased awareness of the world around us and in the value, for problem solving, of learning to look outside a narrow focus. Philip Slater remarks on the nearsightedness of humanity's relation to the rest of the world over the past seven centuries and urges us to be not less but more aware of our surroundings. The more sophisticated our understanding of the world, the less we are able to see human or other beings as existing in isolation. Moreover, if one of the purposes of liberal education is to prepare students for problem solving, in the broadest sense, some study of environment and training in environmental thinking can be justified as broadening the context within which we define problems and expect to come upon solutions to them.

Environment and Literature

In addressing the question of what "teaching environmental literature" might mean, I speak first to the definition of "environmental literature" and then to what it might mean to teach environmental literature environmentally.

Any problems we may have in defining "environment" obviously carry over to the definition of "environmental literature." Rather than discuss them at length, I shall treat "environmental literature" as literature that deals with physical surroundings, most especially biological surroundings, in such a way as to include, tacitly or explicitly, that which is surrounded. "Environmental literature" is presumably to be distinguished from other writing about the environment in possessing aesthetic qualities that make it worthy of consideration for its own sake. While we do not require of environmental literature that it raise moral or political issues, it might be said that, other things being equal, environmental literature that allows for the raising of such issues is to be preferred for teaching purposes over that which does not. As to the category to which environmental literature belongs, I suspect we would not term it a genre, inasmuch as those who produce it do not think of their activity as part of a collective enterprise with a history upon which they can draw. Environmental literature more properly belongs with a kind of course increasingly taught in English departments, in which works are categorized according to subject matter, such as "Travel Literature," "Women's Literature," "The Immigrant Novel."

Teaching environmental literature environmentally calls for special emphasis on its representational aspects. Environmental literature is not a form that creates distance. The narrator of an environmental work is typically an "I" who describes himself or herself as moving to and fro in an environment, observing it and musing upon it. The ideal situation, then, is one in which the student is immersed for some time in a physical environment as close as possible to that of a particular work or group of works. When such immersion extends over a longer period of time, it is desirable to leave much implicit that might otherwise have been drawn to the student's attention. The very fullness of the environment in which the student is immersed, which might at first appear to make for inefficiency, is useful in challenging his or her powers of discrimination. When we take students into an environment similar to that described in *Walden*, there is much for them to experience that closely matches what is described there. At the same time there is a great deal that does not match *Walden*. Sorting this out is one way of getting to understand what sort of a feat it might be to write such a book. A further advantage of fullness is that it is experienced against the instructional leanness of the usual classroom situation. Not only does the novelty of the situation create new opportunities, it also creates new difficulties. Some of these difficulties, of course, have little or nothing to do with literature, but their net effect is to arouse energies that, properly focused, lead to more effective learning. There is a freshness to the encounter with a work of literature when one comes to it in its own environment that cannot be duplicated by a lecturer's description, no matter how artful. There is a sense in which we own any environment in which we have struggled, and this ownership extends also to literary works portraying that environment.

Environmental Literature and Liberal Education

Compartmentalization of knowledge is both strength and weakness in the modern university. What contemporary liberal education gains in intensity it may lose in breadth. One of the advantages of environmental education, as I see it, is that it offers opportunities to work for breadth within the present system. As a method, environmental education enlarges the boundaries of the traditional classroom or else abandons it completely—immersing both students and teachers, requiring of them that they mobilize their energies, encouraging them to clarify the basic purposes of education, withdrawing them for a while from the traditional university environment where so much conduces to the restriction of the learning process within tacit boundaries.

The least we ask of liberal education in the present day is that it offer the student the opportunity to master a particular discipline. This mastery entails assimilation of a certain body of knowledge, a style of thinking characteristic of the discipline, an awareness of the questions deemed important in the discipline, and an understanding of the criteria for judging whether answers to disciplinary questions are satisfactory or not. Along the way the successful college students acquire self-discipline through meeting the institutional requirements placed upon them, as well as a certain social competence attendant on their membership in the student body. These will be of use to them in their careers.

In addition to meeting criteria already stated, a good liberal education does the following: (1) It encourages students to compare the ways different disciplines conceive of and think about their subject matter, it encourages generalization and synthesis, and it promotes holistic approaches to intellectual problems in balance with analysis. (2) It imparts the art of learning how to learn and encourages the student to experience learning as active, adventurous, and chance taking. (3) It cultivates imagination. (4) It provides opportunity and encouragement to merge cognitive with affective and social growth and does not wall off the physical. (5) It fosters the clarification and election of values, i.e., gives students some basis for making moral and political choices. (6) It encourages students to connect learning and living.

A further generalization under which these goals would be subsumed might be contained in the observation that one of the most important things an educational institution can do is to facilitate, or at least not impede, the process whereby students come to see themselves as getting an education, rather than being educated. I am convinced that the teaching of environmental literature, as subject and as method, offers opportunities to forward this.

American Literary Environmentalism before Darwin

Bruce Piasecki

According to the standard histories, environmental writing has descended from Darwin. In the *Origin of Species* (1859), Darwin's example of the relatedness of apparently unconnected organisms correlated the interactions of cats that killed mice that plagued bees that pollinated some clover. Ernst Haeckel, again according to these histories, was the European who capitalized on Darwin's hints and coined the new science of ecology in 1866. But a number of nineteenth-century literary works, upon closer investigation into their assumptions about nature and their sources in the science of the day, evidence significant environmental thinking in America before the advent of Darwin. The earlier "environmentalists" not only fostered an empirical respect for the complexity of humankind's interaction with nature but also generated a variety of concepts in their effort to understand humanity's role in changing the face of the earth.

The careers of various early American naturalists have been studied in a number of recent books, such as Joseph Kastner's *Species of Eternity*, that document the scope and depth of some of the more technical naturalists from the Puritan era to the time of Darwin. Other works, such as Samuel Hays's *Conservation and the Gospel of Efficiency*, reconstruct the preconditions under which the "conservationist impulse" became a leading issue in American social engineering from 1890 to 1920. In addition to these early American naturalists and conservationists, there also exists a large group of American writers, including many prized writers of the American Renaissance and some lesser-known but in their time widely acclaimed science writers whose works display a rich pre-Darwinian climate of opinion.

What follows is a glossary of some of the leading concepts in American literary environmentalism. I have noted where these concepts appear in the editions of Walt Whitman's works and have referred to the editions that were read in Whitman's day, both to illustrate their availability and influence before the time of Darwin and to acknowledge their importance to those teaching in the field. I have used Whitman as an index for these diverse cultural concerns simply out of convenience. I agree with the notion that college courses in environmental literature should have a strong twentieth-century emphasis that on occasion tempers the works of such modern writers as E. F. Schumacher, Leo Marx, and René Dubos with earlier archetypal writers like George Perkins Marsh and Henry David Thoreau. I strongly believe, however, that the many lesser-known and neglected writers mentioned in the following pages may prove equally fundamental to "the literature of nature" and equally profitable to students' historical sense of the issues.

Uniformitarianism

Until the eighteenth century, the geologic forms and movements of the earth were understood in the American colonies in terms of the estimate of nature inherited from the Puritans, whereby the earth was the manifestation of the will of an inscrutable deity that might be benign, orderly, or chaotic at whim but was always beyond the scope of human comprehension. This insistence on an element of the unknowable recurs in various forms throughout American environmental literature, often with a concomitant intensification of the possibilities of catastrophe in nature. In contrast, the "uniformitarian" estimate of nature and the beginning of geology as a science had their origins in an entirely new set of ground rules, particularly those established by James Hutton and popularized by John Playfair in the *Illustration of the Huttonian Theory of the Earth* (1802) under the name "doctrine of uniformitarianism." According to this doctrine, the earth is not arbitrary or capricious but follows knowable, predictable, and reliable patterns of cause and effect. Nature itself is a lawbound system of matter in motion and is understandable by man. The American uniformitarians supplemented this theory with new terrain for geologic evidences. With its promise of exotic and unexplored formations and fossil finds, the immense expanse of the American landscape became the "testing ground" for this new estimate of nature. By 1840, many American scientists and writers had assumed significant roles in the formulation and defense of uniformitarianism.

The cultural implications of this new estimate of nature, as it clashed with the conflicting theory of catastrophism, are evident in Arnold Guyot's *The Earth and Man* (1849). This set of popular lectures, reprinted by Arno Press in their series American Environmental Studies, applied discoveries in comparative geography to the accepted histories of Western civilization. Walt Whitman and other mid-century writers read Guyot and attended his lectures. The American editions of the works of Sir Charles Lyell are also telling. The works of Lyell were well received and thoroughly reviewed in America. Walt Whitman, for instance, clipped out two reviews of Lyell's *Travels in North America*: one from an 1845 issue of the *Quarterly Review* and the other from an 1849 issue of the *Democratic Review*. Other relevant works by Lyell include *Principles of Geology, Lectures on Geology,* and *A Second Visit to the United States of North America.* In 1863, Lyell published his *Geological Evidences of the Antiquity of Man,* which advanced the important question of humanity's status in nature by showing its "immense preparations," to use Whitman's words, in natural history.

Humankind's Status in Nature

Although the relation of humans to nature has been a subject of Western thinking for centuries, the question of their status in the natural universe became a most pressing issue by the middle of the nineteenth century. Then, for the first time, the widely read English philosopher Herbert Spencer linked the idea of social evolution to the idea of organic evolution. "Not until then," writes John Greene in *The Death of Adam*, ". . . would man's progress in history be viewed as a continuation of the progress of nature" (219). Developments within biology itself, such as Louis Pasteur's disproof of the doctrine of spontaneous generation, contributed to an utterly naturalistic conception of universal law. "Thanks to the revolution of the 1850's," writes Robert Bannister in *Social Darwinism: Science and Myth in Anglo-American Social Thought*, "the study of life, no less than the rest of the universe, was put on a thoroughly naturalistic basis" (19).

The question of humanity's status in such a universe became a popular cultural concern by mid-century. Robert Chambers, for instance, in *Vestiges of the Natural History of Creation* (1844), articulated one of his day's leading concerns when he wrote: "A question of a very interesting kind will now probably arise in the reader's mind—what place or status is assigned to man in the new natural system" (262). Thomas H. Huxley, looking back on the progress made in the physical sciences during the first half of the nineteenth century, brought the weight of his authority to this issue when he wrote soon after mid-century:

> The question of questions for mankind—the problem which underlies all others, and is more deeply interesting than any other—is the ascertainment of the place which man occupies in nature and of his relation to the universe of things. What are the limits of our power over nature and of nature's power over us; to what goal are we tending; are the problems which present themselves anew and with undiminished interest to every man born into the world. (71)

In fact, Huxley dedicated an entire book to this question of human status; and in addition to the above quotation, every page of *Man's Place in Nature* (1864) exemplifies the importance of this question for his times. Because this became, in the words of Huxley, "the question of questions" by mid-century, the publications on humanity's status grew in scope and sophistication. Scientists such as Carl Ritter and Sir Charles Lyell used the question to discuss the deep ties between humans and nature, while humanists such as J. F. Herschel and Henry Thomas Buckle employed it to open new fields of study that reassessed natural philosophy, cultural history, and comparative religion.

A fine example of how the question of human status influenced the course of natural philosophy can be found in J. F. Herschel's *A Preliminary Discourse on the Study of Natural Philosophy* (1830). Whitman linked Herschel with Swedenborg, Voltaire, and Rousseau as some of the "foremost actors . . . from 1750 to 1830 both in Europe and America" (*Prose Works* 2: 628). Whitman also clipped out a long review of Herschel's observations of the southern heavens, published in the *Edinburgh Review* in February 1848.

For an instance of this question as it became integral in cultural history, see Henry Thomas Buckle's *History of Civilization in England* (1857). In his introduction, Buckle stresses the variety of environments and their ability to awe and influence humans. Whitman refers to this book in a letter to Alfred, Lord Tennyson. In 1852 Carl Ritter published *Comparative Geog-*

raphy, which employed an all-embracing-design argument to evidence the deep environmental ties between humans and nature across the globe.

Humanity's Place in Nature

As a result of the interest in humanity's "natural standing," many pre-Darwinian thinkers measured the status of humans by placing them in a scale or hierarchy of animal types, with special reference to humanity's relation to other primates. They were interested in humankind's role in nature from the standpoint of its natural lineage or kinship with other organisms: "For it will be admitted," wrote Huxley in *Man's Place in Nature*, "that some knowledge of man's position in the animate world is an indispensable preliminary to the proper understanding of his relation to the universe" (73). Huxley's book illustrates both the concerns and the limitations of most mid-century thinkers and helps to clarify the distinct advancement toward environmental thinking latent in the writers of the American Renaissance. Throughout his book Huxley provides numerous parallels between humans and apes. He notes, for instance, that both orangutans and humans live to be forty or fifty and that they are both long under maternal care. He even documents the remarkable dexterity orangutans demonstrate in building their tree beds. Although Huxley twice refers to the new work of Darwin, his primary interest is to compare humans with primates, with "those singular creatures" whose history he has sketched in many essays before he became "Darwin's bulldog."

E. P. Odum, in *Fundamentals of Ecology*, notes that it took more than fifty years after the time of Huxley and Darwin for most scientists and writers to turn their attention from humanity's natural lineage with the primates to "the idea of man's natural linkage or ecological interdependence with the biota" (512). Yet many American Renaissance writers reveal an incipient awareness of humanity's "natural linkage" with nature, as in section fourteen of Whitman's "Song of Myself":

> The wild gander leads his flock through the cool night,
> *Ya-honk* he says, and sounds it down to me like an invitation,
> The pert may suppose it meaningless, but I listening close,
> Find its purpose and place up there toward the wintry sky.
>
> The sharp-hoof'd moose of the north, the cat on the house-sill, the chickadee,
>   the prairie-dog,
> The litter of the grunting sow as they tug at her teats,
> The brood of the turkey-hen and she with her half-spread wings,
> I see in them and myself the same old law.

Although numerous late-nineteenth-century writers were appalled at Darwin's documentation of interrelatedness, which in the words of Huxley "awakened a sudden and profound mistrust of time-honored theories," Whitman, as well as pre-Darwinian naturalists, conservationists, and transcendentalists, was prepared to accept the idea of the individual's place in nature. These writers revealed a significant modern response to the environment before the advent of Darwin.

Humankind's Relation to the Cosmos

When Walt Whitman describes himself as a "kosmos" in section 24 of "Song of Myself," he is using a word made popular by Alexander von Humboldt. Humboldt's book *Kosmos* surveyed the history of the subjective contemplation of nature in literature as well as the objective understanding of nature attained through science. This book had been widely read in the English-speaking world by mid-century. Like many environmental writers before the advent of Darwin, Humboldt considered both the aesthetic appreciation of nature and the scientific understanding of it essential for the understanding of humanity's place in nature. Whitman quotes two passages from Humboldt in his *Notebooks*.

Many American writers capitalized on this interest in humanity's relation to the cosmos. William Fishbough, for instance, further popularized the concept with *The Macrocosm and Microcosm* (1852). Fishbough's book was favorably noticed in the *Tribune* by Horace Greeley, and acclaimed by the July 1854 issue of the *American Phrenological Journal* as a "remarkable work . . . equal if not superior to the *Vestiges of Creation*." It was compared in the *Philadelphia Sunday Ledger* to the writings of Lord Bacon, Sir Isaac Newton, Dr. Franklin, and Humboldt.

American environmental writers had access to two American and one British edition of Humboldt, each published in 1850. The more ardent naturalists may have read Humboldt's *A Geognostical Essay on the Superposition of Rocks in Both Hemispheres* as early as 1823.

By the Civil War, environmental writers had become even more informed about the career of Alexander von Humboldt, as many of his works were again reprinted and reviewed in America. In 1869 the centennial of his birth was celebrated worldwide, with Louis Agassiz as the keynote speaker for the Boston Society of Natural History. There was also a series of Humboldt festivals at the time. The *Letters of Humboldt* was translated from the second German edition by Friedrich Kapp. Horace Traubel records how Walt Whitman read these with great enjoyment and agreement (3: 446).

The Antiquity of Humanity

The interest in the antiquity of humankind was so widespread in the years before Darwin that numerous magazines established columns and published series of essays on the subject, and a new set of contributors emerged who could serve as intermediaries between the scientists and the lay reader. During the year 1853, for instance, the *Phrenological Journal*, which Whitman and other transcendentalists read studiously throughout the 1850s, ran a series of nine articles, The Natural History of Man, which in the words of the author, William C. Rogers, endeavored "to bring the researches of the most profound Anatomists, Physiologists, and Naturalists, within the reach and comprehension of all." These popular works quoted heavily from other more technical books on the subject, such as J. C. Prichard's *The Natural History of Man* and R. C. Smith's *Atlas of Modern and Ancient Geography* (see Stovall 154–160). These books served as the means by which environmental writers could gain access to the more scientific information. Interest in "the antiquity of man" became increasingly intense throughout the 1850s and 1860s, culminating in works like D. D. Dana's *The Geological Story Briefly Told: An Introduction to Geology for the General Reader and for All Beginners in Science* (1879). Environmental writers invested many hours in reading these popular works; from them they built a solid foundation of fact and the vast structures of time and space found in Whitman's poems and Emerson's later essays (see Stovall 282–305; Gay Wilson Allen 18–19, 81–82; Asselineau, 243–65).

A parallel mid-century concern involved the vast antiquity of the globe. This was noted by Lamarck, the famous paleontologist, when he wrote: "Oh, how great is the antiquity of the terrestrial globe. And how little the ideas of those who attribute to the globe an existence of six thousand and a few hundred years' duration from its origin to the present" (qtd. in Stromberg 112). Many Americans gained access to these "ideas" through Robert Chambers' *Vestiges of the Natural History of Creation*.

Although relentlessly criticized by scientists and theologians, *Vestiges of Creation* was so widely read that it inspired a series of myths about itself. One such myth, according to G. M. Young in his cultural portrait *Victorian England* (1936), claimed Prince Albert had written the book to show the Western world the importance of England's interest in the natural sciences. In a fine review of the controversy that *Vestiges of Creation* stirred in America, George H. Daniels discusses Asa Gray's fifty-two-page review of *Vestiges* that appeared in the *North American Review* (57–62). Daniels discovered that many American scientists became "highly irritated" over Chambers, claiming his errors "not errors of science but merely of inaccurate or outmoded science." Nevertheless, many were in agreement with Chambers' conclusion: "Man, then, considered zoologically, and without regard to the distinct character assigned to him by theology, simply takes his place as the type of all types of the animal kingdom, the true and unmistakable head of animated nature upon the earth" (272–73).

New Standards of Nature

As it became increasingly obvious that the Linnean system of classification was limited in its utility, it became common to call for a "wiser estimate" of nature. In the twenty-year period between 1825 and 1845, for instance, "at least twenty different 'natural systems,' not including the great number inspired by Naturphilosophie, had been published," according to Daniels. One of the most famous of these, published by George Perkins Marsh, reads:

> If man is destined to inhabit the earth much longer, and to advance in
> natural knowledge with the rapidity which has marked his progress in
> physical science for the last two or three centuries, he will learn to put

a wiser estimate on the works of creation, and will derive not only great
instruction from studying the ways of nature in her obscurest, humblest
walks, but great material advantage from stimulating her productive
energies in provinces of her empire hitherto regarded as forever inac-
cessible, utterly barren.   (112)

American Renaissance writers were assuming this same climate of opinion
when they offered their new understanding of nature: this rebirth of a
wiser estimate of nature is at the base of a wide range of nineteenth-century
works. Whitman says as much in the following passage from *Democratic
Vistas*:

> Nature, true Nature, and the true idea of Nature, long absent, must,
> above all become fully restored, enlarged, and must furnish the per-
> vading atmosphere to poems, and the test of all high literary and es-
> thetic compositions. I do not mean the smooth walks, trimm'd hedges,
> poseys and nightingales of the English poets, but the whole orb, with
> its geologic history, the kosmos, carrying fire and snow, that rolls through
> the illimitable areas, light as a feather but weighing billions of tons.
> (*Prose Works* 2: 416–17)

As seen in Whitman's emphasis on "the whole orb," many of these pre-
Darwinian estimates of nature were inspired by earlier works in geology,
which had greatly enlarged the writers' knowledge of the plans and op-
erations of the universe.

The Geologic Sublime

These new standards of nature, especially when they involved a "geologic estimate," did not enter the mainstream of American culture without
significant debate and controversy. The nineteenth century, as studied by
Charles Coulston Gillispie in *Genesis and Geology*, abounds with instances
in which this new geologic estimate of nature makes the earth seem un-
inhabitable and hostile. While Whitman found the "fully restored" sense
of nature sublime and promising, some of his closest contemporaries found
it chilling, as noted by the well-known writer and naturalist John Burroughs:

> How the revelations of science do break in upon the sort of private and
> domestic view of the universe which mankind have so long held! To
> many minds it is like being fairly turned out into the cold, and made
> to fare without shield or shelter the eternities and the infinities of
> geologic time and sidereal space. We are no longer cosily housed in a
> pretty little anthropomorphic view of things. The universe is no longer
> a theatre constructed expressly for the drama of man's life and sal-
> vation.   (3: 225–26)

This fearful reception is understandable, given the flicker of time a human
life becomes in the face of geologic change. If one could speed up any
human's "private and domestic view of the universe" so that mountains

might rise and fall in a month or the seas change like giant tide pools daily, it would be "to many minds," as Burroughs notes, "like being fairly turned out into the cold" (225). But various environmental writers, assimilating the same "revelations of science," found this realization of humanity's precarious existence exhilarating. They read the same evidence as proof of the ultimate generosity of the earth: for nature not only provided human-kind with "shield and shelter" but also permitted its ascent through the work of natural history. This, they argued, was miraculous, considering that a single lapse in the complex process might have cleansed the earth of its living debris. Many of these writers considered the growth of hu-manity's geologic knowledge not as an end in itself but as the means to one of the great enlargements of life—namely, the feeling of being at home in the world.

Whitman's poetry expresses this new emotion, a response to world process that one might call "the geologic sublime." Instead of presenting life as a series of rough approximate adjustments, as a struggle for equi-librium that is seldom established and often challenged, these pre-Dar-winian writers announced, in the words of Whitman:

> Me imperturbe, standing at ease in Nature . . .
>   O to be self-balanced for contingencies,
> To confront night, storms, hunger, ridicule, accidents, rebuffs, as the
>   trees and animals do.   ("Me Imperturbe," *Leaves*)

This captures the smooth exactness of wonder at the core of the "geologic experience," a feeling dramatically presented by Whitman as humanity's new awareness of "the whole orb . . . the kosmos." This feeling of relief is not, for Whitman, a product of intellectual self-possession or repose as much as it is the result of a felt remembrance of humanity's ascending status in the continuum of nature. Moreover, the faculty of clear-sight-edness this experience gives, according to Whitman, comes from forces far more natural than social. David Leveson writes of this modern environ-mentalist insight in *A Sense of the Earth*:

> Awareness of the earth, consciousness of its proximity, of its inescap-able influence—even when not obvious—presents aesthetic and psy-chological possibilities largely overlooked or forgotten. . . . If it can reach him, knowledge of the earth as reality, rock as material of the universe, landscape as momentary expression of natural process, is a rich and vital source of sanity and calm for modern man.   (18–19)

The Law of Succession

A number of early-nineteenth-century writers applied a concept of natural succession to their creative writing and their social thought. The fundamental problem of social science for Karl Marx was to find the law of motion by which any state of society produces the state that succeeds it. Hegel's three main phases of history involved the succession from Asiatic and Greco-Roman civilizations to a synthesis of freedom in the strong state of Germanic-European civilizations. While Marx's key to succession lay in the technocratic and economic sphere and Hegel's key to historical epochs was conceived in the political terms of the state, many pre-Darwinian environmental writers understood both social and political change as part of a naturalistic system. Although political and socioeconomic considerations enter as significant factors in their works, the central explanatory model for these writers was natural succession. Walt Whitman asserts as much when he writes in *Democratic Vistas*:

> Law is the unshakable order of the universe forever; and the law over all, and law of laws, is the law of successions; that of the superior law, in time, gradually supplanting and overwhelming the inferior one. . . .
> It has been and is carried on by all the moral forces, and by trade, finance, machinery, intercommunications and, in fact, by all the developments of history, and can not be stopp'd than the tides, or the earth in its orbit.　(*Prose Works* 2: 381, 390)

For these writers, natural succession represents an orderly process of development that is visibly directional and predictable. John Stuart Mill claimed that "of all truths relating to phenomena, the most valuable to us are those which relate to their order of succession. On a knowledge of these is founded every reasonable anticipation of future facts, and whatever power we possess of influencing those facts to our advantage" (34). Writers in the *Democratic Review* argued that this law of succession governed the "unshakable" sequence from a feudal world to a democratic one. "Dynastic ruin," writes Whitman, is inevitable, for "such democratizing is about the only resource now left" (*Prose Works* 2: 425). This sense of natural succession constitutes, for some of these writers, their most reliable grounds for hope; it contains their conception of human self-reliance and their observations on historical and social change, as well as their insights into previous writers and people of action. Although the advent of Darwin shattered the closed metaphysical system of these earlier conceptions, various literary "environmentalists" applied a concept of natural succession to their social thought long before there was any mention of social Darwinism in America.

Humankind's Role in Changing the Face of the Earth

It is an irony of American environmental history that most wildlife conservation legislation, which restricts and taxes the hunter, has been passed at the insistence of hunters. Leading this conservation movement were men considered the top hunters of their time, such as Teddy Roosevelt, Charles Sheldon, and Gifford Pinchot. A similar irony is evident in the generation of writers before Darwin: as they appropriated the startling "new evidences" about the antiquity of the globe and the uniformity of nature, they also saw, many for the first time, that humankind was a significant geologic agent. Whitman bases many of his poems, such as "Passage to India," on humankind's global longing, on the theory that his age of energy was the first in which humanity could fully transform the world with its railroads, steamships, and transatlantic cables into a new earth governed by human design. Instead of isolating humanity's many attempts to transform parts of the wilderness into select cities of god, these early environmental writers spoke of humankind's destiny to inhabit the entire globe.

Many early-nineteenth-century writers were fascinated by the motility and strength of the human species, and a series of treatises was published on humanity's dominion of the globe. Albert Brisbane summarized the opinion of thousands of land speculators, resource businessmen, and writers when he wrote in *The Social Destiny of Man*:

> The terrestrial Destiny of man is to oversee the globe, which is a vast domain confided to his care. This important trust supposes a general and perfect cultivation of its surface, the fertilizing of its deserts, the draining of its swamps and morasses, the covering of its mountains with forests, the regulating of its streams—in short, the adorning and embellishing of it by every means in his strength and intelligence. (239)

This estimate of nature becomes an undeniable part of America's material culture, evidenced by the gridiron that spread across the West as the natural tool of the land speculator and auctioneer. Many felt this idea of globalization noteworthy in itself: thus a series of pamphlets were written, such as Samuel Tayler's *Treatise on Scientific Method* (1844), that attempted "to give some account of the philosophy of utility—the philosophy of lightning rods, of steam engines, safety lamps, spinning jennies and cotton gins,—the philosophy which has covered the barren hills and the sterile rocks in verdure, and deserts with fertility" (Brush 138).

There was a second strand of American writers, represented by Melville's conviction that the West was being dominated by a false "metaphysics of Indian-hating" (Drinnon, pref.) that maintained that the possibilities of this power and control over nature should be based on trust, not conquest. For them, humanity's exploitation of the earth was accountable to forces higher than self-interest. People were, in fact, responsible to the earth both as an object of worship and as the source of knowledge. Others argued that the construction of the universe was in itself sufficient warrant for profound patience and respect. Although humankind had been given tremendous power to change the face of the earth, our greatest asset, according to writers like George Marsh and Henry David Thoreau, rested in our ability to manage, to restrict, and to deliberate. Elaborating upon the biblical image of the good shepherd, these writers conceived of humanity's place as a stewardship—where the capacities of the appointed "manager" is tempered by a delegated trust. Although a profit is expected from one's time with the earth, the steward must be equitable for he or she may be called upon when least expected. We now recognize that the value of this metaphor lies in its projection of a human-guided rather than a human-dominated nature; but it is ironic that this conception of humankind as a steward of the earth gained ground in American letters at a time when most Americans first dreamed that humanity could be a forceful global agent. The instances of this worldview are rare in the nineteenth century; but they have become even more infrequent since the advent of Darwin.

American Literary Environmentalism, 1864–1920

Frederick O. Waage

As a young man the famous American naturalist and writer John Muir fled from Wisconsin to Canada with his brothers to avoid being drafted into the Union Army. When he returned at war's end, he rejoined a nation moving into a culminative period of tension involving its identity and destiny. A long dialectic of ideology and experience between "wilderness" and "civilization" reached a heated point, with the wilderness of the West being discovered, described, investigated, idealized at the same time that it was being destroyed and with the same energies. Urbanization and technological development accelerated at the same pace as a new critique of the social and economic effects of overcivilization.

This tension between contrary goods seems to have been a creative one in that it launched, as well as imaginative acts of policy that sought to reconcile wilderness and civilization (the establishment of the first national park, Yellowstone in 1872, of the National Forest Service in 1905, etc.), imaginative efforts in literature, painting, and photography to understand and communicate the nature of American nature and its relation with civilization. The following pages discuss some of the major figures and movements in the imaginative interpretation of the American environment between 1864 and 1920.

George Perkins Marsh

Marsh was a Vermont lawyer, entrepreneur, and statesman whose ideal of the Renaissance Man (more appropriately that of Emerson's American Scholar) achieved fruition in his *Man and Nature; or, Physical Geography as Modified by Human Action* (1864). His tenure as American minister to Turkey, 1848–54, and to Italy, 1861–82, combined with voracious scholarship and polylinguistic ability, allowed him to gain a cosmopolitan knowledge of world affairs unequaled in his time. His novelty was to apply this knowledge not solely to political and economic enterprise, nor to traditional scholarly pursuits, but to human effects on the natural world just at the time when a collective and permanent effect of human production and transportation systems on nature could first be observed. *Man and Nature* defines an end and a beginning: the end of any surviving mythology of America (or World) as an unspoiled and unspoilable Eden of innocence and the beginning of a concern for America's (and the World's) land and water as both finite and vulnerable.

Although *Man and Nature* (republished, in somewhat expanded form, in 1874, with its subtitle as title) is not often considered a "literary" work, I believe it is "literary" in the sense that Burton's *Anatomy of Melancholy* or

Flaubert's *Bouvard et Pécuchet* is: it is a nondramatic, conceptually macaronic epic, in which phenomena and ideas, rather than specific individuals, are the heroic and antiheroic movers. It contains a general introduction to human effects on nature; then discussion of effects on four elemental categories of earth phenomena—vegetable and animal life, woodlands, waters, and deserts; finally, a projection of these effects into the human future on the planet. "The whole force of *Man and Nature*," says David Lowenthal, "lies in its assumption that the welfare of future generations matters more than any immediate considerations" (xxvi). Complementing this visionary quality is a language of remarkable precision and eloquence. At times Marsh can take on the learned poetic diction of a Sir Thomas Browne; at other times he can be direct and prophetic.

Marsh's book made a great impression at its publication and in subsequent years; the first acts of wilderness preservation in our country immediately postdate it. In the 1930s and subsequently, the accuracy and prophetic nature of its ecological vision have been fully substantiated.

Powell and the Surveyors

After the Civil War, the conjunction of unemployed military professionals needing new worlds to conquer and new professional natural scientists produced some of the best environmental writing of the nineteenth century. This was through the private and public geological, geographic, and ethnographic surveys of the trans-Mississippi West, which employed the combined labors of physical and natural scientists, artists, and photographers and resulted in descriptive volumes of verbal and visual magnificence. In their public manifestation, these volumes are found in, or associated with, the proceedings and publications of the United States National Museum (the Smithsonian), the bulletins and annual reports of the United States Bureau of American Ethnology, and the annual reports of the United States Geological and Geographical Surveys of the Territories. Since many of the surveyors were both humanistically and scientifically literate and since professional jargon was not yet highly developed, the texts of surveys from the 1860s through the 1890s often combine precision of observation with romanticism of vision and expression.

The vital center of these epical environmental assessments was Civil War major John Wesley Powell, whose daring navigations of the unknown Colorado River in 1869 and 1870–71 made him a national hero and eventually director of both the newly founded United States Geological Survey and the Smithsonian's Bureau of Ethnology.

As well as dominating the political and environmental arenas of western survey and development until his forced resignation from the USGS in 1894, Powell also held a more enlightened view of the stewardship of America's natural resources than did most of his peers. He favored controlled and limited human development of natural areas and a centralized, unified plan for the agricultural and industrial exploitation of the West. Too many interest groups, from individual farmers to state governments to great railroad and mining organizations, profited from fragmented control of this development, and Powell's ideas could not prevail.

Powell is best known as a nature writer for two works. *The Exploration of the Colorado River of the West and Its Tributaries* (1875), chronicling the adventures of his two expeditions, was first published as a series by *Scribner's Magazine* in 1874–75 and, after its more scientifically oriented consolidation in 1875, in expanded form as *Canyons of the Colorado* (1895). More influential and as striking in its writing, although less well known because of its lack of an adventure narrative, is his *Report on the Lands of the Arid Region of the United States* (1878).

Powell's *Exploration* takes the form of a journal, and Powell drew on journals and memories of the expedition's other participants to create its complex sense of immediacy and distance, of involvement in the suspenseful fate of the adventurers and of the timeless indifference of their environment. A single passage in the contemplative mode ("Clouds are playing in the canyon today . . . ," 69) can give a sense of Powell's art. Here, with the overt subjectivity of only a single metaphor, Powell manages to weave observed details into a structure of transcendence, wherein a space of utmost confinement is uplifted into a condition of utmost freedom.

Equally remarkable as a writing scientist was Powell's eccentric, inexhaustible contemporary, Clarence King. After two years of studying geology at the new Yale Scientific School, King went on to a life of incredible adventure and imaginative exploration of the West, beginning where John Muir did—in Yosemite and the southern Sierras. From his early explorations alone and with independent surveys, to his appointment in 1867 to direct his own Geological Exploration of the Fortieth Parallel, to his appointment as the first director of the new USGS, and to numerous subsequent mining and cattle-raising ventures all over western North America, King was rarely still. Although many of his uncollected writings are of great interest, he completed only two books, while always maintaining the unfulfilled desire to be a novelist. One of these is the meticulous textbook *Systematic Geology* (1878), published as part of the final report of the Fortieth Parallel expedition. The other one is a great American nature book, *Mountaineering in the Sierra Nevada* (1872), most of whose chapters were originally published as articles in the *Atlantic Monthly*. *Mountaineering* combines fabulized, suspenseful tales of King's explorations in the Sierra with unequaled nature descriptions and studies of the marginal and migrant native and nonnative human culture surviving "on the edge" along this final frontier. King can dramatize both human and nonhuman nature with a stroke and place human responses in subtle juxtaposition to the outward phenomena the people are experiencing, fusing the scientific and aesthetic perceptions of nature.

The final member of the most prominent trinity of literary surveyors was Capt. Clarence Edward Dutton of the USGS. Of the several reports he collaboratively wrote, the most important and influential is his *Tertiary History of the Grand Canyon District* (1882), the first USGS monograph, prepared while Dutton was one of the four western regional directors of Clarence King's first survey. The *Tertiary History* is a magnificent volume;

Dutton's prose, which makes geology scenic without ceasing to be geology (ix), collaborates with the work of three great western artists: photographer Jack Hillers and artists Thomas Moran and William Henry Holmes. As Wallace Stegner says, "later specialization has eliminated from scientific publications most of the elements that make the *Tertiary History* so charming" (xiii).

Starr King, Muir, and Mills

The dominant and most familiar name among all nature writers of our period is that of John Muir (1838–1914). Muir wrote his first complete book at the age of fifty-six, was elected president of the newly founded Sierra Club at age fifty-four, and was active as a lobbyist for wilderness preservation only in his last two decades. The creative and activist work for which he is popularly recognized today was a late outgrowth of a deeper, lifelong, more solitary immersion in active and contemplative living in the wilderness itself—or, in violent contrast, during his "silent decade" of the 1880s, the first decade of his marriage, of his immersion in commercial enterprise as a fruit grower. Although Muir was deeply influenced by Thoreau's writing, as well as by Emerson's "Nature" and Emerson himself, whom he hosted in a famous encounter at Yosemite in 1871, his transcendental language and vision of nature owe as much or more to the work of his own imagination upon his own experience.

Likewise, although Muir is popularly identified with Yosemite and the contiguous mountains of California, as both subject of concern and literal and figurative homeland, he sought and enjoyed urban and urbane life no less, particularly in his later years. He explored and wrote about different wilderness areas of the United States, although he was not the first writer and publicist to bring the beauties of Yosemite Valley to public attention. His significant predecessor was Thomas Starr King (1824–64), a Harvard-educated Boston Universalist clergyman. As one of many transcendentalizing frequenters of upper New England in the earlier nineteenth century, King wrote an original, expansive, lyrical guide to the White Mountains of New Hampshire, *The White Hills: Their Legends, Landscape, and Poetry* (1860). Then he accepted a call to head a new Unitarian congregation in San Francisco and immediately on his arrival (in the summer of 1860) embarked on an expedition to the western Sierras and the newly discovered valley called Yo Semite. On his return, he composed letters to the *Boston Transcript*, describing with awe the natural wonders he had witnessed (the letters were published together only in 1962, as *A Vacation among the Sierras: Yosemite in 1860*). King's vivid letters created a tremendous response in the East and seem to have given the Yosemite Valley a certain status both spiritual and emblematic upon which Muir could work. As Paul Brooks notes, it was only a few months after King's death, on 25 June 1864, that Congress reserved Yosemite as "inalienable" territory, for public use, "the first such act in our history" (*Speaking for Nature* 42).

John Muir's own publications derived their growing influence on attitudes toward western wilderness from their wide periodical audience.

He first wrote for the influential *Overland Monthly*, after that magazine's demise for eastern periodicals such as *Harper's* and *Scribner's*, and, following his silent period of the eighties, for the *Century* of his friend and ally Robert Underwood Johnson.

Actually, though, his first full-length work was the journal of his famous hike from Indianapolis to Cedar Key, Florida, in 1867, published posthumously as *A Thousand-Mile Walk to the Gulf* (1916), and in fragments, with the photographs of a contemporary retracer, in John Earl's *John Muir's Longest Walk* (1975). This journal, although obviously reworked by the author, already manifests his quality in language and observation of what one might call "mystical precision." It also stands out for its understated, alert interweaving of postbellum southern social observation with that of nature.

Muir's next "book" (in terms of self-conscious composition) was the lavishly illustrated collection of essays he assembled and published in 1888, *Picturesque California and the Region West of the Rocky Mountains, from Alaska to Mexico* (reprinted in 1976, with a preface by Richard Nicholls, as *West of the Rocky Mountains*). Containing essays by Muir and others, including his patron Jeanne Carr, his future Yosemite antagonist John P. Irish, and the notorious poet Joaquin Miller, and more than sixty illustrations, *Picturesque California* was "the first large-scale attempt to present to the American people a thorough description of the mountains, forests, deserts, wildlife, and people of the western half of the nation" (pref.). It may be considered a regional version of the nationalistic "panorama" volume such as William Cullen Bryant's influential *Picturesque America; or, The Land We Live In* (1872–74). With each chapter devoted to one significant western topographical area, it has an aesthetic shape as a whole, verbalizing the cultural and natural landscape from Canada to Mexico.

Muir's alliance with *Century* (and later with Houghton Mifflin) led to a series of complete volumes, composed in many cases of previously published periodical essays. The first of these was *The Mountains of California* (1894; enlarged edition, 1911), the last in his lifetime the autobiographical *Story of My Boyhood and Youth* (1913), which was originally written at the time of his walk to the Gulf. Included in the volume is his only work of fiction, the autobiographical *Stickeen* (1897 version, published in 1909), a narrative of a heroic companion dog that also engages the question of anthropocentrism by challenging the author's own principled aversion to personification.

Muir's *Mountains of California, My First Summer in the Sierra* (1911), *The Yosemite* (1912), and *Travels in Alaska* (1915) are deeply textured descriptive works, fusing accuracy of observation, subjective adventure narrative, and subtle imagistic prose that often focuses so exhaustively on a single phenomenon that, without the slightest recourse to abstract language, the phenomenon becomes epiphenomenal. For Muir, the true spirituality of the natural world could be apprehended only through concentration on the natural world itself, could be approached only from "below." Thus, in *The Mountains of California*, he can describe "snow-banners" in objective language describing specific configurations of the mountain peaks from which the storm winds toss them and in ecstatic incantational language pervaded by the human's emotional experience of the banners (*Wilderness Essays* 100–01).

As Muir's writing evolved, in his last years, toward more sustained literary modes, it also moved with his own orientation toward advocacy and political involvement. There is an intriguing rhetorical tension among the roles of observer, celebrator, and advocate that Muir plays with in later writings. *Our National Parks* (1901) mingles description and advocacy in the stronger interest of the latter. John of the mountains, come down from the mountains to contemplate more transient and humanly modifiable phenomena, sounds much like George Perkins Marsh but speaks in a voice of even greater urgency: "In the noblest forests of the world, the ground, once divinely beautiful, is desolate and repulsive, like a face ravaged by disease. . . . The same fate, sooner or later, is awaiting them all, unless awakening public opinion comes forward to stop it" (5–6). The detailed survey of *The Yosemite* leads up to a strong final chapter against "despoiling gain-seekers and mischief-makers of every degree from Satan to Senators, eagerly trying to make everything immediately and selfishly commercial . . ." (198).

Works published posthumously have added greatly to Muir's canon. These include the writings whose publication he directed himself, the Sierra Edition of his works (1917–24), his life and letters (1923–24), and his unpublished journals (1938). Despite his fame, influence, and extensive literary production, remarkably little study has been done of Muir's actual writings themselves and of his art as a literary naturalist.

More neglected than Muir's, and as interesting, is the writing of Enos Mills (1870–1922), the "Muir of the Rockies" (see Wild 71–80). At fourteen, Mills left his native Kansas for Colorado and built a cabin near the Continental Divide; at nineteen, wandering in California, he met John Muir in Golden Gate Park. Apparently inspired, he returned to the Rockies and began writing and lecturing to urban audiences on the nature of the mountains. Starting in 1905 with the self-published *Story of Estes Park*, Mills wrote sixteen books about American wilderness areas and numerous periodical photo essays, many of which were directed toward young people. Mills wooed the young into environmental consciousness while their parents stayed at his Long's Peak Inn, which was run much in the same manner and on the same Rousseauean premises pursued by Ernest Thompson Seton with his Seton Indians.

A good example of Mills's writing for children is *The Story of a Thousand-Year Pine and Other Tales of Wild Life* (1909). The autobiography of the pine's life through the centuries, told by its rings, is striking and imaginative and, I believe, the source of Aldo Leopold's famous "Good Oak" chapter in *A Sand County Almanac*, which redirects the same device. Mills is a stylist of drama in nature and even in this book paces language and subject in subtle and expressive ways.

An example of Mills's adult writing is his own later version of Muir's *Our National Parks, Your National Parks* (1917). The "your" may suggest the degree of establishment identity the parks had achieved by the sunset of the progressive environmentalist era. Mills's book is an even more interesting mixture of lyrical description, environmentalist advocacy, and epigrammatic polemic: "No nation has ever fallen from having too much scenery" (xi). As Peter Wild notes, Mills compromised Muir's vision of nature's integrity in the interest of seducing a "Victorian" popular audience to support wilderness preservation. Yet as a writer he used personification and sentimental appeals with wit and literary mastery.

John Burroughs

John Burroughs is the equal, and in some ways opposite, of John Muir, though they are coequal as the dominant nature writers of their time. A journal comment on Muir's visit to Burroughs' Riverby house in 1896 suggests some of their empathy and difference. "He is a poet," says Burroughs of Muir,

> and almost a seer; something ancient and far-away in the look of his eyes. He could not sit down in a corner of the landscape, as Thoreau did; he must have a continent for his playground. . . . He has done many foolish, foolhardy things I think; that is, thrown away his strength without proper return. . . . Probably the truest lover of Nature as she appears in woods, mountains, glaciers, we have yet had. (*Journals* 192–93)

Burroughs emulated Thoreau in this contrast. Both in his aversion to extreme experience as source of insight into nature and in his ultimate self-definition as a "writer" on all aspects of culture as well as natural history, he differs from Muir. Yet they were "comrades," shared the same values and commitments, wrote in the same modes, and accepted the same transcendental literary and philosophical heritage. It is not often recognized today that, particularly through his wide adoption as a model in primary and secondary school English curricula beginning in 1887 (see Westbrook 91), Burroughs was for several decades one of the most familiar, famous, and admired of living Americans, at least in his own country. Perhaps the recent diminution of his influence on American attitudes toward the environment is due to his major genre—the essay—and to the lack of a flashpoint of social activity such as the preservationist crusades that made Muir famous.

Also, Burroughs is often more prominent in literary history as an acolyte of Walt Whitman than as his own person. His early and late books on Whitman, *Notes on Walt Whitman* and *Whitman: A Study*, and his tireless praise of and friendship with him were profoundly influential. Burroughs' Whitman, the "poet of the cosmos," is a philosophical naturalist. Since the Whitman he describes contains and understands all of nature, anyone who appreciates nature in a holistic or ecological sense must appreciate Whitman as a modern "mirror of nature." Whitman incarnates, for Burroughs, a union between the realm of human culture, originating in the human imagination, and all that is nonhuman (see, e.g., *Accepting the Universe*, *Works* 21: esp. 322–23).

Burroughs' own career exhibits the inclusiveness of contraries. Born on a New York farm, greatly self-educated, variously employed in rural teaching and clerkships, he wrote first for the urban and avant-garde New York *Saturday Press*. During the Civil War years, the fulcrum of his career, he moved to Washington, consorted with Walt Whitman, and worked for the Treasury Department. Yet it was in the early 1870s, when he retreated to the rural area of his birth, built Riverby on the Hudson shore, and published his first book of nature essays, *Wake-Robin* (1871), that his period of national fame began. In this span of fifty years, to his death, Burroughs issued a continuous flood of books, on multiple aspects of human civilization but preponderately on the natural environment and human relationships with it. The essays in these books rise, as did Thoreau's published writing, from a series of journals as detailed and extensive as his, which Burroughs kept from 1876 to 1921; excerpts from them have been published in Clara Barrus' *The Heart of Burroughs's Journals* (1928). Works particularly directed toward environmental concerns include, as well as *Wake-Robin*, *Winter Sunshine* (1875); *Pepacton* (1881), in which Burroughs reenacts Thoreau's voyage on the Concord and Merrimack rivers on his own rivers; *Signs and Seasons* (1886); *Riverby* (1894); *Ways of Nature* (1905), which elaborates on his position in the famous "nature fakers" controversy of 1903 wherein he, seconded by Roosevelt, attacked Ernest Thompson Seton and William J. Long for "humaniz[ing] the wild life about [them]"; *Leaf and Tendril* (1908); and *Field and Study* (1919).

Mary Hunter Austin

Mary Austin is often considered in a trinity with Muir and Burroughs. Like John Muir, she identified much of her life with the western United States, particularly, in her earlier creative years (c. 1890–1905), with the Owens Valley in eastern California, and in her later ones (1924–34) with New Mexico. Like Muir she was an active environmentalist, engaged in saving Owens Valley water from Los Angeles' water system as he was in saving that of the Hetch Hetchy Valley from San Francisco's; later she was an active delegate to the Second Colorado River Conference on Southwest water resources in 1927. Her first writing, like Muir's, was published in the *Overland Monthly*. Like Burroughs, Mary Austin was a cosmopolite in action: she was a European traveler, an inhabitant, novelist, and playwright of avant-garde New York, and a founder of two famous literary-artistic colonies—Carmel, California, and Taos, New Mexico. Her celebrated familiars ranged from Lincoln Steffens to D. H. Lawrence. She was also, however, something neither Muir nor Burroughs could or would be—an ardent feminist, whose assertion of women's rights was intimately tied to her assertion of universal human dependence on the earth as Mother.

In her strong autobiography, *Earth Horizon* (1932), Austin traces the unfolding of her life as an ordained pattern: ". . . it was clear that I would write imaginatively, not only of people, but of the scene, the totality which is called Nature, and that I would give myself intransigently to the quality of experience called Folk, and to the frame of behavior known as Mystical" (vii). Her childhood moment of revelation under a walnut tree has become famous as a birth of "environmental awareness" (371).

Austin's acknowledged chef d'oeuvre as an environmental writer is her collection of essays *Land of Little Rain* (1903), very similar in organization and intent to *Walden*—only Austin's corner of the earth is dry, the region of Owens Valley, between the Sierras and the Nevada desert. In separate chapters with titles such as "My Neighbor's Field," "The Streets of the Mountains," and "Water Borders," she explores the ecosystem of this desert and the difficulties and successes of those humans who have sought to adapt themselves to it. "Go as far as you dare in the heart of a lonely land, you cannot go so far that life and death are not before you" (13). One of her subjects of meditation in these essays is the role the desert takes on in the human imagination, particularly the "tragic key" it falls into so often—and, by contrast, how full of untragic life it actually is. In this emphasis Austin is the founder of a lineage of desert writers, notably, in two subsequent generations, Joseph Wood Krutch and Edward Abbey.

Not only is there a mirroring of Thoreau's subjects in *Land of Little Rain* (the "neighbor's field" is akin to Thoreau's bean field, and the "pocket hunter," who survives on his own resources, seems to be her version of his "animal man," the Canadian woodchopper), but there is a style as subtle and studied as his that seems worked to communicate the topography, the "earth horizon" of the desert.

As someone engaged in the preservation of a threatened desert, Austin can be ironic about the human actions antagonistic to its survival. But she can also praise John Muir, not for his preservationist activity, but for being a "devout man," a nonintervenor in the actions of the "Spirit moving in the void" (247) to create such things as storms. We must remember of course that this is an ironic Spirit—it is "the experienceable quality in the universe" (*Earth Horizon* 371). In fact, a strong feature of Austin's nature writing is a paradox of both knowledge expounded and ignorance prized.

The skepticism of both knowledge and ignorance of nature ties in with her idealization of Native American life and culture, whose defense was a vital cause throughout her life: "The Indian never concerns himself, as the botanist and the poet, with the plant's appearances and relations, but with what it can do for him" (*Land* 233). The Native Americans' life, like their art, is, as it were, expressionistic, not impressionistic; it is arranged along what in her pioneering ethnomusicological work *The American Rhythm* (1923, 1930) she calls "the landscape line, the line shaped by its own inner necessities" (54). Much of her environmental writing, in fact, explores the harmony of nature and southwestern Indian culture as a touchstone for white self-examination. This is true in her adult novels such as *Isidro* (1905), in children's fiction such as *One-Smoke Stories* (1934), in experimental-primitivist dramas such as *The Arrow Maker* (1911). A remarkable example of interwoven Spanish–Native American cultural history and environmental study is *The Land of Journey's Ending* (1924), based on her work surveying the culture of the Taos area for the Carnegie Foundation (see Pearce 49).

Many of Mary Austin's other writings are expressive of contemporary environmental literature's concerns and of strong literary interest in their own right. *The Flock* (1906) and *Lost Borders* (1909) are prose writings forming a trilogy with *Land of Little Rain*. *The Ford* (1917) is a dramatic novel of ideas based on her experience with the attempt to divert Owens River water to Los Angeles. It is a true "environmental novel" like those of Edward Abbey or John Nichols, dramatizing the issues involved in the choice between development and preservation. Finally, *Outland* (1910) anticipates Ernest Callenbach's *Ecotopia* (1975) as an allegorical vision of a conflict between the Outliers, people who live in harmony with nature, and the House-folk who invade their land.

Easterners

The year 1864, the date of *Man and Nature* and of the reservation of Yosemite from private development, is also that of the climaxing development of Central Park in New York City. The park's guiding hand was that of Frederick Law Olmsted, who also was the first president of the commission mandated to administer the Yosemite reservation. Olmsted and other eastern environmentalists of varying professions and comfortable backgrounds (among them Gifford Pinchot, launched as a forester on Olmsted's Biltmore project) promoted an ambiguously grounded yet deeply influential preservationist direction. Olmsted, the city planner and landscape architect, was caught in the middle between aristocratic preservationism limiting public access and "democratic" uncontrolled industrial development. Similarly, George Bird Grinnell and William Brewster, the Boone and Crockett Club conservationists, were, to differing degrees, part wildlife preservers and part aristocratic gentleman hunters.

Olmsted's aesthetic influence was profound, if ambiguous, even though his own strictly literary output was not great. His most sustained works are three volumes of *Journeys* into the United States interior and *Walks and Talks of an American Farmer in England* (1852, 1859). The latter defined his own ideals and future career. As Alex L. Murray writes, "Olmsted's career as a landscape architect can be seen in part as an attempt to bring joy and pleasure into the everyday lives of Americans through the influence of close contact with nature" (*Walks* xi). *Walks and Talks* sets vivid pictures of rural life and political and philosophical speculation against a background of natural observation. Olmsted might be seen as a respondent to Marsh's argument: human modification of the landscape can and should be done, but it must always be done as a collaboration of human art and nature, or, as he puts it, as an "encouragement" by art of nature to fulfill its inherent potential (*Civilizing* 208).

The relation of planning and natural preservation also emerged with the activities of a group of professional and amateur preservers and destroyers of wildlife in the 1880s. One branch of this development was the sequence of organizations launched with the 1873 founding by William Brewster of the Nuttall Ornithological Club, whose offshoot was the American Ornithological Union (1883). George Bird Grinnell, one of the members of the AOU's Committee for the Protection of North American Birds, was inspired to organize a more completely preservationist "Audubon Society." The society lasted only two years (1887–89), but its precedent allowed the first successful eastern conservation organization, the current Audubon Society, to be founded in 1896 with William Brewster as president.

The other branch was the organization under Theodore Roosevelt's patronage in 1887 of the Boone and Crockett Club, in which Grinnell and other conservationists were moving figures even though its goal was the preservation of game animals for amateur hunting. Nature writing was a central force in the influence these groups had on public environmental awareness, through periodicals like *Audubon* and Grinnell's *Forest and Stream* and through books by individuals and groups, such as *Musk Ox, Bison, Sheep, and Goat*, by Grinnell, Caspar Whitney, and Owen Wister (1904), or *Hunting and Conservation: The Book of the Boone and Crockett Club*, edited by Grinnell and Charles Sheldon (1925).

The individuals prominent in these efforts wrote works of lasting significance. William Brewster's writing was posthumously published in *October Farm* (1936) and *Concord River* (1937). George Bird Grinnell was a prodigious activist and gifted writer. His life's direction inspired by Audubon, with whose family he had grown up, Grinnell became a western adventurer, paleontologist and faculty member of the Yale Scientific School (Clarence King's alma mater), and editor of *Forest and Stream* magazine, from which vantage point he had significant influence on Theodore Roosevelt and American conservation policy. Besides innumerable magazine articles and stories he wrote many books—on wildlife (e.g., *American Big Game and Its Haunts*, 1904), on Native American culture and folklore (e.g., *Blackfoot Lodge Tales*, 1926), and on cultural impacts on the environment (*When Buffalo Ran*, 1920).

While Grinnell favored noncommercial hunting, William Temple Hornaday, the great preservationist and opponent of Boone and Crockett conservation, could write in *Thirty Years War for Wild Life: Gains and Losses in the Thankless Task* (1931), "Ten years ago no man could have convinced the writer that the hardest warfare of his life for the rights of game would be waged with men called 'conservationists,' bent upon maintaining the big killing privileges of millions of game hunters" (ix). Hornaday, director of the New York Zoological Park, in his vigorous writing and lobbying angered many conservative conservationists but anticipated the philosophy and rhetoric of contemporary environmentalism.

Roosevelt

Within the popularly recognized roles of Theodore Roosevelt as game hunter and progressive conservationist is an often-ignored substance of impressive environmental writing, often disguised by book titles such as *Hunting Trips of a Ranchman* (*Works*, vol. 1) that do not accurately characterize the rich nature description the books contain. Roosevelt's devotion to hunting has also been characterized in a polarized context as a blot on his political record, rather than as in harmony with it.

But Roosevelt's interest in natural history took precedence over all others in his life. In his *Autobiography* he writes, "When I entered college, I was devoted to out-of-doors natural history, and my ambition was to be a scientific man of the Audubon, or Wilson, or Baird, or Coues type—a man like Hart Merriam, or Frank Chapman, or Hornaday, to-day" (*Works* 20: 25–26). The literary naturalist became a Rooseveltian ideal: "among those men whom I have known the love of books and the love of outdoors, in their highest expressions, have usually gone hand in hand" (308).

An essay crucial to Roosevelt's literary environmentalism is his 1910

Romanes Lecture, "Biological Analogies in History." Roosevelt's analogies are based on the belief "that as the field of science encroaches on the field of literature there should be a corresponding encroachment of literature upon science. . . . We need a literature of science which shall be readable" (*History* 43). With the premise of this interdisciplinary approach, Roosevelt examines the "strange analogies in the phenomena of life and death, of birth, growth, and change, between those physical groups of animal life which we designate as species, forms, and races, and the highly complex and composite entities which rise before our minds when we speak of nations and civilizations" (40–41). By elaborating on the subjection of human cultures to the same forces that govern the life histories of other organisms in the ecosphere, Roosevelt in effect articulates an "environmental ethic" in advance of Aldo Leopold, Gregory Bateson, et al.

This vision of interdependence informs all of Roosevelt's nature writing. In *Hunting Trips of a Ranchman*, for example, discussion of hunting the black-tailed deer requires a study of the hunter's psychology, the geology and geography of the Badlands, and detailed behavioral observation ("life history") of the deer themselves. It includes a violent attack on the "brutal slaughter" worked by game butchers and skin hunters on the deer (*Works* 1: 12). *Ranch Life and the Hunting Trail* (*Works*, vol. 1) describes in great detail the frontier hunting and farming cultures in their interaction with their environment. *The Wilderness Hunter* and *Outdoor Pastimes of an American Hunter* (*Works*, vol. 2), the latter dedicated to John Burroughs, frame descriptions of hunting expeditions with a celebration of the American wilderness.

Bailey and the Naturalists

Both amateur and professional American naturalists have been traditionally drawn to Theodore Roosevelt's recommended interfusion of literature and science. The progenitor of modern American descriptive natural history is surely John James Audubon, who was in a sense both an amateur and a professional. His journals and the texts of his *Ornithological Biography* (1831–39) and *The Quadrupeds of North America* (1845–53) contain remarkable narratives, strangely neglected by students of nineteenth-century American literature (though not by Robert Penn Warren, who based his *Audubon: A Vision* [1969] on them). Beside Audubon might be placed the writings of "true amateur" naturalists, among them the early and influential *A Summer in the Wilderness* (1847) and *Letters from the Allegheny Mountains* (1849) of Charles Lanman; *Life in the Open Air and Other Papers* (1863) by Col. Theodore Winthrop, Clarence King's youthful hero; and William H. H. Murray's *Adventures in the Wilderness; or, Camp-Life in the Adirondacks* (1869). Later unembarrassedly nonspecialized writers include Frank Bolles (*Land of the Lingering Snow* [1891]; *At the North of Bearcamp Water* [1893]) and Dallas Lore Sharp, whose writings for a younger audience, such as *A Watcher in the Woods* (1903), were as artful and influential as the stories of Ernest Thompson Seton.

American professional naturalists in the later nineteenth century, like the geologists and geographers of the surveys, still retained literary ability. Two ornithologists of different generations might be mentioned: Elliot Coues, whose texts (such as *Birds of the Northwest* [1874]) were published under survey auspices, and Frank M. Chapman, whose *Bird Life* (1900) was illustrated by Ernest Thompson Seton. A later American naturalist of literary pretensions and ability, William Beebe, became famous for global exploits, including his ocean-probing Bathysphere, described in *Half-Mile Down* (1934).

The naturalist whose literary work I find most arresting, though, is Liberty Hyde Bailey (1858–1954), who might be considered the scientific founder of American horticulture. Bailey was a professional writer before he gave his life to agricultural interests; he also maintained idealistic and pastoral attitudes toward the relations of human society and nature. He articulated and promoted vigorously a Jeffersonian vision of harmonious "country life" as materially and spiritually productive in speeches, in the Country-Life Commission, in his *Country Life in America* magazine, and in hortatory texts such as *The Outlook to Nature* (1905) and *The Country-Life Movement in the United States* (1911). Bailey urged a sort of nonregional agrarian ethic, but one placed in the given situation of threatened natural resources. Many of his writings exemplify the inseparability of the practical and the spiritual or aesthetic—from basically scientific texts such as *The Garden of Gourds* (1937) to a collection of poetry, *Wind and Weather* (1916). The latter and a number of his other writings constitute a series of what Bailey called "background books" expounding "the philosophy of the Holy Earth." The jewel in this crown of environmental writings is *The Holy Earth* itself (1915). As its semi-ironic name implies, it is a secular holy book, as it were an ecological sacred scripture, cast as a sermon on the primal text "In the beginning God created the heaven and the earth" and couched, initially, in ironically archaic diction:

> So bountiful hath been the earth and so securely have we drawn from it our substance, that we have taken it all for granted as if it were only a gift, and with little care of conscious thought of the consequences of our use of it; nor have we very much considered the essential relation that we bear to it as living parts in the vast creation. . . . (5)

Bailey, in his scripture, is not naively antiutilitarian. For example, he attacks social Darwinism not as a false philosophy but as a distortion of Darwin's own idea of a struggle for existence that included both mutual aid and enmity. And Bailey praises environmentally conscious technology. He also discusses the issue of environmental literature, arguing in favor of affective scientific writing: literature that is the "expression of personality," not the "product" of "perfected organizations" that "has all the hardness of its origin." It is the former that is "naturally the literature of freedom" (86).

Thoreau's Afterlife

It is well known that Henry David Thoreau's writing had only a limited audience of appreciators in his lifetime and that most of what we today define as the Thoreau canon was unknown and unpublished. Whether accepting or skeptical, all the great nature writers of our period were deeply influenced by the writings of Thoreau and the Concord transcendentalists. But it is striking to observe how, after three decades of partial neglect, Thoreau's writing and writing about Thoreau suddenly burst in great quantities on the American public in the 1890s. It would be hard to prove, but it seems quite possible that Thoreau influenced at this time not only literary folk but the progressive conservationist movement as a whole.

Francis Allen's 1908 bibliography of Thoreau, itself one of the manifestations of this development, tells the story of Thoreau's rediscovery graphically. The first American edition of *Walden* subsequent to the 1854 edition was published by Houghton Mifflin in 1889. Then between 1889 and 1906 nine various editions were issued. *A Week on the Concord and Merrimack Rivers* had three editions up to 1868, then five between 1889 and 1900. A crucial date in Thoreau awareness is 1894, which saw the publication of the Riverside Edition of Thoreau's collected writings. His *Familiar Letters* were published in 1896. In 1906 followed the twenty-volume Manuscript edition and the Walden edition (both edited by the naturalist Bradford Torrey), which included for the first time Thoreau's journals.

Much of the outpouring of writing *about* Thoreau's life and work in the 1890s and 1900s seems, paradoxical though this may appear to us now, to involve the rehabilitation of his reputation. The perfect expression of this collective change of heart is found on the first pages of Alexander Japp's *Thoreau: His Life and Aims* (1901). "Till within a few years ago the name of Thoreau stood to me for morbid sentiment, weak rebellion, and contempt for society," says Japp. Through frequent contact, however, he discovered

> that, in spite of an outer coating of stoicism and protest, he was true and tender of heart; that, though he was sometimes extreme in his expressions of dislike for the artificial make-believes of modern society, he loved individual men, and most that which was individual in them . . . ; that his love of nature and his power over animals, which were so express and characteristic in him, did not lead him to sour retreat from society, but rather to seek a new point of relation to it, by which a return might be possible and profitable. . . . (vii)

Japp's new attitude toward Thoreau might characterize the new progressive environmental consciousness of the time itself: concern with nature as a new way of envisioning society, not as a rejection of it.

As well as interpretive books such as Japp's, there were many other publications of the time devoted to bringing to life the real presence of the "poet-naturalist." Examples of these are Samuel Arthur Jones's *Pertaining to Thoreau* (1901), which reprints rare early contemporary commentary on his work, and Frederick Sanborn's edition of William Ellery Channing's memoir *Thoreau the Poet-Naturalist* (1902). Also to be noted is Sanborn's biography in the American Men of Letters Series (1882), whose successor, in another series with the same title, was by Joseph Wood Krutch, himself a poet-naturalist in the master's vein.

Seton and Others

Lee Clark Mitchell, in his *Witnesses to a Vanishing America: The Nine-teenth-Century Response*, discusses in great detail two (among other) broad categories of environmental writing, rich in works of significance, but which there is no space to discuss in detail here.

The first is white writing about Native American life and culture, from a sympathetic point of view. Mitchell shows how deeply rooted is the pro-Indian attitude among nineteenth-century white writers. An inspiring fig-ure in this tradition is George Catlin, with his paintings and writings such as *Letters and Notes on the Manners, Customs, and Conditions of the North American Indians* (1844). The work that opened the way for associating aggression against American nature with aggression against native inhab-itants was Helen Hunt Jackson's *A Century of Dishonor: A Sketch of the United States Government's Dealings with Some of the Indian Tribes* (1881). The estab-lishment of the Smithsonian's Bureau of American Ethnology (1879) ini-tiated the subsidy of many writings about Native American life. Two other figures worth particular notice are Edward S. Curtis, whose monumental photographic-ethnographic *The North American Indian . . .* covered twenty volumes and twenty-three years (1907–30), and Charles Eastman, who wrote sensitively about Native American life in such books as *From the Deep Woods to Civilization: Chapters in the Autobiography of an Indian* (1916).

A second category of environmental writing in our period is "frontier" narratives. The initiating figure in this tradition might be considered Francis Parkman, with many works to his credit, particularly *The Oregon Trail: Sketches of Prairie and Rocky Mountain Life* (1872). The philosopher of west-ward expansion and frontier creation is William Gilpin (*The Mission of the North American People* [1874]). The elegist is Frederick Jackson Turner, with his famous paper "The Significance of the Frontier in American History," read in 1893 and collected with others in *The Frontier in American History* (1920). In his preface to this volume, written in 1920, Turner clearly sees an end to a particular definition of America involving the domination of nonhuman nature.

A final environmental writer of considerable significance is Ernest Thompson Seton (1860–1946), such a universal man that it is hard to as-sociate him with a particular literary direction or even with a particular life activity. Growing up on the edge of the Canadian wilderness, he developed an extreme preservationist ethic that at times became misanthropic, yet he engaged in much humanitarian activity as well. He was the greatest nature artist of his time, illustrating his own books and those of many other nature writers. Famous now for his children's stories of animals, he was a prolific and talented author of volumes and articles for all sorts of audiences and an indefatigable publicist of environmental awareness. Finally, he founded the Seton Indians, an organization dedicated to bringing young people up in this awareness, in groups modeled on Native American tribal life; his organization—plagiarized, distorted, and co-opted by a British military officer named Baden-Powell—became the Boy Scouts of America. Seton's writing must be studied as "literature," not just as "children's literature," for its expression is mature and complex. Seton may be considered in concert with his fellow Canadian environmental fiction writer Sir Charles G. D. Roberts (*The Watchers of the Trails* [1904]), the American novelist Gene Stratton-Porter (*The Song of the Cardinal* [1903]), his fellow "nature-faker" (in Burroughs' view) William J. Long (*School of the Woods: Some Life Studies of Animal Instincts and Animal Training* [1903]), and the artist Frederic Remington (*Pony Tracks*, 1895); all are fiction writers with an overtly environmental concern.

The Nature Book in Action*

Richard G. Lillard

The traditional nature book is a nonfiction work that is lyrical, informational, and apolitical. As a type it began in the eighteenth century along with the romantic movement, which has never ended, and modern biological science, which is now competing in impact with the inorganic sciences. It has had steady authorship and readership in Western Europe and in North America, especially in England and the northeastern United States. The nature book flourishes anew in the era of environmental concern and color photography. Since it deals with seemingly eternal life processes broader by far than the doings of *Homo sapiens*, it is not obsolescent as perhaps industrial humankind is with its obsession for the immediate moment. The nature book concerns itself with phenomena that take their own time, with self-perpetuating activities that go on without help or notice from human beings.

Nowadays the nature book, newly invigorated, hybridizes with the conservationist battle book and its black-and-white photographs of poisoned mammals in contorted postures, muddy, littered slopes that once held forests, and turgid streams clogged with dead fish, belly up. Mild or embattled, the nature book fits easily into the reading lists and the discussion time of many English courses. It can serve as a basis for separate courses, for interdisciplinary programs, or for richly appropriate colloquiums on humanity's place amid natural things—on its proper role on land, at sea, and in the air.

Examples are Sally Carrighar's *One Day on Teton Marsh*, laid in Wyoming; Joseph Wood Krutch's *The Desert Year*, in Arizona; Helen Hoover's *A Place in the Woods*, in Minnesota; Henry Beston's *The Outermost House*, a Cape Cod classic; Josephine W. Johnson's *The Inland Island*, set on an abandoned Ohio farm; and John G. Samson's *The Pond*, located in rural New York. Though a few nature books like John Kieran's *A Natural History of New York City* deal with urban niches, most take as subject rural or wilderness areas or quasi-wild borders such as the tidal marshes of Florida or Iraq.

The nature book is not a philosophical work like Emerson's *Nature*, although the nature book implies the idea that freedom comes from choosing to live within natural laws. The nature book is not literary analysis like Leo Marx's *The Machine in the Garden* or a case history like Robert Easton's *Black Tide: The Santa Barbara Oil Spill and Its Consequences*; not a taxonomic compendium like Ernest P. Edwards' *A Field Guide to the Birds of Mexico* nor a collection of lore like the entrancing J. Frank Dobie books on coyotes

*Reprinted, with revisions, from *English Journal* (62 [1973]: 537–48), by permission of the National Council of Teachers of English.

and other animals; not a historical work on geological epochs or evolution; not a topical research book, however readable, like W. M. Wheeler's *Social Life among the Insects* or Peter Farb's *Living Earth*. It is not a thesis book built on research and travel, such as Marsh's *Man and Nature; or, Physical Geography as Modified by Human Action* or *Man's Role in Changing the Face of the Earth*, edited by William Thomas.

The astute nature writers do all they can to avoid sentimentality, personification, and the imputation of conscious purpose to natural events. Such teleology, an absurdity, simply means that human values get between writer and nature, writer and reader. Anthropomorphism is the curse of much children's literature, as when animals talk and think and possess proper names. Human judgments distort observation. The "awkward" shape of the lake, says a writer. What is its shape? The "savage" wolverine. What does the wolverine do? The "ungainly" walk of the aardvark. How does an aardvark walk? The "unearthly" screech of an owl. What is the sound? Women and men can make some legitimate pretensions to being able to interpret fellow human beings, but they had better only report about fellow creatures. In the context of nature, nothing is in itself beautiful or ugly. It is functional. It is.

No good nature book imposes on other species any human-being system for aesthetics, morality, economics, comfort, or danger. As Margaret Millar points out in *The Birds and the Beasts Were There*, humans and birds differ in point of view. Humans dislike and avoid a patch of weeds; a goldfinch spends all day in it. Humans hate a pile of trash; there a wren finds a spider, a thrush a worm, a towhee a shelter, a wood rat a homesite. Humans want to fell a dead and therefore superfluous tree; a woodpecker goes to it for luscious larvae and a snug nesting place. Many people hate telephone poles and overhead wires; mockingbirds sit up there and sing.

The nature book is a personal statement, often charmingly literary, told at firsthand by a well-rounded observer who is as much at home in the humanities as in the natural sciences, especially the biological studies. At best, in Darwin Lambert's phrase, the nature writer is "a poetically inclined generalist." He or she is tolerant, eloquent, reflective, well-read, and also freshly and patiently observant. Agassiz, who refused to connect the evidence that pointed to evolution, said, "Study nature, not books." The nature writer studies both books and nature, staying in one place, often a small precinct, instead of traveling over the earth's curvature. And the nature book shows in sharp, specific, sensuous detail how this person lives in harmony with nonhuman nature, adjusts to this nature, examines it—marveling at its features large and small.

The nature book has a place for the Grand Canyon of the Colorado, or Barranca del Cobre in Chihuahua and Sonora, or the Himalayas, but more often than not it celebrates the little things that make big memories. Edmund Jaeger gathered bookfuls of observations from his cabin sites in the Chocolate and other desert mountains. Henry Beston wrote of wildlife and the intricate rhythms of the Atlantic waves as he spent his days and nights at his lonely house on Cape Cod. Jean Henri Fabre pioneered in entomological studies and derived ten volumes from decades of studying one weedy garden in Provence. Fabre illustrates a Park Service yarn: A man asked a naturalist friend how he'd spent the summer. "Well, I started exploring my backyard. I got only about halfway across it."

In *Listening Point*, Sigurd Olson of Minnesota tells how, when he is on a canoe trip amid wilderness, he chooses a camping place for the view, but he remembers it as the site of the little details that in time he notices. Like the Louis Halle of *Spring in Washington*, he wants to snatch the passing moment and examine it for signs of eternity.

Authors of nature books will admit that their presence affects the nature they observe, but they wish to intrude as little as possible. They want to record, not alter; understand, not possess; leave alone, not replace; be in on something already a going thing, not in any way redirect or stop it. They dream of seeing Eden as it was before Adam and Eve ate the fruit—an apricot, probably—before man and woman began to impose human values on nature, such as prudery—denuding a fig tree of leaves in order to hide human genitalia. In the huge world of the naturalist, humankind cannot acquire too much knowledge in the laboratory or in the field, but it can all too soon begin to apply its knowledge to kill animals, cut trees, move earth, and invent lethal chemicals unknown to nature.

In its unmilitant, serious, informed way the nature book celebrates life. It implicitly rejects the notion that nature is dead or obsolete, as now announced by some intemperate technologists. It rejects the idea that in the long run humanity can win over nature. The nineteenth-century paintings called "still lifes" showed apples and quinces picked by humans, draped ducks and grouse shot by humans. The French name for such genre paintings is appropriate: *nature morte*. Human beings can indeed kill individual living things; they can even wipe out entire species and genera, and they are much engaged the wide world over in exterminating species that rode to safety on Noah's cramped ark.

To all the destruction of the life in the environment, the nature book is a heartfelt reply. It adumbrates or states an ethic broader than that of the Sermon on the Mount, for it includes the mountain itself and the native plants, animals, cliffs, canyons, waters—the whole ecological network of relationships. This encompassing, dedicated concern is the land ethic of Aldo Leopold in *Sand County Almanac*, which says we must extend the Golden Rule to all elements in our environment. For technological humankind is now the most powerful, evident, continuous force on earth for change or alteration. It is the leading force in all things hydrological, geological, atmospheric—ecological. It should prepare an ethical impact statement for every proposal for altering the environment of human, beast, and plant—for altering hillside and plain, high sky and ocean deep.

The nature book announces unity, interrelations, the balance of an ecosystem. In *Beyond the Aspen Grove*, Ann Zwinger inventories her forty acres west of the Rampart Range in Colorado; tells about the food chain there; presents much information about insects, fungi, sedges, arthropods, and plants; and laments the absence of wolves, wolverines, and grizzlies, now facing extinction as the activities of human beings constrict and destroy the wilderness habitat. She finds unity on a rock in her lake as she looks around and senses what her place is amid a self-perpetuating natural order.

Gavin Maxwell, whose *Ring of Bright Water* exuberates over the seashore wildness of northwestern Scotland, treats familiarly of rabbits, whooper swans, greylag geese, blue and rorqual whales, and a wildcat. He has fascinating details on the inland migration of elvers—eels—and he is particularly expansive on river otters. There are interludes when he travels to the Near East, to the swamps of the marsh Arabs, and to London, but his book holds to a bay on the edge of the Western Highlands. In the foreword he says:

> In writing this book about my home I have not given to the house its true name. This is from no desire to create mystery—indeed it will be easy enough for the curious to discover where I live—but because identification in print would seem in some sense a sacrifice, a betrayal of its remoteness and isolation, as if by doing so I were to bring nearer its enemies of industry and urban life. Camusfearna, I have called it, the Bay of the Alders, from the trees that grow along the burn side; but the name is of little consequence, for such bays and houses, empty and long disused, are scattered throughout the wild sea lochs of the Western Highlands and the Hebrides, and in the description of one the reader may perhaps find the likeness of others of which he has himself been fond, for these places are symbols. Symbols, for me and for many, of freedom, whether it be from the prison of over-dense communities and the close confines of human relationships, from the less complex incarceration of office walls and hours, or simply freedom from the prison of adult life and an escape into the forgotten world of childhood, of the individual or the race. For I am convinced that man has suffered in his separation from the soil and from the other living creatures of the world; the evolution of his intellect has outrun his needs as an animal, and as yet he must still, for security, look long at some portion of the earth as it was before he tampered with it.   (vii)

Maxwell's statement catches many of the persistent themes of the nature book, including the selection of a specific locale that is a home or a second home or a definite locality where one spends a prolonged and loitering amount of time. In earlier generations of nature writers, in John Burroughs or W. H. Hudson, Enos Mills or John Muir, the locale is always specific, as in the earlier *The Naturalist on the River Amazon* of Henry W. Bates or the still earlier work by Gilbert White, *The Natural History and Antiquities of Selborne, in the County of Southampton* (1789). The reader always knows where he or she is in space. The reader knows this in Dudley Cammet Lunt's *Taylors Gut*—about one estuary in Delaware—or Elna Bakker's *An Island Called California*, about one transect across the state from San Francisco Bay to the Colorado River. Maxwell does not, however, prescribe for himself a definite time frame as many nature writers do. In *This Living Earth*, a pictorial study of one California meadow, David Cavagnaro covers three years, which he calls in turn "Awakening," "Discovery," and "Understanding." A year is a common period, as in Thoreau's *Walden*; Krutch's *The Twelve Seasons*—that is, months—at his Connecticut home; Fred Bodsworth's heartrending *The Last Curlew*; Hazel Heckman's *Island Year*, set in Puget Sound; or Eliot Porter's masterful book of photographs *"In Wildness Is the Preservation of the World"* (1962).

Some writers take the season as their period, as do Louis J. Halle in *Spring in Washington* and Klaus and Elizabeth Gemming in *Block Island Summer*. Allan W. Eckert takes only three weeks for his *Wild Season*, set at a lake on the Illinois-Wisconsin border, and Sally Carrighar takes twenty-four hours for *One Day on Beetle Rock*. Straight-line annalistic history through the years is human-invented and human-imposed on astronomy, geology, and human history. Nature works in cycles—the day, the season, the year, the life cycle, the succession of plants and animals in a certain ecological niche or ecosystem, the evolution and devolution of species; and though some present-day nature books are built on the old principle of the diary or journal, the fresh ones use the cycle, which parallels the recycling of waste material that at present is fashionable, and properly so. In nature, beginnings and endings go in all directions in concentric circles in cubic relations. The great chain of being, more intricate than a stack of coats of mail, forever vibrates and rustles.

Before 1859 and the *Origin of Species*, as after, nature writers identified God and religion with natural beauty and perpetual balance in the ecosphere. For the John Burroughs of *Wake-Robin* (*Writings*, vol. 1), for the Walt Whitman of portions of *Specimen Days* and for the Gene Stratton-Porter of *Freckles*, there was a grand spiritual design to nature. Nature was a she who taught lessons. She renewed one's health. She provided a sanctuary, a retreat for communion and exaltation.

A specimen of nature writing at the transition point between metaphysical fantasy and field observation is Susan Fenimore Cooper's *Rural Hours*. This enduring minor work, published in 1850, revised in 1887, and reprinted in 1968, concerns a year in Cooperstown, New York, and the vale occupied by Lake Otsego. The author deals largely in specific detail. She is conscious that writing on nature objects "is now much less vague and general than it was formerly; it has become very much more definite and accurate within the last half century" (226). Her topics, taken up during the round of a single year, are weather phenomena, animals, trees, and flowers. Throughout the book Cooper reports and comments on historic intrusions into the original natural balances of land and lake. The wood bison are gone. Wolves, panthers, and bears are scarce. Carolina parakeets grow rarer and rarer, as do passenger pigeons, for no longer in 1850 does she see "large unbroken flocks several miles in extent succeeding each other" (7). The Indians are almost all gone, though she presents one touching vignette of three Oneida women—Awa, Cootlee, and Wallee—who come to the Cooper house and beg for bread and meat. Local anglers have introduced pickerel to the lake. The pickerel is "a good fish though inferior to some others in our lake" (21). Cooper is critical of people who insensately strip the forest of noble pines, who waste wood and saplings, and who stupidly cut down every tree instead of thinning the groves and leaving all the trees on knolls or along stream banks—who see a tree only as an enemy or a source for dollars.

Cooper is noting an unbalanced ecosystem half a century and more ahead of such exotic plagues as Chinese chestnut blight, Dutch elm virus, and Siberian white pine blister rust, and the Japanese and European gypsy moth. She speaks out like an early forest conservationist, but she is concerned only in passing. Except for her pages on how people mistreat trees, her overall tone is without protest. Clearly she accepts the concepts of material progress and of the superior civilization of the non-Indian North Americans. And she proclaims the "immeasurable goodness, the infinite wisdom of our Heavenly Father," though this does not correlate with the extirpation of species and the vandalism among the trees. She finds an orthodox comfort in the words of her God in the Bible and in his works which are the natural scene. A beautiful sixteenth of May throws her into several pages of post-Calvinist rhapsody ("What have the best of us done to merit one such day in a lifetime of follies and failings and sins? . . ." [44]).

An unquestioned faith in God enables Cooper to avoid any anxiety about the future. There is a parallel in *Hidden Valley of the Smokies* by Ross E. Hutchins, a ranger naturalist, who tells of his favorite haunts along a creek called Little River in eastern Tennessee inside Great Smokies National Park. He concentrates on insects, mammals, flowers, and trees. He is sad about the extermination of chestnuts by the blight, for it deprives bear and squirrels of food and has reduced their population, and he mentions the danger of invasion of the park by Ural Mountains Russian swine, escaped from a North Carolina hunting preserve set up in 1912. But he shows no worry, not because he believes as Susan Cooper did in Almighty God but because he believes that the Mighty United States will guard and protect national parklands.

But faith in any deity or any government now sustains few nature writers. World War II with the atomic bomb was a turning point. The bomb—the brutal, fateful symbol of applied science and governmental technology—marked a new era in nature writing as in foreign policy. With the big bombs and the big earth-moving machinery, the helicopters and the chemicals, with all the new technology for war against human beings, insects, and coyotes, neither wild nature nor isolated native tribes, not even the remotest organisms and peoples of the Amazon jungle, were safe from destruction. It was no longer possible merely to study nature or to eulogize it.

Conservation groups, once devoted to happy expeditions into wilderness, now fight back against technology and development. A prime example is the Sierra Club with its lobbyists in Sacramento and Washington, D.C., its battle books, and its many legal actions. The Scenic Hudson Preservation Conference has worked to stop Consolidated Edison and save Storm King, the noble mountain upriver from Con Edison's facility serving Manhattan. GOO (Get Oil Out) and other organizations engendered by the Santa Barbara oil spill and similar disasters the world around have influenced legislation and public administration at all levels of government and affected deliberations of the United Nations. The Nature Conservancy buys and protects unspoiled or relic tracts "supporting the best examples of all elements of the natural world" in all the states (3). The Conservation Foundation, active in many directions, produced Rice Odell's *The Environmental Awakening: The New Revolution to Protect the Earth*.

Authors of nature books are in the fight, too, especially in books that have appeared since 1960. Active defense of unspoiled-terrain natural relations appears, for instance, in Edward Abbey's *Desert Solitaire: A Season in the Wilderness* and in Adolph Murie's *A Naturalist in Alaska*. In one passage Murie defends the Alaska wolves as part of the total natural plan that includes Dall sheep, caribou, and moose. He says the wolves add "immeasurable richness and wilderness spirit to the landscape" (196). Sigurd Olson defends bobcats against Minnesota bounty hunters, just as long ago John Muir, a one-man early conservation movement, defended alpine wildflowers and tundra sedges against rapacious sheep ranchers. In *Yellowstone: A Century of the Wilderness Idea*, Ann and Myron Sutton celebrate an immense variety of contiguous and extraordinary ecosystems astride the Continental Divide. Unlogged, unmined, unfarmed, the park is by intent a living display of primeval America. Yet the Suttons make clear that Yellowstone's officials face the problem of modifying human behavior: of preventing overfishing, any feeding of deer and bear, and all attempts to kill predators; of getting all housing facilities and autos, even all horses, outside the park; of reversing the "vandalism of improvement" (157)—a point developed further in Frank Craighead, Jr.'s *Track of the Grizzly*.

Defense of the coyote, now found wild from coast to coast, appears in two sympathetic firsthand reports, Hope Ryden's *God's Dog*, and François Leydet's *The Coyote: Defiant Song Dog of the West*.

Alarm shows all the way through books like the highly artistic *Inland Island* of Josephine Johnson, whose home on an old, abandoned farmsite has two streams. One, pure, rises on the farm and supports a hundred species; the other, blackish, bubbly, odoriferous, and dead, drains sewage from the nearby town. Throughout the author is critical of hunters, trappers, and vandals who despoil the wildlife on or near her wooded acreage. Hazel Heckman protests steadily in her *Island Year*, set in Puget Sound on Anderson Island, which is six by three miles in size. She is in agony over ruthless, careless deer hunting and roadside spraying. Heckman writes:

> Anderson Island is no Grand Canyon, no Everglades, no redwood forest, to arouse public indignation. It is only one of the "little wild places," one endangered island in Puget Sound. But great losses are made up of small losses. We cannot shrug this off as *progress*. Nor is it just we who have lost. America has been deprived. Our children and our children's children have been cheated out of that wildness that should have been their heritage. (230)

Justice William O. Douglas, like many other writers, combines lyrical description with tough out-and-out counterpropaganda. In *My Wilderness: East to Katahdin*, which describes eleven varied locales from southern Utah to central Maine, he lambasts those public officials allied with private commercial interests who drain natural waters and dry up the Everglades, who drop poisons from planes over Bridger National Forest in Wyoming and kill every creature in the food chain that eats meat, including foxes, martens, coyotes, bears, hawks, and eagles. Forest Service and Bureau of Land Management workers spray herbicides on willows and sagebrush in order to augment stream flow and grass growth—all to help ranchers—and wipe out trout, moose, sage grouse, and much else. Books like Douglas' have led to the beginning of revised federal policies. Douglas' chapter in *A Farewell to Texas* on the pillage and heartless exploitation of the remarkable Big Thicket in eastern Texas has given hope to Texas conservationists. A sequel is *The Big Thicket: A Challenge for Conservation* by A. Y. "Pete" Gunter, professor of philosophy at North Texas State University.

In many new nature books dismay over present trends shows particularly in the final chapter. Heckman calls her last chapter "Rape." David F. Costello ends *The Desert World: Plant and Animal Life of the American Desert* with a chapter called "Man and the North American Deserts: History and Future." His pessimism and protest are in startling contrast to his earlier loving chapters on plants, animals, desert scenery. He objects to housing-tract eyesores, used-car lots, trailer courts, industrial plants; to jet planes and their condensation trails; to dune buggies, campers, vans, trailers, motorcycles, and ghetto campgrounds; to pipelines, strip mines, city and industrial dumps; to smog, which now accumulates in Phoenix and Las Vegas; and to dams, war games, and trophy hunting.

John Hay and Peter Farb in *The Atlantic Shore* concern themselves largely with natural history from Long Island to Labrador. They are legitimately rhapsodic over what was there when Capt. John Smith first explored: "the high standing trees, the wild turkey, the otter, the wolf, the great auk, the sweet prodigality of these spring shores." But they admonish at once that "we may now be close to realizing that what is left will be kept only if we admit our need of it" (20). In their final chapter, "The Shore in Human Hands," they report "the shadow of the former reality" (212): the shad and salmon and alewife reduced to small numbers, the shorebirds few and far between, bald eagles scarce, ospreys doomed, headlands bulldozed, marshes filled in, shellfish beds polluted, freshwater tables falling, and salt water penetrating underneath the land. Hay and Farb end on a bitter note: "Ours is an experimental civilization, experimenting with its own 'progress,' experimenting dangerously with its mother earth" (220).

Dudley Cammet Lunt, a conservationist hunter and activist in the prolonged fight to save Delaware's shoreline of marshes and estuaries from a combine of big oil companies and the federal government, devotes a late chapter in *Taylors Gut* to "The River Road," once a lane between rows of blue chicory and hedges sweet with the scent of honeysuckle, a lane with views of white egrets at rest, great blue herons borne on pumping wings, and the miracles of iridescence called wood ducks. "The countryside would be alive with birds."

Then came the year 1955.

> In the spring of that year bulldozers appeared and they and their twin engines of destruction, the dirt carriers, began snorting through this countryside. This rich rolling river country, its trees, its spacious dwellings, the broad fields, the long lazy vistas of marsh and river, all were destined to oblivion. In the leveling, in great clouds of dust and smoke, they all disappeared. Swiftly mounds of topsoil began to squat here and to squat there. Derricks towered. Wire fences ran harsh and hard. Circular storage tanks began to take form.

And—

> Today this stretch of the River Road is lined on either hand by the ugly
> tubs and tanks and, rising against the sky, the vast convoluted plumb-
> ing and towering stacks of an oil refinery, touted by the Tidewater Oil
> Company as the most modern in the world. Overhead, day in and day
> out, a myriad of stacks pour forth fumes into the sky. Thereabout the
> air smells. Satellite enterprises have burgeoned and continue to prolif-
> erate, and the whole 5,000-acre area has become an ugly industrial
> wasteland comparable to the familiar disfiguration of the once lovely
> Hackensack Meadows in Northern New Jersey. (286)

In despair conservationists and crusading ecologists often write books with gloomy titles: *The Exploited Eden* (Robert J. Gangewere), *Silent Spring* (Rachel Carson), *The Frail Ocean* (Wesley Marx), *The Darkening Land* (William Frank Longgood), *The Closing Circle* (Barry Commoner), *America the Raped* (Gene Marine), *Road to Ruin* (A. Q. Mowbray), *Our Plundered Planet* (Fairfield Osborn), *The Empty Ark* (Philip Kingland Crowe), *Last Chance on Earth: A Requiem for Wildlife* (Roger Caras), *The Silent Sky* (Allan W. Eckert), *Slaughter the Animals, Poison the Earth* (Jack Olsen), *The Pesticide Conspiracy* (Robert Van den Bosch), or *Lifeboats to Ararat*, Sheldon Campbell's account of how many animals will probably survive only in zoos. The authors of such books, prodding people to action, see humankind (that is, wage-oriented labor and profit-oriented capital) as living shortsightedly by the idea of a struggle against nature, a drive to conquer nature—an idea that now in an age of overpopulation and overexploitation points to defeat for the human species.

In contrast to the embattled crusaders, the quieter nature writers who only protest present an ordered world in which humans and nature must work together as necessarily permanent parts of an organic-inorganic process operating through time in an ever-modulated harmony.

Both the nature writer, with a benevolent outlook and vicarious imag-ination, and the conservationist writer, with a determination to conquer human nature's brutal, greedy side, can help humanity to correct its myopic economics, walleyed politics, blindfolded education system with its vo-cational and monetary bias, and environmental bad habits, which shock the eye even as they offend the nose and ear. The mind is properly horrified by illogical and senseless annihilation. The heart properly holds to natural beauties, wild creatures, and self-perpetuating life.

We teachers of English at any level can make telling use of nature and conservation books in courses in composition or in courses dealing with portions of eighteenth-, nineteenth-, or twentieth-century literature. Such books fit into a course in report writing or intellectual history. There can be a course called "Books about Nature" or "Literary Controversies in Conservation." Books by writers like René Dubos, Barry Commoner, Gar-rett Hardin, Loren Eiseley, Paul Sears, Peter Farb, Raymond Dasmann, or Rachel Carson raise central issues that involve teachers and students along with everyone else. There is solid, useful history and science in Donald Worster's *Nature's Economy: The Roots of Ecology*. If our primary task is to teach writing, reading, thinking, and discussion, we can use informed, highly charged books on nature and the environment just as we use literary classics and contemporary literature, films, and phonograph records. An excellent general text, provided with a reading list, is Paul Brooks's *Speaking for Nature: How Literary Naturalists from Henry Thoreau to Rachel Carson Have Shaped America.*

We English teachers have the large body of established nature literature to draw on—including Thoreau's *Walden* but not B. F. Skinner's *Walden Two*—and we have a growing library of new titles to make use of in the everlasting effort to hold student attention and enlighten future decision makers. The negative power of our technology cannot destroy all life, but it could set back evolution by wiping out just about everything alive this side of the algae and of our most successful rivals, the insects. The nature book, in its positive way, celebrates life, living, continuity, successful adjustment, and survival from one set of individual life cycles to another. The anonymous author of Ecclesiastes, a philosopher ecologist, has this to say: "One generation passeth away, and another generation cometh: but the earth abideth forever."

PART 2:

Environmental Literature
in the Classroom

Introduction

The essays in part 2 all describe courses wherein reading is the primary educational experience and the traditional classroom the primary learning environment. Since environmental literature is inherently interdisciplinary and (as essays in later parts will demonstrate) often requires nontraditional situations in order to be experienced fully, inventive strategies are necessary to enable the classroom space to work with and not against it.

The courses described in part 2 can be presented in terms first of their concerns and second of their techniques for presenting these concerns. They can also be distinguished by their differing premises about environmental literature and about the most productive ways of experiencing and learning from it.

Ralph Lutts, in "Views of Nature," assumes the subjectivity of individual interpretations of nature—his interpretations, those of his students, and those of the literary creators whose works are studied. He structures his classes around the dynamic of these varying interpretations of the environment and the resulting diverse aesthetic embodiments of these interpretations.

Lutts's concern—like that of other contributors—is therefore equally with the phenomena of nature and with the ways in which these phenomena are perceived. Lutts uses subjective techniques such as a journal and simulation exercises. Students in their journals of experience in nature play off their own perceptions against those of the works they are reading. In the simulation exercises, personal experiences and imaginative visions (e.g., the student's "ideal home") are played off against those of others and against possible "realities" that they distort or ignore. Despite the relativistic premise of his course, Lutts insists on reading and textual interpretation of nature writing as starting and ending point, on the classroom as basic learning environment, and on the necessity of covering nontraditional material in a traditional setting.

Barbara Currier Bell, in "Environmental Literature: An Approach Emphasizing Pluralism," attempts to draw her students to a sophisticated and tradition-mediated mode of environmental perception. She has established a typology of human roles in relation to nature, roles manifested consistently through human history: Humanity as Sufferer, Defender, Steward, etc. Complementing this structure, which in a way transforms Lutts's individualistic views into persistent collective views, Bell used a team-teaching situation.

A goal of both the typology and the team teaching is to counter a "gloomy" or "deterministic" view of humans' relation with the environment by showing that human treatment of nature has varied and been subject to change in the past and is in the present. Her discussion of interdisciplinarity in teaching and the use of cross-cultural material (which contrasts interestingly to the experiences of Weatherly in this part and of Christensen and Vonalt in part 5) emphasizes the difficulty the literary humanist faces when confronted by the narrowness of his or her own training. Precisely because it presents material involving the basic issues of human survival in the world, environmental literature requires poly-mathic qualities that many teachers of literature do not possess. Yet the sharing of teaching with others in scientific disciplines can lead as much to rivalry as to a tolerance of complementarity. It can also lead the literature teacher to feel, rightly or wrongly, that his or her turf is being taken over; whereas the science member(s) of the team may, despite the best of in-tentions, experience the literary qualities of the materials as impediments to understanding their content and may communicate this attitude to the students.

Bell's difficulties with, and reflections on, typological organization and interdisciplinary technique say much about the application of what can be learned in literature classes to the problems of the "real" world. Such difficulties arise only when a teacher is venturesome enough to attempt, through interdisciplinarity, to make such an application. The readings for Bell's course were taken from many genres of writing, none generically "environmental." If so much of the world's literature has applied itself to environmental concerns, is there not an obligation, in order for this liter-ature to be known and taught fully, to present it in terms of the different disciplines and cultural values that are so deeply implicated in it?

Science fiction is a literary genre that bridges two cultures. In "Some Necessary Heresies Revisited," Felicia Campbell describes her course "Eco-fiction." Campbell's concern is more outwardly directed than that of the previous writers, since her course is an adaptation to literary materials of the science and social-policy questions covered in a nonliterary multi-disciplinary course from which she got her initial inspiration. The imagi-native construction of future worlds in science fiction provides a perspective from which the certainties of contemporary industrial society can be per-ceived as subjective at best and destructive at worst. Science fiction presents "heretical" ideas to challenge students to examine unquestioned beliefs. Campbell's essay suggests what possibilities may lie in the exploration of other "popular" literary genres, undertaken with an environmental slant.

Joan Weatherly's course, described in "Pastoral: An Ageless Form of Environmental Literature," combines the concerns and techniques of Bell and Campbell. By focusing on a single mode of perception and expression, definable as both genre and archetype, she seeks to incorporate and make coherent a great diversity of environmental perceptions viewed histori-cally—particularly as they have been translated into aesthetic terms in visual art, music, and literature. Weatherly treats the pastoral as a privi-leged genre because of its basis in tension between "ideal" and "real." It is instructive to compare her course with that of Lutts. The confrontation of ideal and real is common to both. Lutts, however, takes as ultimate object of concern his students' own individual views of what they are or where they would ideally be. At the other extreme, Weatherly has her students gain self-knowledge by responding to the persistent theme of the pastoral, which is outside themselves, manifested in the works of art they examine.

Weatherly collaborates with a musicologist in presenting "Landscape in Art, Literature, and Music" and avoids the "two-cultures" difficulties that Bell discusses. She uses a traditional classroom format but also multimedia resources (films, recordings, artworks). Her course is structured in a historical sequence of what might be called "aesthetic phases"—although the categories might be applied to all modes of thought—from classicism through romanticism and existentialism to contemporary pre-ismatized expression. In each phase, her "sister arts" are studied together, interrelated. Throughout, the pastoral motif of "dispossession" is traced as a continuity—the shepherd's exile by technology from a green world of harmony with nature—and its psychic and cultural analogues are evoked.

Jack Kligerman's " 'Nature' and the Classroom: Outdoors and In" describes a course that moves further away from the classroom itself than do any others in this part. However, it uses as a theme the contrast between the classroom as a learning space and the natural world outside the walls as a classroom—the issue of pedagogical environment discussed in "What Teaching Environmental Literature Might Be" (part 1). Kligerman's classroom embodies the necessary limitations of his urban students' backgrounds, and by objectifying it as space he can overcome some difficulties in presenting "nature" to an audience more familiar with it as concept than as experience. Kligerman's course, complementing reading with expeditions out from and back to the city and classroom, imitates the figurative and conceptual history of "nature": " 'Nature' was born of the city, so what better place to start from on an expedition into what, for my students, was an unknown land, a wilderness. . . ."

Kligerman emphasizes that his course, "Nature and the Nature Essay in American Literature," continually changes, as he does while learning from his experience with it. But it retains a complementary content of traditional course material—nineteenth- and twentieth-century nature writing, photography, and art—and journal keeping or essay writing by students based on their field trip experience outside the city. Kligerman combines a history-of-ideas approach to nature as concept with an experiential approach to nature observed and sensed. He places the greater importance on his students' discovering by observation and writing how they themselves give "nature" conceptual and figurative meanings and how this process of meaning giving embodies the struggle between given and new interpretations of nature. Unlike Lutts, Kligerman integrates his students' journal writing tightly into the traditional sequence of his course. As students read, weekly, nature texts based on observation and go on field trips to natural areas that they can observe in terms of the texts' approaches, they also refine and redefine their own nature writing based on these inside- and outside-classroom experiences. Their journals evolve into self-consciously directed texts in their own right and are periodically shared with, and critiqued by, fellow students.

Certain techniques and concerns dominate these different approaches to teaching environmental literature in the classroom environment with primary emphasis on traditional pedagogical materials. All the courses attempt to strike a balance between literary and extraliterary presentations of nature, and all of them employ a chronological, historical framework for sequential discussion. All of them evoke and work through a consciousness of change—whether it be retrospective or prospective, change in the natural world itself or change in the individual or collective human perceptions of that world. All of them, to varying degrees, use interdisciplinary contexts, personnel, and/or materials and challenge themselves and their students to deal with thinking in terms of a synthesis of different modes of perception.

Views of Nature: An Interplay of Personal Reflection and Literary Natural History

Ralph H. Lutts

Most environmental studies courses dwell on the externalities of our environment—on the engineering, medical, ecological, economic, and other aspects that are amenable to more or less scientific analysis. I have often felt, though, that there should be an opportunity for students to examine some of the internalities—the expectations, presuppositions, biases, and delights that they and their culture bring to and find in the world around them. Our environment *is* ourselves. It is a product of our own creative, mythic, neurotic, and aspiring selves. We, in turn, are a product of the world around us. We have evolved within it and have been shaped by it at least as much as it has been shaped by us. We, humans and environment, are the product of a mutual interplay of opportunities, constraints, and expectations.

Those who are involved in environmental studies often see themselves as agents of social and environmental change. As change agents, though, we need to have a grasp not only of the material options that are open to us but also of the individual and cultural biases that both limit our perception of options and distort our decisions and that render some options more personally and culturally satisfying than others. If we are out to save the world, we must take care to save a world worth living in. We need to become aware of our own deep personal environmental agendas and become able to transcend them, rather than succumb to a narrow and biased view of the world.

Much of my teaching has been motivated and informed by this perception. One of my courses has focused on gaining an awareness of our own environmental presuppositions and has made extensive use of the writings of literary naturalists such as John Muir, Henry Beston, Aldo Leopold, and Loren Eiseley. It has gone under a number of titles, most often that of "Views of Nature." The title reflects the idea that although each author brings a great love of and commitment to the natural world to his or her writing, each views that world through a different window. It is too easy for students to account for the differences in the positions of the "pro-" and "anti-" environmentalists in terms of good and evil, right and wrong, and other such broad and value-charged categories. This tends to give them a false sense of security in their own environmental positions—after all, it is the other guy who is to blame for our problems. Focusing on the images of nature represented in nature literature allows students to take a much more subtle look at their own approaches to their environment, because their positions in response to this material are no longer defined by opposition to those of an enemy. They can begin to ask, "What, then, are our views of nature?"

There is another value in working with nature literature. The task of the literary naturalist is to report his or her experiences of nature to the reader. The report must faithfully record careful and accurate observations of nature. This alone, however, is not sufficient. The author must also be faithful to the *experience* of nature. What is reported is nature as it has touched the heart and mind of the writer. It is not simply an objective report; it is also an expression of a creative interplay between author and environment. The literary naturalist is one of the few people professionally required to combine the perceptions of both scientist and poet. A study of nature writing is a study of this interplay. A student who steps out of the woods, sits down, and writes a piece of literary natural history is engaging in this interplay in an educationally profound manner, for he or she is beginning to integrate thoughts, feelings, and actions. This is a step toward reuniting the rational, emotional, and physical aspects of our being, among which our culture long ago drove a wedge. This reunion is an important and necessary step toward dealing with our environmental problems.

My course is taught at Hampshire College, a small, private, experimenting liberal arts college in Amherst, Massachusetts. The college is somewhat unorthodox. Academic progress is measured by the successful completion of a series of independent research projects and an individualized program of study designed in collaboration with a faculty committee, rather than by a transcript listing prescribed courses and graded credit. Much of the teaching at Hampshire occurs not in the courses but in meetings of the students' individual project committees. The faculty on these committees often come from a variety of disciplines and find this educational process nearly as instructive as do the students. Courses exist as resources to assist students in developing the skills and knowledge necessary to pursue their projects. For this reason there are no formally required courses. The students who take a course tend to be highly motivated, since they have chosen to be involved in structuring their own education. Classes are generally small, the college does not require final examinations, there are no academic departments in the traditional sense, and student evaluations are in the form of a narrative, rather than a letter grade. This academic structure creates an unusual teaching situation.

"Views of Nature" is a product of this unusual situation. It has been taught through the college's Outdoors Program and the School of Natural Science. The Outdoors Program is an outdoors recreation program that has also tried to link outdoors activities with the formal academic program of the college. The School of Natural Science has long had a commitment to environmental studies and to exploring the interface between science and society. Many Hampshire students have designed programs of study that integrate elements such as outdoors pursuits, outdoors leadership training, environmental education, American studies, environmental sciences, psychology, political science, and literature.

"Views of Nature" examines the character and history of literary natural history, surveys many of its significant American authors and works (with an emphasis upon those of the twentieth century), and helps students to examine their own views of nature through values clarification exercises, writing assignments, and class discussion. We also try to have a good time; this is important, because a relaxed, semiformal atmosphere is conducive to the kind of candid reflection that I try to promote in my students.

In the following pages I will review the readings that we use, course expectations and method of evaluation, and teaching methods and activities. The course has been in continuous flux, and there is no fixed syllabus. For this reason, I will not provide one. Rather, I will review what I do and the thinking behind it. This should prove much more useful to someone who is interested in adapting what I am doing to his or her own academic context.

The Readings

This course requires a good deal of reading. My students read about a book each week, plus selections from a variety of sources. I want them to gain a good grasp of the range of nature literature, its diversity and significant themes, and its important books and authors. The amount of material covered, though, places quite a burden upon them, and I have found that I must highlight specific parts of each book for them to focus on; otherwise it is difficult to insure that they will be properly prepared for each class. It is also helpful to suggest specific study questions to have in mind as they read. The following books and articles have often been used in the course, although not all have been used each time it was taught.

We have generally begun with Aldo Leopold's *A Sand County Almanac*. I assign only the "Almanac" section. This is an enjoyable and accessible piece, and many of my students are already familiar with it, which makes it easier to begin analyzing the themes and structure of the writing. With this as an example of nature writing, we can begin to ask, "What is a literary naturalist, and what is he or she trying to do?" In preparation for this discussion, I have my students read John Burroughs' introduction to *Wake-Robin* (Riverby ed.), Joseph Wood Krutch's introduction to *The Best Nature Writing of Joseph Wood Krutch*, and the introduction to John Steinbeck's *The Log from the Sea of Cortez*. In the future I may include chapter 1 of Donald Worster's *Nature's Economy*. I also distribute a collection of definitions of "naturalist" that I have culled from a variety of sources. I underscore the distinction between literary naturalists, research naturalists, and interpretive naturalists.

Since I want my students to use the literature as a vehicle for reflecting on their own experiences of nature, I employ a number of books that nclude biographical or autobiographical elements. Paul Brooks's biography *The House of Life: Rachel Carson at Work* concentrates on Carson as a writer. A substantial part of the book consists of excerpts from her work. Sally Carrighar's autobiography *Home to the Wilderness* follows her life to the writing of her book *One Day on Beetle Rock*, which we also read. *The Night Country* by Loren Eiseley includes a good deal of autobiographical material, as does much of his writing. Many of the other books that I have used, although not written as autobiography, include the presence of the author who is reporting his or her experiences and thus include tacitly autobiographical material. It is relatively easy to turn the discussion of these books to the students' experiences by asking questions such as "Does this ring true in terms of your experience?" and "Have any of you experienced something like this?"

I have also found it useful to contrast works and authors. John Burroughs and John Muir, for example, were nature writers, contemporaries, and friends, yet they differ considerably in what they write about and in writing style. Muir strides across glaciers and mountaintops, while Burroughs stops at the edge of a country road to contemplate a flower. Edwin Way Teale's collection of Muir's writings, *The Wilderness World of John Muir*, is a good anthology. I have not found a satisfactory collection of Burroughs' writings and have relied on selected essays from various volumes, kept in reserve at the library. Henry Beston's *The Outermost House* provides a good contrast with *A Sand County Almanac*. Beston's approach to nature is largely aesthetic, while Leopold sees it through an ecological eye. Another good contrasting set is Annie Dillard's *Pilgrim at Tinker Creek*, Edward Abbey's *Desert Solitaire*, and just about anything by Loren Eiseley—I have generally used either *The Immense Journey* or *The Night Country*. Dillard's breathless natural theology, Abbey's macho and misanthropic ecoanarchism, and Eiseley's immersion in geological time and the plight of consciousness provide a great deal of material for discussion.

Interest in homesteading and back-to-the-land movements provides an opportunity to explore pastoral themes and examine some of the literature of rural life. The material that we have used includes Henry Beston's *The Northern Farm* (1–9), Hal Borland's *Countryman: A Summary of Belief* (15–37), John Burroughs' *Leaf and Tendril* (45–50), and *Adventures in Contentment* (3–40, 97–118), by David Grayson (pen name of Ray Stannard Baker).

The last book that I assign for the course is John Steinbeck's *Cannery Row*. This is not a work of literary natural history, but it incorporates most of the themes that are likely to have been developed in the course. My purpose in assigning this book is to connect the specialized context of the course to the wider body of literature that my students will encounter and to demonstrate that they do not have to limit themselves to works of literary naturalists in order to discover an author's views of nature. The essay "*Cannery Row*: Steinbeck's Pastoral Poem," by Stanley Alexander, is quite useful in helping students to understand what Steinbeck has done.

At some point in the course I try to include in an assignment a particularly syrupy, sentimental piece of writing that, although relevant to the theme of the assignment, is just awful. My students generally share my feelings about the piece, although they are often reluctant to criticize it, thinking that it must have some merit if it was assigned. A discussion of this reluctance helps to loosen their tongues and gives them some confidence in their own opinions. The reading also provides an example to which I can refer when they write equally syrupy and sentimental essays of their own.

My library reserve list contains scholarly works related to nature writing, attitudes toward nature, and environmental history, including Norman

Foerster, *Nature in American Literature*; Philip Hicks, *The Development of the Natural History Essay in American Literature*; Hans Huth, *Nature and the American*; Leo Marx, *The Machine in the Garden*; and Roderick Nash, *Wilderness and the American Mind*. The most comprehensive, although popularized, review of American literary naturalists is Paul Brooks's *Speaking for Nature*. I also include published journals of a number of authors, including Emerson, Thoreau, Muir, and Burroughs. I do not specifically assign any of these books, but I do refer to them in my lectures and tell my students where they can be found. The assigned readings and other books by and about the authors that we discuss are also placed on reserve.

Expectations and Evaluation

Hampshire College does not have a grading system, not even pass/fail. Evaluations are provided in a narrative form. A student who wishes to receive an evaluation must submit a written self-evaluation to the instructor. The instructor writes an evaluation of the student, and both are placed in the student's evaluation portfolio maintained by the college. The instructor's evaluation generally includes a description of the course (its objectives, methods, and content) and a detailed description of the work that the student did and its quality. At the beginning of each course, the instructor must specify what he or she expects of students who want to receive an evaluation. My expectations for "Views of Nature" are as follows:

Participation. Each student is expected to attend classes on a regular basis, keep up with the assignments, and participate in class discussions.

Journal. Each student is expected to maintain a personal journal in which he or she reflects on experiences in nature and responds to the readings and class discussions. There are two general categories of entries. The first includes all entries that are generated on the students' initiative. I encourage them to use the journals in whatever way will help them to reflect on the course and their thoughts and experiences related to the course content. The second category includes those entries made at my request. Sometimes, for example, I give specific study questions to reflect on in their journals in preparation for a class discussion. The journals, however, are theirs, and they should not feel constraints upon what they enter into them. I explain that they will be evaluated only to determine that a sincere effort is being made to maintain the journal and that they will not be evaluated on the quality of their writing or spelling or on the details of their contents. I also suggest that they might want to look at some of the published journals on the reserve list.

The journals are given to me two or three times during the semester. I explain to my students that I will respect the confidentiality of their journals and that they may remove pages if they feel that the contents are too personal. (Some students prefer to keep the journal in a loose-leaf format, which makes it easier to delete material and allows them to continue writing in it while I am reviewing some of the pages.) I examine their journals to make sure that they are making a serious effort to maintain them, not in a critical manner. The comments that I do make are of three kinds. I may find it necessary to encourage a student to make greater use of the journal and suggest ways of disciplining oneself to do this sort of writing. Other times I may point out sections of a journal that provide good material for a nature essay. Finally, I point out particularly good sections of writing. Many of my students, if not most, have difficulty writing polished essays. It is surprising, though, how much good material appears in their journals.

Biographical Presentations. My students are expected to take turns preparing biographical presentations about the authors that are going to be discussed. This is not a written assignment, although they should prepare a good outline. The students act as teaching assistants during the discussion of their particular authors. In effect, each is our resident expert on a particular writer. At an appropriate point in the class discussion, I ask the student to make his or her presentation. I try to give each student the assistance necessary to locate useful biographical sources and to prepare an effective presentation. Generally this is more time-consuming than if I did the presentation myself, but it is often of considerable value to the student. It is important to have a final meeting with each student about a week before his or her presentation in order to go over the presentation and ensure that it is properly prepared. A variation of this assignment has the students preparing summaries of the reviews of the books that will be discussed.

Childhood memories. Each student is expected to write an essay evoking the memory of a childhood experience in nature. I will go into the details of this assignment later in this paper when I examine teaching methods and activities.

Nature writing. Each student is expected to produce a polished piece of nature writing. Their journals can be very useful sources of ideas and material. I ask them to write about a personal experience in nature—it is not a science paper, although it must be factually accurate. That is, it must be grounded in experience rather than in theory. When I receive the papers, they are placed in a folder on reserve in the library, and the students read each other's work. Allowing them to read each other's papers motivates them to put extra effort into their work and provides an opportunity for the students to learn from and to evaluate their own work in relation to that of the other class members. A class discussion of the essays attempts to identify common themes and to relate the students' work to that of the authors whom we have been reading. I do not permit them to pick each other's work apart.

Research paper. Each student writes a polished research paper on a topic related to nature literature that is of interest to him or her. The biographical presentations and journals may provide ideas and material. They are asked to speak with me about their ideas before they get too deeply into it. Again, the papers are placed on reserve in the library, and the last few classes are spent discussing them. In this case, each student is expected to prepare a class presentation that summarizes his or her paper. I organize the presentations in a sequence that seems to make sense and promises to keep a discussion going.

Methods and Activities

Much of the class meetings consists of discussions of the readings. I try not to lecture very much, and when I do, my lectures are relatively short and designed to set the readings in a broader historical or literary context or to expand on issues raised in the conversation. From time to time, I introduce a change of pace by employing exercises designed to help my students explore their own values and by getting them outside the classroom. I will dwell on these in the following descriptions of some of the methods and activities employed in the course.

Ideal home. In one of the first class meetings, I employ a values clarification exercise in which my students fantasize about their ideal living situation. The purpose of this exercise is to help them to recognize their own landscape biases. I begin by explaining that I want to ask them some questions about their ideal style of living. First, however, they must all put some thought into just what that ideal might be. I ask them to sit back, relax, close their eyes, and picture themselves in the situation that I am going to describe. When they are ready I begin to talk them through a fantasy trip to their ideal home. It is important to explain to them that this is their own fantasy and that there are no "correct" images as long as they are making a sincere effort to participate. I have found that it is helpful if I, too, close my eyes and try to visualize my own ideal home as I guide them on their trip. This both helps me to pace my monologue properly and makes me a fellow participant.

My directions go something like this:

> You are walking along a walkway toward your ideal home. You cannot see it yet, but as you are walking look around you and see what your surroundings are like. Look at the ground, the near distance, the horizon, if you can see it, and the sky. What is the weather like? (A rhetorical question. They are not expected to speak until after the trip.) Try to picture these things and the whole area around you as clearly as possible. (pause) As you are walking you see that your home is becoming visible. You are coming closer to it. As you approach it, study its exterior. How is it shaped? Of what material is it made? What are its texture, color, shape, and design? What feeling does it evoke in you? (pause) Walk to the front door, reach out your hand, and open it. Step inside and look around. What do you see? What room are you in? How does it feel? (pause) Now begin to walk around your home, passing from room to room. How many rooms does it have? As you enter each room, take note of its contents, its function, the way it makes you feel. (pause) Are there other floors? If so, explore them also. Does it have a basement? (pause) How many bedrooms are there? (pause) Is there anything that you have missed? (pause) Now walk toward an exit, the back door if you have one. Open the door and step outside. What do you see as you step outside? (pause) Take a walk around your home. Look at the house, the land around it, and off into the distance. Do you have any possessions outside? What are they? Do you have a car? A garage? Is there any recreational equipment? (pause) Take one more look and turn back to the door you just stepped through and return into your home. Take one last quick tour. Is there any recreational

equipment inside? Picture the inside of your home as clearly as possible. (pause) Now walk back to the front door, open it, and step onto the walkway that originally brought you here. Move back down the walkway. After a while, stop, turn around, and take one last look at your home. (pause) When you are finished, continue walking away from your home until you have returned back here in the classroom.

While leading them on this walk, I try to get my students to picture the scene as vividly and in as much detail as possible. At the same time, I try to avoid providing them with details that will impose my own images upon their fantasies. Thus, I say "walkway" rather than "sidewalk" or "path." Also, I use "home" rather than "house," since it is conceivable that someone might be in a cave or teepee. It is impossible to completely avoid imposing images. I caution my students about this problem and ask them not to take my directions too literally.

After they have finished their fantasies, I ask them to pull out pencil and paper and write down their answers to a number of questions. The papers will not be handed in, although they should add them to their journals. My purpose in asking them to write is to help them to remember their responses for our discussion that will follow. The questions I ask include: What was the appearance of the exterior of your home? Summarize it in one word. How did it feel when you walked into it? Again, summarize this in one word. What was the first thing that you saw as you entered your home? How many rooms did it have? What was the landscape like around your home? Characterize it in one word. How many people share your home with you? How far away is your nearest neighbor?

I begin the discussion by asking people to volunteer their answers to the first item. After a few responses are out, I get things going by asking people to elaborate upon their responses. I have gone through the fantasy, too, and make sure to share my own responses. As I go down the list of questions, it is possible to begin to identify differences and similarities among people's fantasies. This is generally a lively and enjoyable conversation. After the discussion has gone through their responses, I ask a few questions designed to introduce the intrusive presence of reality: What was the most expensive piece of recreational equipment at your home? (Do not forget your stereo.) What is your annual income necessary to support this style of life? What do you do to earn this income? My students tend to feel uncomfortable with this line of questioning and become evasive. For this reason it is best to introduce these questions only after discussion of the earlier ones.

Most of my students have a strong orientation toward wilderness that is reflected in their fantasies. They often visualize themselves living in a wilderness or semiwilderness, either alone or with one other person. Their nearest neighbor is generally half a mile to twenty miles away. It is quite a shock to them when I point out that this image of how to live is alienated from the life experience of the majority of people on earth. I may ask questions such as: What is the value of social life for you? Of the urban environment? To what extent do the things that you value in your fantasy depend upon these things for their existence? What percentage of the earth's population could this life-style support? Would your parents have responded to this exercise in a similar way? Your grandparents? Your peers? Someone from another country?

The purpose of this exercise is not to point a finger but to clarify values. As a coparticipant in the exercise, I can point to the characteristics and implications of my own ideals, which helps to squelch any paternalism on my part. Some students may protest that the exercise was too artificial and did not elicit a full picture of their ideal life-style. This is likely to be correct, but it does not devalue the exercise. The next exercise is a good follow-up to this one, and the results of both are often consistent with each other.

Picture show. In preparation for this exercise, I ask my students to search through their collections of snapshots and slides and select five photographs of places that are special to them—that have happy or pleasant associations. They are encouraged to select slides, but other kinds of photographs, including magazine pictures, are acceptable. They are told to bring them to a specific class meeting. If this is done as a follow-up to the ideal-home exercise, I have them make their selections before that exercise. If possible, both exercises are done during the same class.

The exercise begins with the students taking turns showing their photographs to the group. This is most easily done with a slide projector, which is why they are encouraged to bring slides. If there are a lot of small photographs and the group is large enough, I have them divide into smaller groups within which the pictures are shared. In any event, we begin first with the slides. I let each student present his or her photographs and explain how they were selected. The presentations often stimulate conversation, comments on the qualities of the photographs, and discussion of the places pictured. I try to keep this experience light and enjoyable, taking care to give each student a chance to make his or her presentation.

After the presentations, I broaden the discussion by asking questions such as: What are the general similarities and differences among the pictures? Were people present? Crowds? If so, what were they doing? Were there buildings present? If so, what was their function in relation to the people and the landscape? What relationships between people and nature were represented in the photographs? What pictures would you have brought had you been asked to bring ones with sad or unpleasant associations? If this is a follow-up to the ideal-home exercise, I ask my students to identify the similarities and differences between their responses to each exercise.

Both exercises should be wrapped up by explaining that their purpose was to help the students become aware of their values and biases regarding their images of preferable environments. It is important to be aware of them, because they will help to shape the students' responses to the literature that they will be reading. This may also open the question of the authors' biases.

Two books that are helpful in planning and leading values clarification exercises are *Values and Teaching* by Raths, Harmin, and Simon and *Values Clarification* by Simon, Howe, and Kirschenbaum.

Childhood memories. A number of the readings that I use include the authors' reminiscences of their childhoods. It has been useful to follow this reading with a discussion of my students' childhood involvements with nature. Writings that can lead to this discussion include Loren Eiseley's *The Night Country* (3–27); Pablo Neruda's *Memoirs* (5–28); John Muir's *The Story of My Boyhood and Youth*; John Burroughs' *My Boyhood*; Ernest Thompson Seton's *Trail of an Artist-Naturalist* (3–49); and Elizabeth Coatsworth's *Personal Geography* (3–35).

Prior to the class, the students are assigned selected readings and told to review relevant parts of the readings that have already been discussed. I ask them to pick a specific time and place in their childhood during which they felt very close to nature and write about that experience in their journals. Also, they are each asked to prepare a large map on which they depict the landscape of that experience as they knew it *as a child*. The objective is not to prepare an accurate representation of the landscape as it would be if they visited it as an adult but to be faithful to their subjective childhood experiences. What landmarks were important to them? What were the important paths and routes of travel? (These need not have any relationship to the roads and sidewalks of the adult world.) Did their childhood landscape have special places that they visited and special hide-outs? Were there imaginary places and characters? They are asked to depict all of this graphically on a single *large* sheet of paper that can be shared with the class.

The class begins with the students taking turns displaying their maps and describing their childhood landscapes. Each student can conduct a guided tour for the group. An alternative approach is to have them all pin their maps on the wall, and as one half of the group stands by their maps, the other half wanders around examining them and discussing them with the mapmakers. After a period of time, the roles are reversed. The discussion that follows can touch upon questions such as: What are the similarities and differences between the various childhood landscapes? How do you account for them? (This might include conversation about differences in family and ethnic histories, unique geographical qualities, personal temperament, and archetypes.) What relationships are there between the childhood landscapes and those preferred as an adult? (Refer to the ideal-home and picture-show exercises.) What are the similarities and differences between the class's reminiscences and those of the authors? In what ways does or does not the adult reflect the child?

The personal reflection and conversation generally stimulate a great deal of enthusiasm. I take advantage of it by asking each student to write an essay in which he or she evokes in the reader the special qualities of the childhood landscape that make it personally significant. In writing the essay, they may draw upon their journal entries, maps, and the class discussion. This writing assignment was first made at the request of my students—an indication of the enthusiasm that the exercise can kindle.

The nature fakers. I have been particularly interested in a debate during the first decade of the twentieth century over the disputed accuracy of the natural history reported by a number of literary naturalists. William J. Long, who is now forgotten, received the brunt of the criticism, although some was also directed toward Ernest Thompson Seton and a number of other authors. John Burroughs and Theodore Roosevelt were the chief architects of the debate, which has come to be known as the "nature fakers" controversy. They accused the nature fakers of fabricating tall tales, which they represented as absolutely true, in order to appeal to public sentiment and sell their nature books. Long heatedly defended himself, standing his ground before every attack.

An examination of this affair provides an excellent opportunity to discuss the literary naturalist's responsibilities as both an observer of nature and a creator of literature. The line between who was right and who was wrong was not as clearly defined as Burroughs and Roosevelt thought, and classroom discussion can become quite lively. One of the underlying issues of the debate was just how much we can empathize with animals. Another was the extent to which a literary naturalist can take liberties with facts and observations. There is bound to be disagreement on these issues in any group of students.

Relatively little has been written about the controversy. *The Life and Letters of John Burroughs,* edited by Clara Barrus, reviews the controversy from the perspective of a biographer who adored Burroughs. Paul Russell Cutright's *Theodore Roosevelt: Naturalist* emphasizes Roosevelt's role. Mark Sullivan ignores Burroughs' role in *Our Times: The United States, 1900–1925.* Unfortunately, none of these books gives proper attention to Long's side of the debate. My own review of the controversy, "The Nature Fakers: Conflicting Perspectives of Nature," attempts to give a balanced review of the affair and to identify its underlying issues.

Getting outside. It is often useful to get out of the classroom and into the primary source—nature. This both provides a welcome and refreshing break in the course format and grounds the class in the reality underlying all of the words. Since I have a background in natural history and ecology, I generally take my students on nature walks around the campus. These walks can build upon their interest in the literature, particularly if I am able to show them things in nature about which the authors have written. I have found, though, that I must take care not to overwhelm my students with information. Rather, I try to use a Socratic approach, encouraging them to make their own observations and discoveries. I try not to give them the idea that they must be "experts" before they can find things of interest and material for a nature essay. I have been surprised by a few students who were "put off" by the "expertise" of Leopold and Eiseley, whom they called "show-offish." In addition to the walks that are a formal part of the course, I have also conducted a series of weekend trips, and the college's Outdoors Program conducts a series of backpacking trips that my students are welcome to join.

I also have my students do some "Seton watching." This practice, which is named after Ernest Thompson Seton, has each of them find a private place to sit quietly and watch the natural world around them. This is the passive counterpart to a nature walk; they wait for nature to come to them. During a period of about thirty minutes of quiet sitting, they become aware of the sounds, sights, scents, and small events that they usually pass by. I encourage them to write about their observations in their journals. These entries might provide material for an essay. A modification of this exercise involves writing haiku about their observations and thoughts while Seton watching. Most students find haiku less intimidating than other poetry and can write haiku with relative ease. Before sending them out, I read some haiku to them and explain its form. When they finish their period of Seton watching, the students share their journal entries or poetry with the group.

This varied assemblage of books, exercises, writing assignments, and class discussions is held together by continual reference to some basic questions: What is the author's special view of nature? What is that of the individual students? What are the implications of these views? What alternatives are open to us? The books, exercises, and writing are all used as data that can inform this discussion. In a sense, this is not a course on natural history, literature, or writing, although these are important facets of it. Rather, its core lies in the students' personal reflection upon their own views of nature.

Environmental Literature:
An Approach Emphasizing Pluralism

Barbara Currier Bell

The course described here, "Humanity in Nature" (or CSiS 212), was offered by an interdisciplinary program at Wesleyan University called the College of Science in Society. CSiS 212 aimed to examine, through readings from literature, a variety of views about the relation of humanity with the natural world. Consciousness raising was not the primary issue. Instead, CSiS 212 was designed to demonstrate plurality, to show that, given the importance of the question about humanity in nature, the answers suggested have been many.

One important tool for this job was what I have called the "typological" organization of the literary material: that will be explained in the next section. Beyond that, comments on the course's problems and rewards are given frankly, in the hope that these may be helpful to colleagues.

Premises

CSiS 212 was taught in alternate weeks by myself and another professor, a biologist. The purpose of this arrangement was to expose students to both the humanistic and the scientific ways of thinking about the relation between humanity and the natural world. When we were planning the course, my colleague and I decided independently on the subjects we wanted to cover and made up our own reading lists. We attended each other's classes and participated occasionally in those, but we did not collaborate on the course in the true sense. Nonetheless, we hoped that just as many of the commonalities as of the disparities in our disciplines would be evident to students, especially since I planned to end my part of the course with a unit of readings on scientists' rationales for their work. The problems that came up with this arrangement will be mentioned later; suffice it to say here that most of the present article concerns only the part of the course I taught, which, indeed, was conceptualized as a course in itself.

The readings for the literary part of the course were structured around seven distinctly different views of the relationship between humanity and nature (Sufferer, Defender, Steward, Master, Sharer, Seeker, Skeptic). Three views were subordinate to the Sharer view (Challenger, Seed, Solaced). "Scientist" was a category rhetorically similar to the others but was not meant to subsume a separate type of view. The overall categorization of views was my own and differs from the categorizations most familiar to teachers of environmental literature in cutting across both culture and chronology. I did not, for instance, present a "romantic" view of the relation between humanity and nature, a "Christian" view, an "Enlightenment" view, or an "American" view. I tried to identify universal "types" and consequently to choose literary examples reflecting each view from several different periods and countries.

I adopted this typological approach to environmental literature partly because I needed to try something new and partly to justify my own favorite readings. Fair enough. Another premise had to do with the raw material of literature itself. Pace Marxist and other contextualist critics, everyone can agree that writing literature is a human activity that presses particularly strongly against the fences of time and place. New Criticism lives. As for the rest of my premises, I believe that the conventional approach to environmental literature is gloomy. It is deterministic. It makes us feel as if humans at certain times and in certain places cannot see their relation with nature differently than they do. A plurality of views, according to this frame of mind, can only exist *among* peoples, and if so, the possibilities for change are drastically limited. If, on the other hand, views of nature transcend culture and period, then a plurality does or can exist—whether consciously realized or not—*within* people. Put another way, various views are available here and now, and humanity is liberated to change. Such moral masonry, arguable as I realize it is, lay beneath the structure I chose. I have dealt in "Humanity in Nature: Toward a Fresh Approach" with the philosophical questions and debates that I know swirl around most of the foregoing points, but an extensive rationalization would not be suited to the pedagogical purpose of the present essay and, besides, would be too long.

Many of the samples on the reading list were comparative rarities in literature in that they expressed a view of the relation between humanity and nature that was "pure." Very few secondary works were on the reading list because few were suited to my unconventional types. The only two scholarly studies included were used to challenge the cultural and chronological stereotypes instead of to support them.

From the perspective of one examining many environmental literature courses, the structure of CSiS 212's reading and the particular sort of reading list that structure dictated are the course's most distinctive features. A second type of reading supplemented the assigned list, however. It was student-initiated and linked with the following format for class meetings. The class was meant to be the "growing edge" of the course. For about a third of every meeting, I would outline the chief features of the view(s) illustrated in the assigned readings for that time and everyone would discuss them. During the last two thirds of the meeting, according to a schedule worked out at the semester's start, students would present their own papers. Their assignment was to describe the view of the relation between humanity and nature they had found in a work of art (literary work, film, painting, sculpture, musical piece) or felt in some personal experience. The "raw material" was open (although, in fact, most students chose to study literary works), nor were the students required to cast their reports in terms of the types of views defined by me; they had to address those in some way, however. They made the relevant readings available beforehand to their classmates, so that after they had finished their presentations everyone else could comment.

Turning now to outcomes, I will steer away from those judgments about CSiS 212 that would be relevant only at Wesleyan and comment, rather, on those pedagogical features of the course that can readily be shared with other environmental literature teachers.

Problems

1. Interdisciplinary Teaching

I and my colleague had thought that, purely for the sake of variety, the students would like switching from one teacher to another in alternate class meetings. We found they did not; they felt unsettled, and the alternation actually exacerbated their sense of the difference between our separate disciplines.

At an intellectual level, the approach of alternation failed more importantly. My colleague and I went off in different directions. Of course, we did so partly because of the pressure we felt to cover twice as much material as in a conventional disciplinary course. That reason begs the question, however. More fundamentally, although we both sought to treat the subject of humanity's place in nature, we started out by defining humanity differently. I thought in terms of humanity's purpose—of humanity as agency; he thought in terms of humanity's function—of humanity as mechanism. This difference is so familiar and so intricate that it need not and cannot be addressed much further here. Two second thoughts only. One: the problems with interdisciplinary teaching prove no less troublesome for their predictability. Two: the popular "Do your own thing" school of teaching is especially unsuited for interdisciplinary teaching.

Second thoughts aside, the reader can see plainly why most of the comments that follow apply to my part of the course as if it were an independent entity.

2. The Typological Approach

Many students who enroll in environmental literature classes are activists. As such, they consider culture and history the key determinants of human conduct. An approach to literature that seeks to transcend culture and history bothers them. Thus, much of the time in my class was spent debating the premise for the syllabus or assuming a different one rather than getting through the material as planned. Put another way, since the structure for the readings in CSiS 212 was so different from what the students expected, the course pulled in the direction of being a course in literary criticism instead of a course in literature. As a person whose field is criticism, I was not unhappy with that turn of events, but I overestimated the students' ability to deal with literary-critical issues. A suggestion for improvement would be to add some introductory reading about the relation of literature to society to the syllabus and discuss it at the outset. Also, the course's novel approach could be tested on the students themselves. Asking them to articulate right away, however sketchily, their own personal views about humanity in nature would confront them with data contrary to their antitypological expectations that would be hard to ignore and easy to discuss. A final suggestion would be to spend an early class on two sets of three or four short readings, six to eight in all, that would be especially well controlled. Subject matter and genre would be held constant for both sets, while theme and writer's background would be varied independently to give as succinct a challenge as possible to the conventional categories for views of nature.

Another problem with the typological approach was that it seemed artificial. The first stage is to identify the types. As mentioned elsewhere, single-minded, short, and quite often unrepresentative sorts of readings are chosen for this purpose, of necessity; thus the job seems simple and rigid. The second stage comes in applying the types to more complicated works of literature. At this point, the job seems enriching. CSiS 212's schedule was planned so that students would spend part of each class identifying types and part applying them. Yet the shift tended to confuse the students about the difference between the two jobs, and, if anything, they thought the first was supposed to predominate over the second. Although class members slowly became more adept at handling dialectical shifts of view in literary works—two of them, for instance, collaborated well to explicate one of feminist Robin Morgan's poems as a statement of the ideal relation between humanity and nature—they did not seem prepared to handle subtler counterpoints, such as the irony in Tournier's *Friday*, a book I had assigned for an earlier version of CSiS 212.

A final problem with the typological approach is the necessity of demonstrating similar views expressed in literary works from different cultures and periods. Most so-called humanities teachers' ability to come up with a reading list sufficient to this purpose will be limited, as mine demonstrates, because of the relatively narrow training they receive. Broader training is the solution most often advocated, but I think ensuring sufficient breadth would be impossible for one person; rather, more frequent collaboration with people who know literature from other cultures would help, and they can be found not necessarily in a literature department but in an area studies program or in a religion or anthropology department.

Rewards

1. Eclecticism

A syllabus for a course like CSiS 212, emphasizing plurality, can include some of the greatest works literature has to offer. Very little is ruled out. I have compiled a long list of alternative readings—some better ones—to illustrate each type. Similarly, the possibilities for creating new types to order the readings are numerous. This is not a specialist's course. It is the sort of course where—raw materials being abundant for student and teacher alike—creativity can have a heyday. The degree of eclecticism may be indicated by listing the subjects of a few student papers: "*Black Elk Speaks* on Nature," "The View of Nature in Taoist Writings," "The Chief in *One Flew over the Cuckoo's Nest*," "Nature's Influence on Humanity: An Eskimo Myth," "Selective Writings about the Desert: A Spectrum of Views about

Humanity in Nature." The students' enthusiasm for picking a variety of works balanced their frustration with simple types. One woman commented: "What I liked best about the course were the students' papers. People were into so many different kinds of reading." Indeed, encouraging students with different ethnic or academic backgrounds to write about works they know are unfamiliar to their classmates would also help counter the teachers' limitations mentioned earlier.

2. *Impact on Values*

Any view about the relation of humanity with nature has an obvious and important ethical dimension. A course in environmental literature that emphasizes plurality can stir students anew to confront certain of their own "oughts." For instance, I found students to be less familiar with values different from theirs regarding nature than they were with values different from theirs regarding people. Genocidal statements from rulers like Idi Amin or Heng Samrin did not shock them (however much they disagreed), but images of crusaderlike enmity against nature did. Ethically, what the pluralistic environmental literature course has to offer students is a fresh chance to debate their criteria for determining right and wrong.

At another level, an environmental literature course may demonstrate how values carry over from one part of human life to another. Students quickly grasped the idea that one's treatment of nature may be reflected in one's treatment of other people. (William Leiss's *The Domination of Nature* was widely read among CSiS 212 students, even though Leiss analyzes only one case of the general thesis.)

Finally, the second-level question mentioned earlier about the proper theoretical approach to any subject has ethical dimensions too. Our class became too prickly over method; but another time around, that bramble patch could yield a pedagogical rose.

3. *Adaptability*

A course like CSiS 212 is potentially adaptable in many ways. Because the readings are so varied and accessible, because the structure allows for easy cuts or additions, and because the theme is so engaging and broad, the course can be taught in a variety of departments and at a variety of levels. For instance, it could be made part of an introductory ecology course to stimulate thought about the variety of reasons for studying ecology (say, to establish species' identities, to increase a sense of sharing among species, to give humans more control over ecological systems, to increase knowledge for its own sake, to encourage awe). It could be taught as a humanities course, either at the introductory level, for its engaging theme, or at the second level, to play off against a version of the progress of human thought along cultural and chronological lines. It could be taught in an English department at an introductory level simply to stimulate reading or as an upper-level course where especially challenging texts could be studied, from *The Tempest* to *Moby-Dick* to "The Idea of Order at Key West," or where questions of critical theory, such as the worth of thematic criticism, could be raised. It could be adapted for use in history, philosophy, religion, or anthropology departments to provide supplementary thematic material or to compare with the less typological approaches of those disciplines. Of course, its appropriateness for interdisciplinary programs such as ours at Wesleyan, whose numbers are growing, is obvious. Limits on its adaptability were described in my earlier comments about interdisciplinary teaching; nonetheless, the niche for such a course seems spacious.

All the rewards just listed have associated liabilities. Eclecticism can cause confusion; challenge can cause closure; adaptation can cause crises in character. More determinative, in CSiS 212's local circumstances, were demands on staff time in a climate of shrinkage and consolidation. The CSiS 212 described here is no longer being taught. Its supporters hope the budget will allow it at some future time. Meanwhile, we continue to believe that the concept of courses relating literature and the environment is worthwhile, that the particular kind of environmental literature course described here offers promise, and that shared experience in this area of teaching can profit everyone involved.

Readings

1. Humanity as Sufferer (Stephen Crane, "The Open Boat"; Sylvia Plath, "Blackberrying"; Richard Wright, "The Man Who Saw the Flood")
2. Humanity as Defender (*Beowulf*, part 1)
3. Humanity as Steward (Shakespeare, *Troilus and Cressida* 1.3.85–126; Gerard Manley Hopkins, "Pied Beauty"; E. M. W. Tillyard, *The Elizabethan World Picture*; René Dubos, "Franciscan Conservation versus Benedictine Stewardship" [*God Within* 153–74])
4. Humanity as Master (Daniel Defoe, *Robinson Crusoe*; Genesis 1.1–23)
5. Humanity as Sharer (Henry David Thoreau, *Walden*, or Annie Dillard, *Pilgrim at Tinker Creek*; Lillian Hellman, "Turtle" [*Pentimento* 263–83]; Hopi tribe, "The Meaning of Corn"; Avilik Eskimos, Carvers' chant [Dubos 12])
6. Humanity as Challenger (Ernest Hemingway, "The Short Happy Life of Francis Macomber"; N. Scott Momaday, *House Made of Dawn* 197–204)
7. Humanity as Seed/Solaced (John Steinback, "The Snake"; Paul Radin, "The Winnebago Trickster Cycle" [*Trickster* 3–60]; African folk tale, "How the Earth Was Peopled" [Hogins 9]; "Northern Mythology" [Hogins 15–17]; Katherine Anne Porter, "The Grave"; Jean Toomer, "Karintha" and "Song of the Son")
8. Humanity as Seeker (Albert Camus, "The Adulterous Woman" [*Exile* 3–33]; Margaret Atwood, *Surfacing*)
9. Humanity as Skeptic (Robert Frost, "Design")
10. Humanity as Scientist (Francis Bacon, selections from *The Great Instauration* and *Novum Organum*, *The New Atlantis*; Gerald Holton, Introduction to *Science and Culture*; Lewis Thomas, "Hubris in Science"; Franklin Russell, "The Running Eiders" [*Secret Islands* 28–37]; Janet W. Brown, "Native American Contributions to Science, Engineering, and Medicine"; Aeschylus, *Prometheus Bound*)

Some Necessary Heresies Revisited: Science Fiction as Environmental Fiction

Felicia Florine Campbell

Imagination is our most valuable and least exploited natural resource. Without the solutions that may come through its free play, the future may be indeed grim. Yet few of us would deny that the traditional, narrow academic process too often reduces imagination and stifles creativity.

Studying science fiction in conjunction with another discipline can help to stimulate imagination and creativity both in the classroom and outside it. For example, Robert A. Heinlein coined the word "grokking" in *Stranger in a Strange Land* to describe a psychological state of total assimilation of something through understanding, feeling, empathizing with, and identifying with it. Heinlein's hero Smith came equipped with the sophisticated personal equipment he needed for "grokking" the new reality into which he had been thrust. Lacking this sophisticated personal equipment, we can turn to science fiction as one way to help us "grok" alternative futures and the alien reality into which we have been thrust. Thus we can see our problems more clearly in a context out of the traditional one that too often blinds us through our very familiarity with it.

Let me illustrate from my experience with "Ecofiction," a course I developed several years ago in response to a request from the environmental studies program. "Ecofiction" deals with both cultural and physical environmental problems as they are predicted, illuminated, and sometimes solved in fiction, primarily science fiction. The course grew from a lecture entitled "Science Fiction as Fact" that I delivered in 1970 to a several-hundred-student class in "Man and the Environment," an interdisciplinary course dealing with such problems as pollution, overpopulation, and depletion of natural resources.

I based the lecture on the concept that those of us in the industrialized nations who are environmentally aware are "strangers in a strange land." We have been taught that industrial "progress" is good, that it is our duty to consume so that we may produce so that we may once more consume. The result (as we are becoming bitterly aware) is that we have defiled the earth, bringing ourselves to the brink of annihilation. Choking in our own waste, consuming pounds of untested chemicals in our foods, we are becoming truly alienated from our own planet, afraid to breathe the air, drink the water, or eat the food. The media, which could be a device for environmental reeducation, instead seem bent on creating C. M. Kornbluth's overpopulated society of five billion persons with an average IQ of forty-five. Even Kornbluth, with his invention of *Take It and Stick It* ("Marching Morons"), a television program aimed at the morons, was unable to come up with anything more inane than *Let's Make a Deal* or *The Dating Game* or, more recently, *That's Incredible*. In the course, I touched on this and a half dozen more works, ending with a discussion of ecological principles as illustrated in Frank Herbert's *Dune*, in which the ecology of the planet plays a role greater than the role of any of the major characters.

The lecture was very successful, and my colleagues in science and social sciences asked why it had been so much easier for me to make an impact with my presentation than it had been for them in their fact-filled doomsday lectures.

A large part of the answer, of course, lies in the nature of fiction and of the literary process: science (and *any*) fiction is more than a mere vehicle to carry an idea. It humanizes the idea, making the general specific, and allows us to suspend our disbelief long enough for the impact of that idea to hit us. This is particularly important if one is attempting to convey a large and unpleasant truth, such as the danger of overpopulation and mass starvation. Graphs and statistics may provide an accurate picture, but it is one that is really difficult for many people to identify with. Science fiction, however, because it deals with people, whether earthlings or aliens, can, perhaps, carry many more of us into the midst of a starving, overpopulated world and cause us to live there for a while.

Science fiction also frees us to be heretics, releasing us, on occasion, from traditional logic and from at least some of the "truths" of traditional science and social science. While heresy is fundamental to the intellectual and imaginative process, it is no more popular with the establishment than it has ever been. The irony is that without heretical approaches we cannot hope to explore many of the dimensions of the human condition, whether present or future. Without heresy, we are in danger of becoming dedicated to a single "truth" like Sherwood Anderson's grotesques, and similarly warped.

At the beginning of every "Ecofiction" course, I warn the students that it is a course in heresy and that many of their most cherished ideas will come under attack. As I deal with both physical and cultural environmental problems, the areas of attack are almost limitless, and I vary the texts from semester to semester to keep myself from going stale.

Further, that all certainty is ultimately uncertain is a precept of future study as I perceive it. While we must prepare, insofar as we are able, for the futures projected by professional societal and technological forecasters, we must also make use of what I call the "what if" factor to project as many alternatives as we can conceive, no matter how far-out these alternatives may seem. The works that we study are selected to act as catalytic agents for creative thought.

C. S. Lewis' fairy tale *That Hideous Strength* illuminates the conflict between two cultures. In it we see the sellout of the universities and the humanities to a coldly dehumanized science, and Merlin himself has to return to restore a natural balance. Spin-offs in discussion range from the ethics of grantsmanship to the warpings of the researchers' findings to keep the grantors happy. Such discussion, I might add, has a tendency to make students march off to my colleagues demanding to be told that it isn't so. It also has a tendency to seriously annoy said colleagues, who often feel that such topics are best left undiscussed.

Ethical problems of gene manipulation and cloning are raised by Frank Herbert's *The Eyes of Heisenberg*. In it he not only projects a world governed by gene manipulators but illustrates the Heisenbergian principle of randomness, which, of course, is a major factor in examining any alternative future and invalidates all certainty but its own. Kate Wilhelm gives us a different look at this principle in *Where Late the Sweet Birds Sang*.

Ursula K. Le Guin takes us in *The Left Hand of Darkness* to the planet Winter where we can explore a truly androgynous society. Understanding each other's sexuality is difficult at best, but moving the discussion to another world and another culture seems, at least temporarily, to defuse some of the biases of some of the discussants. This is important, since the relations that human beings have with one another are, of course, central to environmental problems. All value systems and methods of perceiving must be called into question. While this can be done in only a very limited sense in such a course, it is possible that the students may retain the habit of questioning once they have left it.

Colin Wilson's *The Mind Parasites* is a translation into science fiction of his *The New Existentialism*. With its stress on humanism and on the potential for humans to grow beyond their present limitations by utilizing the usually dormant ninety percent of the brain, developing to the point where technology as we know it becomes irrelevant, it provides an alternative to Skinnerian determinism and to traditional existentialism. Wilson's *Philosopher's Stone* takes us a step further in human evolution as the major characters develop psychometry. In addition to traditional works of science fiction such as those mentioned, I have recently added Hofstadter and Dennett's *The Mind's I*, a marvelous collection of science fiction, fantasy, and reflections dealing with relationships of mind, body, and environment. This book is an excellent resource for provoking the modes of thought I am attempting to foster.

My "Ecofiction" students not only read and discuss but create. They design projects either collectively or individually and present them to the class. My only stipulation is that the projects be serious and environmentally oriented.

The first time I taught the course, the class produced a 120-page illustrated magazine called *Ecofriction*. More recently students have produced films, designs for ideal homes, artwork of all types, musical scores, short plays, a futuristic banquet, numerous short stories, cartoons, one novel, and, of course, a few standard research papers.

Flexibility and willingness to entertain all sorts of alternatives are, of course, essential to the success of the course. My students continually bring new works to class (science fiction readers *read*), and in one class we may touch on both time travel and Capra's *The Tao of Physics*. I make the grading system flexible also. Students may opt to be graded on the basis of traditional examination or to contract with me to be graded on the basis of a special project or the combination of a special project and examination.

Finally, I find "Ecofiction" rewarding because there is such a diversity of new material that one needn't worry about burning out. Along with the flood of science fiction on the market, such periodicals as *Omni* make extensive use of both scientific knowledge and science fiction. Let us hope that with science fiction's new found acceptance in academe, science fiction writers are not seduced from their heresies by keeping one eye on the critics and the other on course adoptions.

Pastoral: An Ageless Form
of Environmental Literature

Joan Weatherly

When, after twenty years of fragmentary teaching of environmental literature in all my classes, I at last had the opportunity—through Memphis State's University College—to develop a course exclusively on the subject, I could find no better approach than pastoral to place ecological problems in historical perspective. Deeply ingrained in Western culture from Greek times and in all human experience through the Edenic myth, to which it is closely related, the pastoral motif affords a means of discussing without sentimentality humankind's place in nature and its chances for survival, America as an extension of the westward movement, and the successes and failures of the old Jeffersonian agrarian dream. Viewing pastoral in its broad historical perspective shows that environmental problems are age-old, though they may have accelerated in the last century. The real-ideal tension innate to pastoral is an excellent means of comprehending the paradox of artistic creativity, and the pastoral characteristic of celebrating life through art in the very face of encroaching mechanization permits diachronic and synchronic analysis of the humanities-technology dilemma.

And for teaching pastoral, its numerous versions (see Empson) and post–industrial revolution manifestations in Western art from Greece to Disneyland, there was—and is—no better model than Leo Marx's "middle landscape pastoralism" as presented in *The Machine in the Garden*. The basic paradox of Marx's title—the machine in the garden—relates economically humanity's attempt to fuse the machine into the environment. Although Marx deals primarily with nineteenth-century American literature, his archetypal paradigm—"the middle landscape" as a pastoral setting between the civilized and the primitive—soon seizes the imagination of students, who begin to think creatively as they see its innumerable manifestations in Western culture, particularly their own.

To the call of the interdisciplinary MSU University College for a course emphasizing humanity's attempt to form a coherent place for itself in the world through the humanities, I responded with a course proposal combining pastoral painting and landscape literature. Unable to find an available art historian to team-teach the course, I expanded the emphasis on pastoral music and was joined by Douglas Lemmon of the MSU music department. He compiled the entire discography for the course, for which I had already developed the main outline, defined the scope, and written the narrative sections for the syllabus.

Taught first on the sophomore level as University 1210, "Technology and Aesthetics in the Fine Arts," and later tightened into upper-division Thematic Studies 3506, "Landscape in Art, Literature, and Music," the course retained its general outline and much of its specific content. The main change made in the syllabus each time the course underwent revision was the dropping of some of the longer literary works and the addition of a few more pertinent musical works, such as Henze's *Muses of Sicily*, based on Vergil's *Eclogues*. Gradually the syllabus has been trimmed, the key pastoral works from each major era being retained.

The pastoral motif proved an ideal means of considering environmental problems in an interdisciplinary class and of fulfilling the University College requirement that courses be centered around a theme. The course was structured largely around my adaptation of Marx's concept of middle landscape pastoralism and what I call the dispossession archetype, both based on Vergil's eclogue 1 (see Weatherly). The key elements of the archetype are the "shepherd figure" who has been displaced or threatened; the middle landscape setting—the idealized landscape located between urban civilization and primitive nature—in which the shepherd's position is threatened, debased, or lost; and the counterforce—some materialistic, technological element causing the dispossession.

The abundance of related pastoral materials made selection difficult, but generally pieces by famous writers in key periods were chosen, mainly to show that a pastoral stage often marks a writer's entry into the traditional "progress of poesy." Usually concerned with ecological problems, these great writers, beginning with Theocritus, nearly always have deep roots in their native regions and find regeneration in the myths they weave around their native landscapes. The overall structure of the course was historical, with emphasis on the development of the pastoral motif from classical Greek times through the present. Study of key works from each period showed how pastoral has developed through adaptation and mutation, always keeping the basic town-country contrast feature even in satirical pieces. Hence the chief problem was selecting from the great body of pastoral compositions. The greatest desperation came each term on the first or second day when students realized how much material there was to cover. The second most serious problem was keeping the focus on the pastoral theme—easily done in literature and in painting, but more difficult in music—and its interdisciplinary nature and relation to environmental problems. A third and far more easily solved problem was to dispel the notion that pastoral is a mere sentimental, escapist, hopelessly idealistic genre synonymous with primitivism.

Both of the required papers had to treat the pastoral motif, and at least one of them had to be a comparison involving at least two disciplines (history, literature, music, painting, philosophy). Students were required to keep a journal recording reactions to the works, citing varied examples of middle landscape pastoralism, and listing possible topics for papers, an especially productive activity for upper- and lower-division classes.

For the students, the papers, which were shared with classmates, proved to be rich and highly rewarding experiences, confirming my premise that the pastoral motif is a genuinely universal archetypal phenomenon. It was particularly inspiring for students to begin seeing the middle landscape paradigm in all sorts of places—in gubernatorial candidates' advertisements; art (Japanese flower arrangements); music (especially Joni Mitchell, environmentalist crusaders, and musical comedies); literature; photography; and the "real" world (one written assignment required students to describe a remembered middle landscape). Once the students got past the abstract concept of pastoral and started looking at their environment and at literature and art, they had little trouble choosing topics. So pervasive, indeed, is the motif that students began to find it everywhere, but its infinite diversity ensures that the search for it never seems repetitious.

The Henze musical version of Vergil's eclogues 1 and 9, which was not used the first time we taught the course, was especially helpful in defining the basic tension created by motion in pastoral—the tension exemplified in eclogue 1 in the contrast between Tityrus' reclining in the shade and Meliboeus' prospect of dispossession. Listening to this twentieth-century composition based on ancient material effectively clarified the paradoxical nature of pastoral. Discussing the relation between the ancient literature and the modern music focused attention on what Monroe K. Spears calls the "psychic landscape." It became apparent that the natural world is reflected in the spiritual world of art and that it is possible to study the various modes of perceiving art and nature in all times and places. Films, especially Bryan Forbes's *The Mad Woman of Chaillot*, were consistently effective in emphasizing the environmental slant. In both the lower- and upper-division versions of the course, it was the reading of *The Blithedale Romance* and the viewing of *The Mad Woman* that brought home the relationship between ancient pastoral and modern environmental interests. Hawthorne's novel—like so many of the works exemplifying pastoral—at once embraces and satirizes the motif's tendency toward idealism. The three films used, even after budget cuts, were Paul Czinner's *As You Like It*, François Truffaut's *The Wild Child*, and *The Mad Woman of Chaillot*. The taped musical selections were placed in the library for the students' convenience, and some of them made copies for themselves.

Field trips are, of course, a must for any environmental literature course: almost any park will suffice for *seeing* a middle landscape, but in Memphis we were extremely lucky to have a huge park—one recently saved from destruction through the rerouting of a proposed interstate highway— with virgin timber in the middle of town. Arrangements for our main field trip to Faulkner country and my farm in Mississippi I made myself with very little expense but highly productive returns for the short time we were able to spend.

Among the students in the dozens of racially, sexually, and chronologically integrated classes with whom I have discussed literature in the last two decades, I find environmental problems to be the chief concern among the popular—and unpopular—issues. And I find the pastoral theme to be the most efficient way to approach those problems diachronically and synchronically. The pastoral motif offers a workable paradigm for teaching belles lettres as environmental literature without sentimentality, and so productive is Marx's theme of middle landscape pastoralism that were I ever to teach a course on environmental literature alone, I think it would be called "Middle Landscape Pastoralism in Western Literature."

That environmental literature is closely related to music and art has become clear to me now: I find that I can no longer teach literature without bringing in these arts. I am convinced too that love for the environment and one's place is a potent source of inspiration for all artists, for art is always about landscape, literal and psychic, and the attempt to get back to the garden.

Note: Any reader wishing to obtain more information about the course may write to me in care of the Memphis State University Department of English, Memphis, TN 38152.

Readings

(Required texts have included *The Norton Anthology of Poetry*, ed. Eastman et al.; *The Exploited Eden*, ed. Gangewere; and Van de Bogart, *Introduction to the Humanities*.)

1. Classicism (Vergil, Theocritus)
2. Medieval (excerpts from Chaucer's Nun's Priest's Tale, *Sir Gawain and the Green Knight, Romance of the Rose, Morte Darthur, Song of Roland, Divine Comedy*)
3. Renaissance (Shakespeare, *As You Like It*; Sidney, More, Marlowe, Raleigh, Spenser)
4. Baroque (Marvell, Herrick, Morton, Bradford, Irving, Milton)
5. Neoclassicism (Pope, Thomson, Gray, Goldsmith, Crèvecoeur, Franklin, Dwight, Paine, Jefferson)
6. Romanticism (Hawthorne, *Blithedale Romance*, or Hardy, *Far from the Madding Crowd*; Wordsworth, Coleridge, Byron, Shelley, Keats, Emerson, Thoreau)
7. Realism, Nationalism, Postimpressionism (Tennyson, Twain, Arnold, Browning, Whitman, Morris, Mallarmé)
8. Impressionism, Symbolism, Expressionism, Imagism, Cubism (Yeats, Lawrence, Hopkins, Faulkner, et al.)
9. Wasteland, Dadaism (Eliot, Toomer, Crane, Hemingway, Wright, et al.)
10. Surrealism, Despair (Hesse, Fitzgerald, Agee, Steinbeck, Mann, et al.)
11. Existentialism, Psychic Landscape (Tolkien, Ellison, Mailer, Levertov; Adams, *Watership Down*, or Vonnegut, *Breakfast of Champions* or *Slapstick*)

"Nature" and the Classroom: Outdoors and In

Jack Kligerman

I first taught a seminar on nature and the nature essay in American literature during the spring semester, 1975 (see Kligerman). Then as now, I was teaching at Herbert H. Lehman College, CUNY, located in the Bronx. The school, bordered on one side by a parking lot and reservoir and on the other by the "El," encroached on from the south by an urban blight reminiscent of London after the blitz, seemed an improbable place to explore such a subject as "nature." As it turned out, however, the Bronx was just right. After all, "nature" is a concept, a container into which civilization has poured its ideas and experiences of the natural world. "Nature" was born of the city, so what better place to start from on an expedition into what, for my students, was an unknown land, a wilderness: "nature"—a concept that looked to them like the edges of a forest, serene, safe from a distance, separate from themselves, capable, as it seemed, of being held in one's hands like an enclosed small terrarium.

A few students in the 1975 class had some hiking or camping experience, but for most of them "nature" existed only in imagination or in city parks. Some were readers, but for the most part what they had read had little to do with the nature essay. They were uniformly individualistic: the seminar was offered in a special college program designed for self-motivated students. Surprisingly, not all of them had visited the New York Botanical Gardens, a fifteen-minute walk from Lehman College, but they all had seen bears in the Bronx Zoo. One student would graduate that June and enroll in a summer program in Woods Hole, Massachusetts, at the Oceanographic Institute. Another would graduate three years later and begin an M.S. degree in botany at Cornell. A third is currently a Ph.D. candidate in English at Columbia. A fourth dropped out.

Nature for them was birds, trees, flowers, mountains, rivers, sunshine, sky—all nouns in the plural or what John Locke called "ideas of simple sensations." Their natural world was a "virgin land" in perpetual late springtime, where birds sang, where one tripped barefoot in the greensward, wore no boots, sweaters, or rain gear, carried no provisions or insect repellent, and wandered safely in the company of one's friends or lover. I am not exaggerating. Ask a class, as I did, to write down twenty-five associations on the word *nature* and see what you get. Except for one student, they knew nothing of hypothermia, of sore feet, of dangers on a trail: this one student had taken a bad fall climbing Kaaterskill Falls in the Catskill Mountains, two hours north of the Bronx.

They hardly thought of disease or of earthquakes, flood, fire, or famine as natural; the mistral did not exist for them. Neither they nor myself knew anything at the time about mitochondria, nor had the new biology or our genetic kinship with the world "out there" penetrated our conception of "nature." Their fears, except perhaps in dreams, were of muggers, of getting lost in "bad" neighborhoods, of having the lights go out on the subway or getting a flat on the East River Drive. Their dragons were dealers, addicts. They obviously had a mythology quite unlike the one I would introduce to them.

At the time I knew some things; others I have learned only since and have incorporated into the seminar. I came to the course from a dissertation on James Fenimore Cooper and an acquaintance with the "languages" of natural description in Western literary tradition and in art. I could explain the principles of the beautiful, the picturesque, and the sublime. I knew some warblers when I saw them, though only in spring and with the aid of Peterson's guide, and had hiked in the Yosemite high country and over Knife Edge on Mount Katahdin in Maine. In teaching the seminar I was hoping to do for myself what Robert Frost had advocated at the end of "Two Tramps in Mudtime": "to unite / My avocation and my vocation / As my two eyes make one in sight."

In truth, I could present a conventional course in the "nature essay" and act as pathfinder for my students in their explorations of both "nature" and the natural world. I did not know in 1975, however, that the seminar's greatest value lay not in its traditional academic material but in the struggles the students would have in becoming the keepers of their own journals and the writers of their own nature essays. Although I knew "nature" had a history, I had to learn a great deal outside "English" to bring it up to date. Furthermore, I needed my own kind of fall to find my Self a wilderness full of surprises, a land containing wild beasts and rivers and mountains without end, to know in my heart that writing about the natural world is writing about oneself. Finally, I discovered that the more nature is felt as a metaphor and not thought of as an idea with a history, the closer one gets to the Truth it contains. My seminar had changed in time.

I still keep the same basic objectives and course structure that I had when I set out, however. They have proved useful. The readings include books and essays on nature in American literature, with more emphasis now on contemporary writers than on the nineteenth-century tradition and English background. Supplementary material embraces landscape painting and photography, though I am now willing to bring in creative problems with my own black-and-white photographs. We continue to add practical experience and a scientific point of view through field trips, though possibilities open and close depending on the composition of the class: in my 1980 seminar, half of the class was older than I, half younger, and it was the elder half that participated most actively on field trips. In 1975, a backpacking trip to Slide Mountain in the Catskills ended the term. For my most recent class, hour walks were all several students could handle. A typical program of field trips, spaced two weeks apart during the semester, is this: (1) The New-York Historical Society and/or the Metropolitan Museum of Art; (2) the New York Botanical Gardens; (3) The Pine Barrens of New Jersey; (4) Van Cortlandt Park, New York City; (5) Jamaica Bay Wildlife Refuge, New York City; (6) Ward Pound Ridge Reservation, Westchester County, New York; (7) the New Jersey Palisades and the Hudson River of New Jersey and New York; (8) a backpacking trip to Slide Mountain, the Catskills, New York.

I now make keeping the journal the major writing task of the term; students may write a formal essay if they wish and receive an extra college credit for their labors. I take it upon myself to interject traditional matters into class discussion: the English background, especially Wordsworth; eighteenth-century aesthetics; the pastoral tradition in Western literature and art, as well as brief forays into Chinese and Japanese painting and poetry; metaphor and the ways language both frees and enslaves one's perception of the natural world; ecology and the polemics of nature; and so on.

But even as I take one or another of the above paths, I keep bringing my students back to the central concern of how difficult it is to be an observer and to write down what one sees. I stress the fact that observation involves a constant interaction between self and the natural world. I teach that the journal is both a record of what one sees and a revelation of one's self in the act of seeing. In the journal assignment, the class was asked to find one place in the natural world that was accessible and could be visited about two to three times a week. Their task was to observe what they saw around them and to make regular entries in their journals, the length determined by the particular matter at hand. Students could put in their journals whatever came to mind: straight observations, meditations, or metaphysical flights of fancy. In the meantime, the class began its readings with selections from Thoreau's journal, in order to get a sense of the possible directions journal entries could take. When students had trouble saying what they saw—in a strict sense, naming objects—I helped them out with my experience or with references to numerous field guides, with which I wanted them to get acquainted.

What proved extremely valuable to the students was the perpetual struggle with vocabulary, with the attempt to describe without interpreting. I collected the journals about once every three weeks, both to check on the students' diligence (alas!) and to make suggestions regarding how to expand or otherwise enrich the entries. I also had students read their journal entries occasionally in seminar meetings, so that their fellow students could both share their experiences and see other possibilities for writing in their own journals. One student was astonished on noticing that the world she saw was usually five to ten feet away: never closer, rarely beyond.

When we now read nature essays, I wanted my students not just to learn what the concept *nature* meant for various writers but to see that other writers' problems in seeing and writing were no different in kind from their own, that each of them, in truth, could be his or her own Thoreau, John Muir, Joseph Wood Krutch, or Annie Dillard. I really believe this.

I still refer students to the following texts for a historical view of "nature": John Conron, *The American Landscape*; Hans Huth, *Nature and the American*; and Roderick Nash, *Wilderness and the American Mind*. But I require only the book by Nash and have my students read selectively from it. I deemphasize the historical tradition for two reasons: (1) I do not want my students to be intimidated by the interpretations of others, and, believe me, they are very easily intimidated; (2) I want to counteract the tendency to equate education with learning facts à la Gradgrind. To accomplish this latter end I stress the interaction of inner and outer worlds so obvious in the nature essay, a process basic to any kind of thinking.

When I concentrate in class on how a writer's language, especially through metaphor, projects an interpretation of the natural world on that world, it is because I believe an understanding of the metaphoric *process* more important than the intellectual content alone of the metaphors. To sharpen one's students' perception of this process is to force them to recognize how arbitrary some words are and how arbitrary good writing should not be. Students read Thoreau and others not as models of what they should write but as examples of how difficult the writing process is. The texts are seen, then, less as documents for the cultural historian and more as end products of a very human struggle toward self-expression and self-realization.

To help my students concretize the central struggle of nature essays and the major concern of the course, I bring in examples of paintings and photographs of the American landscape. I show how a painter like Thomas Cole projects the same outlines on "real" and imaginary landscapes, how he and others of the Hudson River school saw the American scene within the confines of an eighteenth-century European tradition of spatial organization. In the 1975 class, for instance, we looked at the paintings of Asher Brown Durand to see how the contraction of space within a canvas—the movement toward close-ups—challenged conventions and began to construct a different kind of artistic space. We turned to the early landscape photographers T. H. O'Sullivan and W. H. Jackson (*The Photographer and the American Landscape*, ed. John Szarkowski) for a radical departure from painterly conventions. To be sure, these men selected their point of view and framed parts of an unbounded natural world, but they nonetheless succeeded in letting into art the wide-open spaces of the American West. The tension in Albert Bierstadt's landscape paintings between natural world and convention was seen to illustrate perfectly the challenge all these visual artists faced.

With this visual experience behind them, the students could turn to Joseph Wood Krutch's *The Desert Year* and Edward Abbey's *Desert Solitaire*. Little prompting was needed for the students to recognize that, yes, the Sonoran Desert near Tucson, Arizona, and the canyon country of southeast Utah do in fact differ. But so, they discovered, did the worlds of Krutch's and Abbey's minds. Moreover, it was an easy step to see that the writers had created the worlds of their books, much as the students themselves were creating worlds in their journals. When they got to read Annie Dillard's *Pilgrim at Tinker Creek*, they were amazed to discover what freedom with place Annie Dillard had. Her mind was metaphysical: extraterrestrial, even. In their own writing, in their reading, the students were discovering that "Things as they are / Are changed upon the blue guitar." They learned, also, the power and obligations of language.

In order to stress how mind imposes self on nature, the syllabus and field trips were arranged with an eye to furnishing the greatest variety of "nature-essay writing" as quickly as possible. Accordingly, the first field trip was to the New-York Historical Society, which has a fine collection of nineteenth-century American landscape paintings. The next time I teach the course, I will follow up immediately with a visit to the Metropolitan Museum of Art, whose American Wing is now open and whose European painting collection includes many impressionist and postimpressionist landscapes. Thoreau's journal, of course, headed the list of readings, so that students could see quickly "how it was done."

Although the first year I taught the course I arranged the readings chronologically in order for students to see how concepts of nature changed in time, as the subject matter clarified for me I took to juxtaposing texts very much unlike each other. I eventually placed Joseph Wood Krutch, whose mind is methodical and whose metaphors develop linearly, next to Annie Dillard, who, as Yeats said of himself in "The Tower," has an "Excited, passionate, fantastical / Imagination." Thoreau himself, of course, ranges from being a down-to-earth to a metaphysical poet, so his journal set the stage for these other writers extremely well.

As the term progressed, I considered it helpful to have my students read a book about a place they could visit, so that they might be able to see what "imagination" does to "reality" in the act of composition. So the second time I offered the seminar, I had them read and discuss John McPhee's *The Pine Barrens* around the sixth week of the term. Then, on our next field trip, we piled into my Chevy van and headed south into central New Jersey, down the Garden State Parkway. We had brunch at the Chatsworth general store, which McPhee had mentioned; then, during the length of a cold, misty afternoon, drove off the main highways onto country and gravel roads, to see the pine barrens from the inside. A walk at Batsto State Park got us thoroughly chilled and damp, cutting off our enthusiasm for stopping at the Brigantine Wildlife Refuge before heading north again. On this trip the students, all with inner-city backgrounds, entered a world they could not have imagined, and McPhee's words were given substance, magically as it were. I felt at this point that the students had been launched in their reading, in their writing, in their experience of the natural world and its images in art, as well as in their understanding of how the "blue guitar" of the mind records and transforms the world. However, I did not try to say all this to my students.

We, as teachers, should hesitate to draw conclusions about what and how much students learn from us or even *how* they learn. Learning occurs in unpredictable ways and often cannot be measured. I would like to illustrate this point by closing with an example of what happened on the last field trip the last time I taught the seminar.We had gone to Ward Pound Ridge Reservation, a county park in Westchester County, New York, to meet a cousin of my wife's, Allen Kurtz, who knew where barred owls nested.

It was an hour's walk in from the parking field, through bare woods of early spring. The only wildflowers up were the hepaticas, among the earliest of all. On the way we came across the remains of a goshawk's kill. When we got to our spot, Allen turned on his tape recording of a barred owl's call: "hoohoo-hoohoo . . . hoohoo-hoohooaw." Silence. Nothing in return. He repeated the call. Nothing. For over ten minutes, Allen continued, adding his mimicry to the recorded call. Students got restless, skeptical, smiles all around. Silence.

Then, from off in the woods, an answer. Allen called again. Another response, this time closer. Again the call, again the answer, even closer. Then the owl swooped into view and disappeared. Allen called again. Nothing. We had had all we were to get of the barred owl. The owl must have seen its mistake, but what do I know of what owls know? Enough to say we were granted a glimpse of a barred owl. We could tease an owl out of hiding, but beyond that was up to it.

What did we learn? Perhaps not much. Perhaps nothing at all. I like to think, however, that the owl was demonstrating what the new biology and modern genetics were showing in other ways. We used to think, as Lewis Thomas phrased it in *The Lives of a Cell*, the last book on the term's reading list, that "the earth was man's personal property, a combination of garden, zoo, bank vault, and energy source, placed at our disposal to be consumed, ornamented, or pulled apart as we wished. The betterment of mankind was, as we understood it, the whole point of the thing. Mastery over nature, mystery and all, was a moral duty, and a social obligation" (103–04). But, as Thomas instructs us, "we had it wrong. We still argue the details, but it is conceded almost everywhere that we are not the masters of nature that we thought ourselves; we are as dependent on the rest of life as are the leaves or midges or fish. We are part of the system" (104).

Perhaps this is what the owl was signifying as it took one look and swept silently back into the woods. But if this instance of "commonage," of space occupied in common, as equals, is true, then it forces us to revise much of what we have read that "nature" meant in the past. The implications of the owl's disappearance force us to feel once again, to start the age-old battle once more, to rethink all the old metaphors. The natural world instructs us, but we shape our response and our attitudes and create the world of "nature" we inhabit. Once again the owl was forcing us to revise our understanding of ourselves and our relation to the natural world. In truth it seems we have become part and parcel of the whole in a way that Emerson, using these words in *Nature*, never even imagined.

PART 3:

Nature Writing

Introduction

The major concern of the essays in this part is the teaching of writing. Although the academic settings of these courses are diverse—an interdisciplinary "experimental college," a major state university, an urban junior college—all three present the experience of writing in a context of subject-generating experience with nature. The great diversity of students—varying in age, background, class level—successfully engaged with writing through the courses described here indicates the wide applicability of nature-focused writing courses at the college level. Nature in many geographical areas of the United States is a "text" that a whole class can "read" together and is also one that can be "read" by individuals as experience, not as words on a page (for this concept applied, see May T. Watts's *Reading the Landscape of America*). It can thus combine the best features of two limited resources for invention, generally called on separately, particularly in lower-level writing classes: personal experience (rarely shared by all of a student's writing classmates) and rhetorical models (rarely connected directly with individual students' experiences when derived from a college reader).

Betsy Hilbert's experience in "Teaching Nature Writing at a Community College," which initiates this section, has much in common with Kligerman's experience in " 'Nature' and the Classroom." To college students in Miami and New York, "nature" is often known only as a media-interpreted concept, and the teacher has to introduce details of both the reality and the interpretation of it to them. Hilbert has to deal with more disadvantages, though, in that she does not have access to outside-classroom space and her students are both poor and strongly vocation-directed; the experience of nature has no inherent place among their personal goals.

Hilbert emphasizes that her concern is therefore not only teaching writing but also conveying a justification for things (and attitudes) that cannot usually be justified in her students' prior frames of reference. Hilbert considers that nature writing provides the best models for such students, for several reasons. Its creators, so often iconoclastic mavericks, contradict her students' values, forcing them to think. It illustrates the creative problems of writing very clearly in its methods of transforming aesthetically unmediated observation. It encourages originality in writing because it rarely conforms to generic formulas.

Because of her teaching environment, audience, and freshman composition framework, Hilbert uses primarily prose nature writing as material, supplementing it with audiovisuals, visits from nature writers, and student "journals of observation." One effect she notes is that, because of the diversity of subjects and issues that nature writing calls up and the diversity of its genres, her course becomes virtually an "introduction to literature" class without losing track of its major goal of competency in prose expression.

Paul Bryant's nature-writing course ("Nature Writing: Connecting Experience with Tradition") is addressed to senior-level students. Despite his more advanced audiences, he emphasizes the same fundamental problem and challenge as Hilbert does as the source of difficulty and power in nature writing: the combining of objective reporting and subjective artistry, without betraying either. Bryant's concern is to teach experientially based nature writing through a knowledge of literary tradition and of the cultural history of human views of nature. One half of his course thus becomes a "crash course in Western civilization," but he structures it so that this part, covered historically, leads through and is eventually taken over by a "laboratory" section of student observation and writing. This "laboratory" runs concurrently with students' reading of twentieth-century environmental literature. Aldo Leopold, Joseph Wood Krutch, and others are examined as models of rhetorical technique. The actual writing is done in weekly two-hour writing workshops that include field experiences. As the historical survey was structured chronologically, the writing section is structured in terms of a progression from subjectivity to objectivity as possible rhetorical poses of an author. The students learn progressively how to employ style, rather than personal reference, to direct readers' subjective responses. This progression is complemented by a sequential focus on four modes of discourse: description, appreciation, interpretation, and persuasion.

Despite his eclectic format, Bryant, like Hilbert, places a great importance on rhetorical technique, such that the elements of his course could be adapted to many advanced-composition or creative-writing offerings. As pedagogy, it makes an interesting contrast to Margaret McFadden's "The I in Nature," which follows, since McFadden's concerns are somewhat different, though her material and technique are similar. McFadden is more concerned with observing and writing about knowledge for self-observation and values clarification. For her, the "I" is always a subject of nature writing, as it is for Lutts (part 2).

Although McFadden's course was prepared as part of a specialized college's curriculum, its texts and procedures are applicable to any interdisciplinary course in which students are creative participants. Indeed, if exact replication of a course like "The I in Nature" is impossible or even undesirable in particular institutions, elements of its materials, technique, or teacher-student interaction can be profitably introduced into more limited teaching situations—even ones that have subject matter unrelated to environment or literature.

The reader of McFadden's essay will also find a strategy for incorporating a concern for student as subject with a demanding structure of course work. A limited number of environmental literary texts are examined in great detail, and the writing activities in the class, focused on self-exploration, are also detailed. The "'I' in Nature" journals she requires students to keep is the most subjective element of a rigorous course plan that includes five full-length essays on environmental literature; the journal itself is written in a disciplined framework of review and revision and is structured around defined writing assignments. Its goals are both self-knowledge and expository skill. The group field experience that climaxes the course does not exist just as experience but as experience described and communicated in writing. Such courses as hers are not enemies of literacy and disciplined intellect; they are the direct opposite. They seek to reinforce the presence of literacy and disciplined intellect by showing how necessary they are to validate and render meaningful any experience of self or nature.

Teaching Nature Writing at a Community College

Betsy Hilbert

I meet the honors class in freshman composition, entitled "Writing about Nature," three times a week, under the blue wink of fluorescent lights in a windowless, air-conditioned classroom. Like most community college classes, this one contains a various mix of people, most of whom are poor, bright, ambitious, and pragmatic. They were chosen for our honors program largely on the basis of high school grade averages. Many are the first in their families ever to go to college; most are just scratching their way out of ghetto and refugee status. Their ambitions run to sports cars and business degrees. As their teacher, I will somehow have to help these students learn to question and challenge, to stop regurgitating stuff out of books and trust their own experiences, to read thoughtfully and to write with style and grace. Teaching nature writing is one of the best tools I've found to help accomplish those aims.

When a community college is working as it should, its processes derive from its population. That is, in the main, how community colleges differ from universities: the orientation at the universities is generally toward subject matter, and energies go in the direction of research and publication. Our concern, on the other hand, is with our people. When I design a curriculum, the choices of content, methods, and procedures—everything we will do over the course of the semester—must be grounded in who the students are, what they need to learn, and how they go about the learning process. "Writing about Nature" is the theme of this class not because it's my specialty or a rewarding area of literary studies and not because this study is central to some of the most crucial issues of our civilization—though all of those things are true—but because the study and practice of nature writing helps my students learn the things they need to know.

Community college students are generally a much more diverse group than the usual crop of university first- and second-year students. Many of our students have been out of school for several years or several decades, and they return to the classroom bringing a wealth of experience—sharp minds and rusty academic skills. We also get many students just out of high school, most of them too young, too broke, or too badly prepared to go off to a four-year college. We see refugee and foreign students of all kinds and refugees, too, from the ghettos of Miami, all of them convinced that somewhere in the halls of our college they'll pick up a one-way ticket to the American dream, or at least a job in computer programming.

Out of the general diversity of Miami-Dade's students, the honors class is a somewhat more coherent group. The honors students read and write fairly competently, so that the range of our readings doesn't have to be limited. (It would be fascinating to plan this class for, say, a group of adults reading at eighth-grade level.) They are acquainted with term papers, and they've heard about Plato. They trust what their teachers tell them and do as they're instructed.

Why choose the theme of nature for a required composition course with these students? For one thing, a solid dose of John Muir or Edward Abbey is just the thing for a classful of people whose overwhelming ambitions are to marry well and to become accountants. Nature writers have by and large been a bunch of mavericks—independent, tough-minded, much more inclined to explore Afghanistan or the creek behind the house than to settle into a regular job. Some may have passionately desired the good opinion of the world, but few have been willing to make the necessary compromises to get it. For another thing, nature writing exemplifies the writing skills that freshman composition is designed to teach, illustrating the challenges and problems faced by the nonfiction writer. At its heart, a nature book is a work of science—precise observation and clear explication. In form, it is of course a work of art—the carefully worked-out selection and presentation of material, the planning toward a certain kind of effect. Nature writing brings into careful balance the relations between content and medium, the ways that experience of the natural world gets transposed into literary work.

One of the best things about using nature writing in teaching beginning composition is that there really is no single, firm definition of the genre. William Wordsworth, Wendell Berry, Sally Carrighar, and Barry Lopez all fit in. That breadth of example is an excellent thing to have when one is trying to encourage beginning writers to develop their own individual styles.

Because so much breadth is available in the literature, the class readings can be chosen to reflect a variety of styles and approaches to writing about nature. Readings change every semester, as the populations of the classes shift, and the piece that works brilliantly one semester may fall flat the next.

Performance-based objectives and competency-based curriculum design are—once you get past the jargon—enormously useful in establishing a flexible syllabus. First, the goals of the course are developed in terms of expected student skills. For example, a general competency to meet the freshman composition requirements might read: "The student must prove that he or she is able to appraise critically and evaluate pieces of nonfiction prose, with attention to content, organization, and style." Specific performance objectives can then be built on that structure, and course syllabi can be changed semester by semester.

Though there are probably as many ways of arriving at the course objectives as there are students in the class, the constant emphasis is on learning to write. Because this class is a composition course meeting a general education requirement, not an elective class in environmental literature, we concentrate on methods of invention and rhetoric more than on critical analysis, history of the literature, or environmental issues. It's sometimes hard to keep in mind that I'm teaching writing, not ecology or environmental studies, theories of nonfiction prose, attitudes toward wilderness in American literature, or any of the other five hundred absolutely essential topics that are far more interesting than anything a rhetorical textbook has to offer. I keep reminding myself that learning how to write is an activity entirely different from listening to an English professor explicate Thoreau or even watching that same professor slog through a swamp.

Nature writers themselves are excellent examples to set before a writing class. They write from direct experience, about things that are close to life. They have learned the techniques of balancing idea with detail, general with particular, and those are among the hardest skills to teach in composition. Above all, good nature writers have learned the value of clarity and precision.

For teaching the craft of handling point of view, I've found nothing better than Archie Carr's chapter "The Snake" from *Ulendo*. For demonstrating comparison and contrast, there are Thoreau's and E. B. White's separate pieces on Walden; for clarifying the structure of argument, the essays of Wendell Berry (see Additional Significant Works) and Aldo Leopold. For showing careful attention to descriptive detail, any single sentence by Rachel Carson.

Besides, if the methods of nature writing are technically useful to a composition teacher, the content adds life to classroom discussions. Natural history brings a sense of adventure and excitement into my dull beige classroom. The students take to the material like cage-bred rabbits to a field of wildflowers, intrigued and dubious at the same time.

Nobody ever sent *these* kids to camp. They work at places like Burger King to pay the insurance on their old cars. They're intensely curious about the natural world, having known pollution and parking lots all their lives and suspected all along that there might be something better.

The class presents some interesting challenges when we get on such subjects as, say, the wilderness ethic. People who teach elective undergraduate courses or graduate seminars in environmental literature are most likely to have students already somewhat committed to appreciation and preservation of the wilderness; those kinds of students want to learn more about a subject that already interests them. But people who are desperately clawing their way into the bourgeoisie don't want to hear about failures in bourgeois value systems. A common reaction to Thoreau in my class, for example, is that he's interesting but terribly impractical.

I do not mean to disparage either these students' intelligence or their ambitions, but I do want to point out that we face in class what the preservationist movement itself faces constantly: the attempt to praise and justify the existence of things that cannot be justified by money alone and to convince people for whom the financial aspect is primary because it has to be. The problem is akin to that of trying to convince a hungry villager that the large chunk of meat that constitutes an elephant really ought to be left alone to stomp around and chew trees. It's not easy.

Over the course of the semester, however, there is a decided swing in attitudes. Partly, of course, this must be laid to the students' easy acquiescence to authority—in this case, mine. But something else seems to happen too, something that is more a result of the readings than of anything I say or do. Intelligent people, even the most ambitious and pragmatic, have serious questions about who they are and what their lives should be. Intelligent people who are also adolescents, like many of my students, consider those questions most intensely. And they discover in nature writing a direct concern not just with the things of the natural world but with their own place as part of that world.

Not quite everything we do in class is high-minded discussion of life or literary theory, however. There are still semicolons to be explained. The class runs pretty much like any other freshman composition course taught with a thematic unity. We read good nature writing (and some bad) and discuss it. We take field trips and write about them. I warn the students about the dangers of the passive voice and the Slough of Despond. They write; I grade. Sometimes I lecture: on Muir or Dickinson, environmental ethics, what to do with a thesis statement . . . whatever. Once we had a whole class period on The Ellipsis, and another time one on Don't Drink the Local Water.

One of the problems created by poverty is that we have to be careful about the cost of materials. Textbooks are limited to works available in paperback, which excludes many things I'd really like to discuss. Ann Zwinger's *Run, River, Run,* for example, is probably the best-crafted work of natural history by a contemporary writer in its balancing of scientific and historical research with fine writing techniques—but it's simply too expensive in hardback. The problem of finances also comes up when we consider the field trips. To spend a Saturday exploring a cypress dome in the Everglades is to miss an entire day's pay.

Material about the local environment is vital to a course such as this. A high point is usually the visit of Marjory Stoneman Douglas. Not only is her book *The Everglades: River of Grass* one of the best works written about the South Florida area; she herself is an example to us all: both a committed, disciplined writer and an untiring fighter for the conservationist cause. Small, old, and now nearly blind, she is still hard at work on a biography of W. H. Hudson and still battling the unthinking development that threatens our coastal and central Florida regions. Local, practicing writers provide a fine resource for a nature-writing class. One needn't look too far for them, either. The class had an excellent session with a member of the college's biology department, a herpetologist and anthropologist who brought copies of one of his published papers and talked about writing.

The college has a good budget for audiovisual materials and excellent delivery service for showing films and videotapes in the classroom. Besides viewing the professional films, the students are encouraged to make their own audiovisual presentations. There are cameras and other equipment for loan, and the school can also offer some help with the cost of film and processing. An experienced audiovisual technician is available to help students create their presentations. Audiovisual presentations are, of course, compositions, requiring many of the same kinds of skills as essays. Material must be selected, organized, and developed, and the result evaluated and edited. Our acceptance of different media of expression also points to another defining characteristic of higher education at the community college level: a commitment to learning through a variety of cognitive styles and methods.

Teaching nature writing is a strategy for achieving the aims and objectives of what could be any introductory English course. Nature is the subject, not the content, of the class. Not only is natural history useful in providing examples and subject matter for compositions, but it engages the students in dealing with some of the most central issues of our age, questions of their relations to one another and to the world. The writings introduce people who are struggling in one world with the fact that other, broader worlds exist. Above all, teaching nature writing helps to fulfill a community college's first commitment: a concern for the variety of its students and the various ways in which they learn.

Nature Writing: Connecting Experience with Tradition

Paul T. Bryant

Nature writing offers English teachers invaluable opportunities for connecting subject matter, experience, and tradition. In a number of ways, this literary genre can be related to the student's own writing, to the student's own experience, and to some of the major problems of contemporary life. It can tie modern concepts and attitudes to the historical tradition from which they have developed. Perhaps most important, it can help students see significant relations between the abstract world of the intellect—of "ideas"—and the physical realities of the material world as they are experiencing it.

This is a lot to claim for the study of a minor, little-recognized literary genre. The claim is based on the experience of three years of teaching a senior-level college course in nature writing. This essay proposes to describe that course and that experience.

Definitions

A necessary first step is to define some terms. "Nature" means, in this course, natural processes or the natural world not affected by human manipulation or at least not primarily determined by such manipulation. This definition becomes a question of degree without precise limits: "wild" nature may intrude upon the most carefully regulated garden, and human influence such as air pollution and acid rain may occur in remote wilderness areas.

"Nature writing," then, might seem simply to be writing about nature, but there are more specific requirements of style and content. People were writing about nature at least as early as the Old Testament and the ancient Greeks, but the literary genre of nature writing in English is generally considered to have begun in the eighteenth century (see Krutch, *Great American Nature Writing* 2). Perhaps a useful working definition of nature writing might begin not with saying what it is but with saying some of the things it is not. It is not fantasy, it is not fiction, and it is not a scientific report. It is not a taxonomic list or a collection of folklore. And it is neither a moralizing fable nor a philosophical metaphor. The nature writer avoids sentimentality, personification, and teleological assumptions (see Lillard).

Having set some limits with negatives, we can consider what nature writing is. At the core of the definition lie two basic characteristics that create a productive if sometimes difficult tension: nature writing must remain true to the objective facts of nature, but at the same time it must present the human response to nature. Thus nature writing must maintain the physical accuracy required of the scientific writer and, at the same time, present the human imagination and emotions with the integrity of the creative writer.

Attention to such dual requirements can help the student gain new understanding and respect for both the sciences and the arts, demonstrating, in the process, that science and art are not necessarily antagonistic or mutually exclusive. Rather, both play a valuable part in our culture. The variety of students who take this course makes the reconciliation of the views of science and the arts especially appropriate. The course is populated by students from forestry, the natural sciences, engineering, agriculture, landscape architecture, philosophy, art, the social sciences, and English. These students are juniors, seniors, and graduate students. Their maturity and the variety of their backgrounds make for lively and productive discussions in which the professor can easily learn as much as any student.

Structure of the Course

In this course, the study of the literary tradition of nature writing is combined with writing assignments that require the students themselves to do nature writing from their own experience. To accomplish this double purpose, the course has two lecture-discussion periods and a two-hour laboratory-workshop period each week. The laboratory period makes the course unusual for an English department. Although there is considerable overlapping, particularly later in the semester, the lecture periods are generally devoted to the study of the literary tradition and the laboratory periods to writing, peer criticism, and a few modest field trips that provide common experiences to be used in the writing.

The Tradition

The study of the literary tradition is conducted much like a literature survey course, with emphasis on the cultural and intellectual history underlying the development of the genre. An important goal of this part of the course is to help the students understand how a given piece of writing can grow out of the assumptions the writer makes about the human relation with, or place in, nature. Conversely, the intelligent reader can work backward from the writing to the assumptions. Either way, each illuminates the other.

To place these ideas in a historical context, we begin with a brief consideration of the Old Testament and compare it with the ideas of the ancient Greeks. If nature is a set of special creations, regulated and caused to function by God's special will, which may alter at any given moment, possibly for reasons unfathomable to humans, then the natural world might be a place for wonder, worship, and poetry but not one for rational analysis or systematic study. On the other hand, if, as at least some of the Greeks assumed, nature behaves according to regular "laws" even though "the gods" might on occasion interfere, then rational analysis may be both possible and profitable. If, as the Book of Genesis says, the natural world was created as a dominion for humans and put totally at our disposal for whatever uses may seem fit at the moment, our attitude toward resource exploitation might be different from that of those ancient Greeks who saw us as an integral part of nature, part of an interrelated system and not superior beings standing above it. Conversely, however, the Christian doctrine of stewardship may provide a theological basis for conservation and careful use of the earth.

Even the landscape in which these ideas originated can be shown to play a role in these assumptions. For example, the Old Testament presents the "wilderness" as a barren desert, a life-threatening place without water or vegetation. "Good" places for humans (Paradise, Eden) are gardens, oases, green pastures, and still waters. Wild nature is harsh, punishing humanity for its transgressions. If one is to rest in the shade of the willow trees, someone must first plant the trees and cultivate them carefully.

In northern Europe, however, wilderness is forest, and safety and ease lie in the clearings. As the American plant ecologist William T. Penfound used to remark to his students, humans are park animals. Where they find lots of trees, they cut most of them down. Where they find no trees, they plant some (see Shepard 65–118).

Once we have considered the attitudes toward nature fostered by the Judeo-Christian tradition and those of the Hellenic tradition, we begin to follow the interaction of those two through the development of Western civilization. We spend little time on the Middle Ages other than to note some of the beliefs that prevented the occurrence of nature writing as we define it. Although in the Renaissance there was still no nature writing, some time can be well spent studying the writings of explorers, colonizers, and the forerunners of modern science. The sense of wonder conveyed by some of the explorers in an expanding and increasingly varied world, the utilitarian optimism of would-be exploiters, the arcadian propaganda of colonizers and promoters of colonies, the tensions in the Christian tradition between wilderness as Eden and wilderness as stronghold of Satan, the Cartesian separation of humans from other creatures, and the beginnings of scientific observation and analysis are all to be found in the Renaissance. And all these ideas continue to echo through English and American nature writing today.

The New England Puritans of the seventeenth century contributed much to our complex modern attitudes toward nature. As Hawthorne recognizes in such stories as "Young Goodman Brown," the wilderness for them was Satan's domain, a lawless region over which the godly order of civilization had not yet been extended. As such, wilderness was a foe to be "conquered," subdued, replaced by towns and cultivated farmlands.

At the same time, and perhaps paradoxically, the Puritans' doctrine of typology made natural events a part of God's plan and handiwork and perhaps also symbolic messages that could determine the fate of the Puritan's immortal soul. If the Book of Nature was second only to the Book of Scriptures as a means by which God might communicate with humans, natural events should be observed very carefully and accurately. This made many Puritans good natural scientists, as evidenced by some of the scientific writing of Increase and Cotton Mather and later of Jonathan Edwards. Edwards' essay on spiders is a classic of careful observation.

During the late seventeenth century in England, in the meantime, a revolution occurred in aesthetic attitudes toward nature. As Marjorie Nicolson has so well demonstrated, wild nature (in particular mountains) was no longer perceived as horrible; in place of the horror there developed an aesthetic of the sublime. This, of course, was a major step toward making nature writing possible. If students can understand this change, they will have a deeper understanding of the beginnings of romantic writing about nature in the eighteenth century. Since that time the romantic element in nature writing has never disappeared, so this step in the course can be crucial.

With the advent, in the eighteenth century, of nature writing as a literary genre, we see the flowing together of the dichotomies that we originally identified in our definition. On the one hand, Copernican astronomy had been fully accepted, and thus humans had been removed from the center of the universe. Newton, in turn, had presented the universe as a gigantic machine that operates by mathematical rules that can be understood by reasoning humans. The deists even generalized religious beliefs into universal patterns, and, to use Jefferson's term, reason became the "only oracle."

This elevation of reason as the primary path to understanding and this vision of nature as patterned, logical, and knowable through rational inquiry can clearly be related to the modern scientific approach. At the same time, there were developing the aesthetics of the sublime and the picturesque. As interest grew in England in landscape architecture (and as India and the new industrialization produced the necessary concentrations of capital), the walls were removed from English gardens and the landscape became an extended garden, suggesting that nature was a garden and therefore benign rather than savage. In England such landscape architects as Capability Brown and Humphrey Repton became famous and wealthy. In America such naturalists as William Bartram (some of whose writing the students read at this point in the course) could find in the American wilderness gardenlike scenes as well as images for Coleridge's "Kubla Khan" along the Altamaha.

This interest in the picturesque of course helped emphasize the visual perception of nature, at the expense of the other senses. Visual emphasis was further stimulated by the development of photography in the nineteenth century and especially by the later development of the inexpensive, easy-to-use box camera. This emphasis on the visual carries over into the writing of description and is taken for granted by most students until the possibilities of presenting the other senses are suggested to them. A further consequence is even more disturbing and new to them: if nature is reduced to the visual—turned into a picture—then it becomes something separate from the observer. Nature as picture is not a milieu, not an environment in which the writer (and therefore the reader) participates. Nature as picture is nature as seen through the window of a drawing room or air-conditioned automobile. We do not sense nature's temperatures, its winds, its odors, its sounds. We do not really participate. This is a legacy of the eighteenth century that still influences our nature writers and our society's attitude toward nature.

From the rationalism of the deists we move on to the imagination and emotion of the romantics and then the idealism of the New England transcendentalists. Comparing such writers as Bartram and Jefferson with Emerson and Thoreau again makes clear to the students how important it is to understand the beliefs and attitudes that lie behind the work of any given writer.

Thoreau on Cape Cod leads readily to Stephen Crane's "Open Boat," which might not strictly be nature writing but certainly illustrates an attitude toward nature that influenced the literature of the late nineteenth and the twentieth centuries. Nature for Crane, too, is a force not bound to be kind to humans, but after Darwin's *Descent of Man* the assumption was that humans were a part of nature rather than superior beings that stood above nature, given dominion over it by God. Thoreau's intuition that the animals are merely our fellow creatures is confirmed through scientific logic and evidence. We are all fellow creatures, related biologically by the fact of being alive. Before *The Descent of Man*, however, *Origin of Species* had for many replaced the benign nature of the romantic with nature red in tooth and claw, a series of nonconscious inexorable forces that hear neither supplication nor repentance.

Still, in the nature writing tradition romanticism remains strong, as illustrated by John Muir, who can rejoice at the forces of nature even in the midst of storm or earthquake. It is important for the students to understand the ideas both of Crane and of Muir because both views still influence our present attitudes. Often, in fact, the students will entertain both attitudes on different occasions without being aware of their contradictions.

We will have reached this point in the tradition less than halfway through the semester. In effect, the students have not only been reading intensively in the nature writing tradition, they have also been going through a crash course in Western civilization. For some of them this has been disturbing because they have been forced to examine their own assumptions, in some cases assumptions they were not even aware they had been making. It is common for a student of science or technology to say or write something like this early in the semester: "The romantics emphasized the imagination and the emotions. The realists saw things as they *really* are." Sometimes it takes a bit of discussion to get such a student to understand the assumptions that lie behind that "really."

With this background absorbed, however, the students are well equipped to spend the rest of the semester reading nature writers of the twentieth century. In addition, the writers of this century can be used as models and sources of writing techniques for the writing the students are themselves doing in the laboratory. Consequently, from this point more attention is paid to matters of style, organization, rhetorical devices, and such, as well as to ideas and subject matter. For example, the limited range of Teale's "Night in the Garden" (in Conron 497–502) can be contrasted to the sweep, both physical and intellectual, of Kerouac's "Alone on a Mountaintop" (in Conron 509–18). The limited scope, in both time and space, of Sally Carrighar's *One Day on Beetle Rock* can be contrasted to the range through history and space of Sigurd Olson's *The Lonely Land*. All four of these pieces

are effective, but in different ways and for different reasons. Skill at analyzing those ways and reasons can help the students become more sophisticated writers.

A sampling of Ann Zwinger's *Wind in the Rock* gives the students a
model of clear, pure, direct, beautiful style dealing with a region with which
most of them are familiar. As they read Zwinger, many can identify personally with her experience and can think in terms of how they might have
presented that experience in comparison with how she has done so.

Our reading of Aldo Leopold provides a series of rhetorical techniques
for our examination and at the same time becomes an introduction to some
of our present environmental concerns. In Krutch's *Desert Year* the students, now initiated into the tradition, can hear the voice of Henry Thoreau
speaking to them across the intervening century or more. Students already
familiar with the work find greater depth and richness in it as a result of
their new awareness of the tradition out of which the book grew.

By the time the students read Eiseley's *The Immense Journey* they are
prepared to believe that a respected, highly competent scientist can have
a mystical experience floating down the South Platte River. On the same
basis, a fossilized skull can convincingly tell its discoverer something about
himself or herself and not be merely another source of empirical data to
be tabulated.

Finally, having worked our way through the tradition, we are able
fully to appreciate Edward Abbey's *Desert Solitaire*. His "industrial tourism"
can now be related to the Grand Tour of England and America in the
eighteenth and nineteenth centuries. His fellow feeling for the creatures
of the wilderness fits well with the vision of Henry Thoreau, if not that of
Gilbert White. We understand more fully the sources of the anger expressed
in his polemics. And I think we understand ourselves and our own attitudes
toward nature more clearly.

Doing Nature Writing—Laboratory

While the students have thus been studying the literary tradition of
nature writing and the cultural history it has grown from, they have also
been busy doing nature writing of their own. The two-hour laboratory
session each week has become a workshop for writing, exchange of criti-
cisms, and brief trips into the field.

Using a two-hour laboratory period rather than a third "lecture" hour
each week has a number of advantages, in addition to the obvious one of
providing time for field trips. By asking students to work on a specific
assignment at a given place and time, in a workshop setting that may
include discussion of techniques and exchange of critical comments, we
can emphasize that writing is a craft that involves the conscious use of
describable techniques. We can demonstrate that revision is not only desirable but essential for even the most polished writers. And we create a
situation in which students, in reacting to and offering helpful analysis of
the writing of classmates, become far more perceptive in reviewing their
own writing.

Two progressive frameworks are used in laboratory, more or less simultaneously through the semester. One progression is from the stance of personal expression by the writer through a gradual distancing of the writer from the work until the emphasis is less on personal expression and more on giving the reader a new experience of nature through the medium of writing. In achieving this progression we discuss such concepts as Keats's "negative capability" and Eliot's "objective correlative." We consider ways in which we can, as writers, move from a fairly naive impulse to put our feelings into words to a more sophisticated consideration of ways to create in the reader's experience a particular set of reactions. In short, we move from writing as a private behavior to writing as a social act directed toward others.

In the process, students achieve critical distance from their own writing and see it as something that is to be consciously crafted for a given purpose. When students see their work as an artifact that can be shaped and polished for a purpose, rather than merely a blurting out of their own ephemeral feelings, then it is possible to teach them style and rhetorical technique. Then they can adopt a given point of view consciously and create not a naive shadow of themselves but rather a persona to be perceived by the reader.

In the meantime, writing assignments also follow a pattern related to a set of modes of discourse. This set is somewhat modified from the traditional description, narration, exposition, and argumentation of Alexander Bain, but it is based on that well-known quartet. The four we use, in the order in which we take them up, are description, appreciation, interpretation, and persuasion. As you can see, Bain's second element, narration, is replaced by appreciation, and his third, exposition, is called interpretation, really only an elaborated form of exposition. Finally, I prefer to speak of persuasion rather than argumentation because I try to teach my students nonadversarial modes of persuasive writing. Perhaps a brief description of what we try to accomplish under each of these headings will be useful.

We begin our laboratory writing with description. Our first exercise is to go together to a small picnic area on the campus—Sherwood Forest—to prepare two descriptions of the area. One is to be an objective, scientific description written in the style of a professional scientific journal. Such a description will give only factual data concerning size, location, apparent use, species of trees, birds, and mammals present, and so on. This will be the only "scientific" writing done this semester.

The second description is also to give any relevant objective facts about the area, but the speaking voice of the author is to play a part in this description. This description presents Sherwood Forest with the writer as a real, live human being perceiving the forest and reacting to it, rather than as a dispassionate sensing instrument.

As we work on the descriptions together, on the scene, we do various little exercises in perceiving—for example, concentrating on one sense at at time and making notes on the stimuli available to that sense. This can be a useful set of exercises, because most of us are so oriented toward vision that we tend to neglect the other senses in writing description. We do indeed tend to perceive nature as picture.

Among other goals, this exercise is intended to fix clearly in mind the difference between scientific writing and the kind of nature writing we will be doing. All the work on description is intended to encourage the student to perceive clearly, accurately, and in detail, with all of the senses, and to use that perception in presenting a fully human response to what is perceived. By that I mean that the writer is to describe not only from a physical viewpoint but from an intellectual and emotional viewpoint as well.

After perhaps three laboratory sessions on description, in which we criticize each other's work, analyze brief examples of effective description, and revise in consultation and alone, we move on to the writing of appreciation. We have already begun including the observer in the description, but as we work our way into writing appreciation we begin shifting the writer's attention from expressing his or her own response toward creating in the reader a similar response. Such a response may include perception, emotion, evaluation, and it will require both efferent and aesthetic considerations.

In so presenting to the reader an experience that becomes the reader's, the writer inevitably uses both description and narration, thus adding the missing element from Bain's modes of discourse.

During the time we are working on appreciation, we use a laboratory period for a field trip to a small nature center along the Cache la Poudre River near the campus. The area is a wooded floodplain with a variety of vegetation, birds, insects, and small mammals. This again gives the students a common set of experiences from which to write. It also helps those students who have not had a great deal of outdoor experience feel more nearly on equal terms with those who have toured Glacier Bay in a kayak or climbed all the fourteeners in Colorado.

By the time the laboratory work has progressed to dealing with interpretive writing, the reading in lecture will have come up to the twentieth century. At that point, everything in the course begins to come together for the student. In the laboratory, the student has acquired skills in description, narration, and evoking appreciation. He or she can now bring those skills to interpretation, writing that combines rational understanding of processes and relations with the experience of appreciation that is greatly deepened by understanding.

Again to ensure that the students have direct experience from which to write, we devote one laboratory period to a trip to a small state park in the foothills just west of the campus. After a brisk hike up a steep trail we can stop and consider a panorama of mountains and plains. We can see a variety of plant communities; we probably have seen some Abert's squirrels and can consider their relation with the ponderosa pine; there will probably be hawks sailing the thermal air currents above the cliff faces; we may with luck encounter some mule deer or a rattlesnake; and we get a fine view of the hogbacks created from the overlying sedimentary beds when the Rocky Mountains rose. All in all, we have plenty of topics for interpretive writing.

Finally, near the end of the semester, the laboratory work moves onto persuasion. I use this term rather than *argumentation* because I encourage students to see that a reader may be moved to action on an issue (the purpose of persuasive writing) through judicious use of all the techniques of writing we have been developing through the entire semester. A reader who comes to an awareness of the beauty of a peregrine falcon and who understands the role such falcons play in the biological community will likely be persuaded to help save the peregrine falcon from extinction.

I do insist that the student write on a real issue with two arguable sides, but tactics in advocating one of those sides can vary widely.

This succession of modes of discourse is thus made cumulative: description and narration are used in writing appreciation; appreciation is used in writing interpretation; and all are used in persuasion.

Making Connections

As I have already suggested, by the middle of the semester the reading in the lecture has begun to relate to the writing in the laboratory. Not only do the students find in that reading useful models for their own writing, but also, by understanding the ideas and assumptions behind the works they are reading—Krutch's transcendentalism, Leopold's ecological pragmatism, Abbey's dialectic—they begin to become more aware of their own assumptions and to analyze them.

The net result of this course is intended to be a series of connections: perceptive reading connected to effective writing; a whole cultural tradition of the arts and sciences connected to a given individual's perception of the natural world; and close ties, perhaps for the first time, among a student's own perceptions and experiences, that student's own writing, and an established and clearly understood literary tradition.

Readings

(Required texts include John Conron, *The American Landscape*; Aldo Leopold, *A Sand County Almanac*; Joseph Wood Krutch, *The Desert Year*; Loren Eiseley, *The Immense Journey*.)

1. Introduction (Judeo-Christian tradition, Hellenic tradition)
2. Renaissance (Christopher Columbus, Giovanni da Verrazano, Peter Martyr, Pedro de Castaneda, Arthur Barlow, John Brereton)
3. Puritans (William Bradford, Edward Johnson, Robert Beverley; Jonathan Edwards, "Of Insects")
4. Eighteenth Century (William Bartram, Thomas Jefferson, Nathaniel Willis, Horatio Parsons, Timothy Dwight)
5. Transcendentalists (Emerson, Thoreau, Muir)
6. Ways West (Meriwether Lewis, Washington Irving)
7. Nature as Antagonist (Stephen Crane, "The Open Boat")
8. Twentieth-Century Symbiotic Landscape (Edwin Way Teale, Jack Kerouac)
9. Sigurd Olson, *The Lonely Land*
10. Sally Carrighar, *One Day on Beetle Rock*
11. Ann Zwinger, *Wind in the Rock*
12. Aldo Leopold, *A Sand County Almanac*
13. Joseph Wood Krutch, *The Desert Year*
14. Loren Eiseley, *The Immense Journey*
15. Edward Abbey, *Desert Solitaire*

"The I in Nature":
Nature Writing as Self-Discovery

Margaret McFadden

> People go to Nature for various reasons—for solace, sanctuary, renewal; for wisdom, insight, wonder. One of the more satisfying reasons for spending time in Nature is to learn something about ourselves, as individuals. The experience is usually a solitary one, a quest for pilgrimage in self-awareness, exploring the relation of the self to nature, of human to divine.
>
> Many have written of this experience . . . and some of these works have become modern classics. The core of the course, then, will be a series of these works. . . . Our goal will be not only to learn something about "The I in Nature" from people like Thoreau and Annie Dillard, but also to write our own self-in-Nature observations. These observations, written in journal form, will be the result of our reading and study as well as our primary Nature observations.

With these paragraphs I announced to the student body of Watauga College at Appalachian State University my intention to teach a course that would focus on literature of a particular kind—a personal spiritual writing that emphasized the self and, as well, the solitary self's observation of nature. The announcement was a kind of advertisement as well, for students in Watauga College are allowed to choose their own courses and instructors. The course enrolled fifteen students, the maximum, and we were ready to begin.

This course was an outgrowth of two projects I had been working on: research on women nature writers for the American Women Writers series and research for an annotated bibliography of the genre of literary ecology. The course was designed to be interdisciplinary, while at the same time emphasizing literature. Of the three main texts—Thoreau's *Walden*, Annie Dillard's *Pilgrim at Tinker Creek*, and Colin Fletcher's *The Man Who Walked through Time*—only Thoreau is usually read in English department courses. Dillard alludes often to the nineteenth-century naturalist tradition, and her work is structured on philosophical and theological themes; in my view her writing can best be read in the medieval mystic tradition. Fletcher creates a kind of philosophical anthropology for the lay person. With the addition of Georgia O'Keeffe's paintings, we had a course that combined material from literature, art, philosophy, theology, and natural science but with the emphasis always on the writer, the observing or participating self. I wanted the main thrust of the course to be reading and writing; the experiential aspects and the ecological concerns should be natural outgrowths of the reading and contemplation.

This emphasis must be understood in the context of Watauga College, a residential interdisciplinary program for freshmen and sophomores, who take their humanities and social science requirements in this alternative setting. Many of our courses are experientially based, and that kind of course is very popular. This course, however, I envisioned as granting literature or communication credit. If, as I believed, students could be drawn into the experience of literature by the contemplations of a solitary hiker through the Grand Canyon, by Thoreau's pungent philosophizing about individualism, and by Annie Dillard's mystical meditations on the giant water bug sucking the life out of a frog, they would be able to see more clearly, to contemplate their own environments with a knowledge born not necessarily of scientific achievement but of careful observation, and to understand better their own beings and their own place in the ecosystem. I also wanted to focus on the problem of the thinking and writing self, the autobiography of the self and its relation to nature—the literary selves, specifically, of Thoreau, Dillard, and Fletcher. I wanted the students to get used to writing about themselves and their relation to their environments; therefore a large part of the course was the students' own "I in Nature" journals—their own observations on nature and comments on the readings.

The requirements of the course were simple: (1) careful reading of the three texts, some shorter pieces (the last chapter of Sally Carrighar's *Home to the Wilderness*, the first part of Olive Thorne Miller's *A Bird Lover in the West*), and selected poems from such writers as Hopkins, Frost, Hardy, Dickinson, and Maxine Kumin; (2) three short essays on the main texts, one to be written in class; (3) a review essay of four to five pages on another nature autobiography, chosen from a list of possibilities; (4) an "I in Nature" journal (three pages a week) to be collected every two to three weeks, in which students would write their primary nature observations, as well as comments on the readings; (5) a nature activity, to be described in detail in the journal—a bird walk, a camp-out, a mountain climb, a self-sufficiency experiment; (6) a final in-class essay to bring together the materials of the course; (7) participation in a group project or activity.

1. Reading and writing assignments. From the beginning we had some difficulty, because none of the three main texts is easy reading—at least not for freshmen whose reading skills are woefully inadequate.

We began with Thoreau, even though Fletcher is the easiest of the three writers. Since *Walden* is the clear progenitor of the nature autobiography genre and since most students had heard of the book but never read it, there was initial excitement, which quickly turned to difficulty once we began reading "Economy." I refused to let them get bogged down. We worked on structure, on individual sentences, on literary allusions. We followed words and concepts through the chapter; we analyzed grammatically and then diagrammed sentences; I explained literary allusions. The students had never spent time before on a single text and were at first antagonistic. What they wanted to do was debate the idea of "going to the woods" with no one but me to take the opposite side. But as they began to discover the richness of Thoreau they began to appreciate the joys of closely reading a complicated text. Some students were never able to do this, as the essay in class on *Walden* showed; others did improve in this skill.

For variation we read nature poetry—my favorites and theirs. Theirs were inevitably less compact; mine were often Gerard Manley Hopkins, whom I helped them unpack. We read aloud from both prose and poetry— a good exercise, I found. I gave the students little assignments for their journals: write a page describing a single organism in nature that you observe carefully, or write a paragraph on how it feels when it rains, or describe a rock or a single leaf or an ant. We looked at Thoreau or Dillard as examples and models. Some of the journal entries we read aloud and shared, if the student was willing. When I collected the nature journals, I commented fully on descriptive detail, sentence structure, imagery, etc., but I did not "correct" in the text. I often asked that comparisons be made to the reading we were doing. I did not grade the journals until the end of the semester but gave a plus, check, or minus indication of my judgment. If I were to do this again, I think I would judge the journals solely on quantity and not give a grade at all on quality. If the student writes enough, the quality of the writing will necessarily improve. The lack of judgment on the journal writing should remove some of the inhibitions, and the judgment can come with the more formal essays.

In order to keep the students reading carefully, we had weekly oral quizzes on the assignments. The questions were written by the class members—two students each week—and those questions were then submitted and used as starting points for discussion. This worked as well as anything I have found to keep students "honest" and up-to-date in reading assignments. The written essay on *Walden* was done in class and was open-book and notebook. The questions I asked (there were choices) were designed to show how carefully the students had read and contemplated Thoreau; one question gave six examples of Thoreau's use of the word *nature* and asked the students to explain Thoreau's concept of nature. We had spent a class discussion on the problem of defining *nature* and *natural*.

After the discipline of *Walden*, Dillard's religious quest for the meaning of good and evil in *Pilgrim at Tinker Creek* was at least possible for the better students to understand. Her writing is so vivid and forceful, her metaphors so wondrous, that even when the theology was beyond them, the students benefited from the close natural observation. Because the region she writes of is so similar to our area of the Blue Ridge, the students could identify closely with her observations. The chapter on "stalking" was particularly successful. Their "I in Nature" journals were becoming more perceptive, and we talked about Dillard's reasons for reading and writing: "I bloom indoors in the winter like a forced forsythia; I come in to come out. At night I read and write and things I have never understood become clear; I reap the harvest of the rest of the year's planting" (39).

We spent a good deal of time on "Seeing," on the meaning of vision and re-vision, on Dillard's central metaphor of "the tree with lights in it" that the newly sighted can see. We discussed Dillard's "epiphany," the gift of grace that sometimes comes, as in the moments when Dillard sees the clouds and sun on the mountain with new eyes while petting the puppy. How is it that nature offers humanity these timeless moments when our physical senses take us beyond ourselves? For Dillard, the offering is a gift, in spite of the evil in the world, and her book is an attempt to understand chance and evil in the context of traditional Christianity. The poetry of Gerard Manley Hopkins, especially the nature sonnets like "God's Grandeur" and "Pied Beauty" and also "Spring and Fall: To a Young Child," "Binsey Poplars," and "The Windhover," connect well with the discussions on Dillard. One class period was spent on Hardy's "Hap" and Frost's "Design" as two ways of dealing with evil in the world. The writing assignment for *Pilgrim at Tinker Creek* was completed outside class, and the essay choices dealt with such topics as "chance," pilgrimage, and a comparison with Hopkins.

After finishing *Pilgrim at Tinker Creek,* we spent two days on Georgia O'Keeffe, viewing the film about her (directed by Adato, in the series The Originals: Women in Art), looking at prints of her paintings, and discussing the way that an artist views nature. O'Keeffe's inspiration has always been in nature, interpreted with great freedom. She has concentrated her attention on the small, seemingly insignificant natural object, such as a flower or bone, has isolated it from the ordinary and given it new significance. O'Keeffe's eye, as well as her "I" or self, revealed new knowledge about the areas of nature she focused on and her own relation to these areas.

O'Keeffe's life and work in the arroyos and deserts of Abiquiu, New Mexico, led easily to our last text, Colin Fletcher's *The Man Who Walked through Time.* The book begins as a narrative, as an adventure. The students were drawn into this adventure, becoming more interested as we talked about geography and the geology of the Grand Canyon and as they looked at some pictures and a film. Gradually, in the book, Fletcher divests himself of the present and experiences the canyon from the point of view of its various parts and inhabitants over the ages: he *becomes* a beaver, a grain of sand, an Anasazi Indian of a thousand years ago. This process we tried to imitate through journal writing and discussion. One of the essay topics for this book asked the student to make up a monologue in which he or she would *be* the Colorado River, commenting on various aspects of the canyon, its inhabitants, the explorers, the new technology that threatens it.

Near the end of the book, Fletcher quotes a sentence from an ecology paper, saying he might like it to be used as his epitaph: "Organisms themselves are relatively transient entities through which materials and energy flow and eventually return to the environment" (222). His "walk through time" has become, by the end, a kind of vision of the first law of thermodynamics in which the solitary person can identify completely with process *beyond* time. Thus, for Fletcher, the I in nature has lost its uniqueness and become one with that which lies beyond itself. Some students, especially those interested in Eastern religions and mysticism, finally began to understand this process. For some others, Fletcher's journey was never more than an adventure. As he exits, Fletcher becomes an advocate for the canyon; thus the students were led to discussions of what can be done—for the canyon, for other wild places.

2. Review essay. Each student read and reviewed another book from a list of "nature autobiographies." I worked up an "annotation sheet" that asked questions about structure and content and helped to form the impression of the work. Some of the students benefited from this additional reading; for others the completion of the assignment was difficult.

3. Group project. Midway through the course, we discussed the group project; the group decided to have a "natural foods picnic" at sundown overlooking Grandfather Mountain, at a rock outcrop someone knew well. That everyone actually attended this outing was a first for me; we feasted on everything from broccoli quiche to vegetable and yogurt dip to homemade breads and pickles and wine. I asked that everyone bring multiple copies of a favorite nature poem to read and share (it could be their own poetry if they wished). So we sat on the rock at sunset and read poetry and mused; the students loved it and became more of a group than before.

4. Evaluation. How did this course fare? Very well. The course evaluations were generally glowing. One student said that her degree of interest at the beginning had been 0 and now was about 8 1/2. A comment on the teaching: "Good teaching—but hard teaching. But not too hard. So I guess that's what it's all about." Another said, "This is by far the most interesting and personally relevant course of my college career." On the journal writing, one student said, "The journal was an important part of the course. In fact it was my only scholastic opportunity this semester to be creative. Writing assignments were fair in that they required an understanding of the text." Student writing did improve. Certainly the organization of essays and the thinking through of an idea improved greatly for some of the students. Students were positive in their response to the structure of the course, the texts, and the discussions.

5. Prospects for the future. The course was taught only once, since the next year Watauga College changed to a world cultures core curriculum. I did teach a one-hour minicourse on the same subject, using only *The Man Who Walked through Time* and the "I in Nature" journals. That module too was successful, but that class never became a *group.* If I were to teach the course again I might substitute Loren Eiseley's *The Immense Journey* for one of the texts, or I might use the whole of Sally Carrighar's *Home to the Wilderness.* This last work is a fascinating psychological study of a writer, showing, in terms of her own life, why nature study became her profession.

I see a course like this as extremely useful in two contexts. First, it can be offered as an English department course, a possible alternative to the introductory freshman literature course. It deals with literary genres (no fiction, however, in the course I taught), demands close reading and analysis, and requires a good deal of careful essay writing. Second, it can be a prerequisite in environmental studies programs. Most courses in such programs are now either technical (organic gardening, windmill building, alcohol production, aquaculture) or ecological ("Rural America," "Human Ecology," "Man, Energy, and Society"). There are usually no humanities courses.

6. A pitfall to be avoided. In teaching such a course, the pedagogue may be tempted to dwell too fully within the implicit worldview of the literary materials. The achievement of pantheistic consciousness, the reintegration of the self and nature, the resonant symbiosis of personal and natural— these are seductive themes, to be sure. But they are far from self-evidently desirable. The Cartesian-Kantian tradition draws attention to the inevitable transcendence of the self over all natural processes. Human subjects, encountering the phenomena of nature, inevitably examine these by means of such fundamental epistemological categories as mass, shape, velocity, quantity. With what right can a nature so examined then be viewed under the category of person? In studying nature writers, one must therefore ask whether pure human subjectivity, rather than the nature-humanity nexus, is being revealed.

Put another way, it is possible to see nature writers as engaging in systematic self-deception by assuming that they can break out of the prison of subjectivity. If a perspective like this is not raised as this material is studied, then an essential and provocative critical standpoint will be missing. I must confess that in teaching this course for the first time I did not make students sufficiently aware of this perspective.

PART 4:

Environmental Literature in the Field

Introduction

In *The English Curriculum under Fire: What Are the Real Basics?*, George Hillocks, Jr., discusses the dangers in the "back to basics" movement in higher education, which he considers an overreaction to public discontent with "undisciplined" English programs. "Basics," when imposed in a void of curricular imagination, undermines traditional values in English education:

> It specifies content as the learning of particular information and narrowly defined skills, but it leaves untouched the vast domain of learning to use language creatively and critically. It specifies a methodology that results in lockstep drill with teachers directing students through workbooks page by page, but it shuns the give-and-take among students and teachers that can, given appropriate focus, result in learning to use language precisely and effectively. And it implies an ideology of sorts—one which asserts that every question worth considering in schools has a right or wrong answer; therefore, it ignores the most important questions—the ones likely to convince students that language has value beyond the level of the most mundane activities. (3)

The alternative to such a demoralizing effect of curricular restriction is a reimagination of curricula directed to broader goals that involve student creativity and autonomy without avoiding basic competencies.

It is suggested here that "basics," vague and subject to manipulation as a catchword, by being made inclusive and applied to "what we need to know to live in the world" rather than only to the content and techniques of pedagogy, can approach satisfying the needs both of English programs and of their critics; or, at the least, it can give flexible programs credibility in the face of attack.

Such an expanded definition of what is basic can apply both to a knowledge of the world and to a process of knowledge gaining that is not distant from the world. A process of knowing the world is least distanced from the world when it involves action in the world, application of theory to actual problems, an "internship" outside the academic walls guided by processes of knowing learned within them. Encompassing the many individual competencies necessary to live in the world is the synthetic one of knowing how to live in the world without killing it and oneself. Put another way, the competency involves an understanding of how the natural world functions and how it interacts with the sociocultural world of the dominant species—humans. The product of this understanding is the individual's actual skill at surviving in the world while not impeding the survival of other humans and the world itself.

A curricular situation that would teach this basic competency would convey an understanding of how the world functions in terms of individual students' internships in the world. The courses described in this part provide, I believe, this curricular situation. They address the most basic human needs in a practical manner, and they allow students creative autonomy in applying their intellects to them. Indeed, such extramural and integrative courses *are* modes of "basic" education. Although not the only ones of their kind, they can and do exist in interaction with more classroom-based courses to provide the diversity of curriculum necessary to address the diverse needs of humans if they are to survive in an increasingly complex world. These courses apply interdisciplinary approaches to understanding the world, initiated by a study of environmental literature, to the active experience of surviving in the world in controlled situations. Their practitioners actively disavow a naively popular concept of survival that involves physical self-testing in extreme situations. "Survival" refers to the continuous life of humans in human society. Extreme situations, if they occur at all in these field experiences, provide insights useful for surviving and for enhancing life in more mundane situations.

The dominant problem faced by these teachers is to integrate literature and field experience in a meaningful way. John Tallmadge, in "Teaching Wilderness Values to Undergraduates," describes two courses, different in participants and possibilities. In one, a single field trip to Mount Katahdin in Maine was a centerpiece experience. It was preceded and followed by classroom study of wilderness literature, literature whose meaning changes radically once it has been incarnated in a reader's actual experience. In the other, faced with the problem of access (as were Kligerman and Hilbert), Tallmadge uses a debate situation to simulate in class the engagement provided by a field trip. Charles Bergman's "The Literature and Experience of Nature" sets reading and writing *in* a field situation: directed projects and activities, as well as traditional discussion, connect the literature and the experience. Owen Grumbling's "Nature in Midwinter" is a two-week "short-term" course; his readings have a seasonal focus and are carried on throughout the entire two weeks. The first week is taken up with preparation and acclimatization, and only the second involves an actual sustained field experience in a Maine winter. Frank Trocco's Audubon Expedition Institute program differs from the first three in that Trocco does assert that more of what one needs to survive can be learned from experience than from reflection. Like Bergman, he places all learning within the field and outside any classroom—but the institute's program involves traveling through and experiencing many different American environments. Trocco's course could hardly be completely replicated in a conventional university curriculum, but the arguments justifying the institute's approach both demand a constructive response from a nonexperiential point of view and can aid the formulators of any "new basics" curriculum in defining their own goals.

The three university-based programs described here all involve field experiences that do not inherently require heavy expense and long-distance travel—although Bergman's study sites in Minnesota and Arizona are far from his campus. The logistics of organization are discussed in detail by all three, and they emphasize the possibilities of student involvement in organization and methods for avoiding problems of travel, time, expense, and liability. If their field experiences are compared with the more limited ones used in courses described in prior sections—those of McFadden, Weatherly, Kligerman—it is evident that a spectrum of possibilities exists for providing environmental experience in literature courses. It is also evident that field experience can in no way be described as antagonistic to classroom instruction.

All the courses described here involve placing personal experience in a context of intellectual inquiry and demand research-based written work as a result. It might be said that the field experience is a necessary "primary source" among other secondary ones, particularly necessary in environmental studies since the experience of nature is the primary source for most of the imaginative works of literature covered in these courses.

Teaching Wilderness Values to Undergraduates

John Tallmadge

For the past five years I have taught courses in the literature of the American wilderness, using works inspired by intense experiences of place. Writers like Henry David Thoreau, John Muir, and Edward Abbey present highly personal accounts of their encounters with the land, yet they also suggest ways we might begin to develop more viable relations with the rest of the living world. I am convinced that such material ought to be brought into the curriculum, not only because students find it challenging and inspiring but, more important, because it can help change their attitudes toward the land, especially if presented in a way that engages them personally with the ideas and values at stake.

I first became interested in wilderness literature during my tour in the army, when the mountains of California offered a weekend refuge from too much regimentation and the shadow of the Vietnam War. A friend suggested John Muir as off-duty reading, and from his graphic, celebratory essays it was only a short traverse to Aldo Leopold, Loren Eiseley, Clarence King, and other classic wilderness writers. I became aware of a long tradition of narrative and meditative literature exploring the relations among wilderness, American culture, and the individual character. Much of this writing was highly sophisticated, and I began to wonder why I had never heard of it in school: it seemed to have been neglected by literary scholars and excluded from the curriculum with other "nonfictional" genres like the autobiography, the essay, and the travel book.

After leaving the service I continued to visit the mountains and deserts, reading about them between trips, keeping journals, and gradually developing a more or less coherent sense of what the wilderness meant to me and my culture. Here the analytical writings of thinkers like Paul Shepard, Roderick Nash, Robert Marshall, Joseph Wood Krutch, and René Dubos proved highly useful, for I had begun to think dimly about teaching courses in this material and wanted a philosophy that would integrate my outdoor experience with my reading and give me a basis from which to argue before the necessary chairs and committees.

Aldo Leopold provided a starting point. If our environmental problems had grown from what he called our "Abrahamic concept of land" (land viewed as a commodity rather than as a community), then perhaps we could develop a "land ethic" by learning to love the land as Thoreau, Abbey, and other wilderness writers had done. In the army, I had come easily to love the High Sierra and to appreciate John Muir's delight in its wild plants and animals, which served their own vital purposes apart from the economic needs of humans. Wilderness travel, I thought, might give my students a real opportunity for spiritual growth. Combined with the proper readings, it could foster sensitivity and gentleness toward the land, acceptance of an order of creation not dominated by our own imagery, and respect for other creatures as ethical equals, not as objects to be manipulated or consumed.

Besides having spiritual value, wilderness also might promote various physical, intellectual, and emotional values, as noted by Marshall, Dubos, Nash, and others. Wilderness journeys teach self-reliance, courage, discipline, and endurance, and they contribute to health, fitness, and self-confidence. Moreover, they can increase our awareness of history by reminding us of our frontier roots and by teaching the arts of primitive travel. Our intellects are also served by all the disciplines of nature study, which increase our appreciation of the complexity, beauty, and interdependence of what Leopold calls the "land organism." Finally, wilderness can enhance our emotional health by reminding us of our proper place in nature, by providing us with delights and challenges that put our normal anxieties in perspective, and by stimulating all of our senses to a finer appreciation of adventure and beauty.

Back in graduate school I discovered the Yale College Seminar Program, which had been set up during the 1960s to answer student demands for a more relevant curriculum. The seminar format presented both advantages and constraints. With a small class, I could assign lots of reading and advise a long term paper; there was also much opportunity for counseling and discussion. On the other hand, with only one meeting per week, there was little time for lecturing or visual aids, though I did use some slides. I assigned ten primary texts and a background one.

Like any reading list, mine reflects personal interests as well as pedagogical strategy. I chose texts for literary and historical value, and in presenting them I focused on the authors' personae, ideologies, and styles to demonstrate how intense experiences of place are both mediated and conveyed by language. I also illustrated the growth of major themes in the American debate over wilderness values by setting the works in their proper context of intellectual, literary, and political history.

Beginning with the first two chapters of Genesis, which established a moral and theological picture of wilderness that lasted well into the nineteenth century, I set the stage for the American debate by contrasting ambivalent Old Testament and Puritan views of the wild with Emerson's assertion in *Nature* (1836) that a life lived close to the land can lead to moral, physical, and spiritual perfection. Emerson's desire to unite science, poetry, and religion in a distinctively American way leads him to develop the metaphor of the Book of Nature according to a doctrine of Swedenborgian correspondences whereby natural history can be seen as an intellectual and religious discipline. Thoreau builds on these ideas in "Walking" (1862), arguing that the present frontier is the heroic age of our culture and that wildness is necessary to the health of civilization. In *The Maine Woods* he seeks, characteristically, to test his theories by closely observing the character of the settlers and Indians and by climbing Mount Katahdin, one of the wildest peaks in New England. On Katahdin he encounters an environment that is remote, unforgiving, and perhaps even demonic, calling into question the easy pastoralism upon which much transcendentalist nature ideology was based. He also moves from a facile, Rousseauistic view of the Indians toward a more humane and comprehensive understanding as he travels with Joe Polis, the Penobscot chief, down the Allagash and East Branch.

John Muir also responded to Emerson's ideas of natural religion but developed them along significantly different lines. In *My First Summer in the Sierra* (written in 1868 but published in 1911), he imagines the wilderness as paradise, where all creatures, harmoniously and ecologically united, join God in carrying on the happy work of creation. Muir sees the Book of Nature as a kind of sacred history, written by raindrops, rivers, and glaciers, with the naturalist as a prophet interpreting this text for his fallen contemporaries. The geologist Clarence King, however, paints a very different picture of the Sierra. In *Mountaineering in the Sierra Nevada* (1872) he applies Ruskinian aesthetics and geologic catastrophism to portray the range as a Dantesque landscape that assaults both the minds and the bodies of intrepid explorers but that can be overcome by a combination of science, willpower, and brute strength.

Moving into the twentieth century, one finds the lure of exploration and adventure formalized in Robert Marshall's *Alaska Wilderness* with its graphic depictions of self-reliance, remoteness, and primitive travel surviving in a mechanized age. Aldo Leopold presents an ecological view of wilderness in the exquisitely crafted essays of *A Sand County Almanac* enunciating the key concept of a "land ethic" and developing the image of the wilderness lover as a prophet without honor (the wilderness being, of course, his threatened paradise). Leopold's prose style invites comparison with Thoreau's and needs to be examined closely so that students do not miss the rich layers of nuance and understated irony upon which so much of the book's meaning depends. Loren Eiseley's *The Immense Journey* works well as a complement to Leopold's ecological view, introducing evolution as a link between human civilization and primeval wilderness.

With the growth of the preservationist movement in the twentieth century, and especially after the passage of the Wilderness Act and the burgeoning of environmental awareness in the 1960s, wilderness writing becomes more self-conscious, and the major themes are developed to a high degree of sophistication. Edward Abbey's *Desert Solitaire* describes an idealized summer in southern Utah as a kind of vision quest, using the desert's harshness and solitude as ascetic disciplines. The concerns of the wilderness traveler reflect major ideas in Western religion, literature, and philosophy, but Abbey seasons his prose with vivid descriptions and liberal doses of dry humor. Most important here are the temperament and persona of the author and the ideology of wilderness as a spiritual, physical, and political refuge from the various tyrannies of mechanized society. Colin Fletcher's *The Man Who Walked through Time* describes a hike through the Grand Canyon and gives another, less dazzling but perhaps less stylized, view of the desert. During his month in the canyon, Fletcher grows from a mere adventurer to an intuitive naturalist with a deep sense of desert ecology, viewing the canyon not as a physical challenge but as a "living museum." In John McPhee's *Encounters with the Archdruid* a profile of conservationist David Brower demonstrates how images and ideas developed by wilderness writers affect current environmental politics.

The most significant feature of the Yale seminar was a field trip to Mount Katahdin, which we undertook after reading Thoreau's account. Here the primary aim was to give students an intense and personal wilderness experience in a place described by one of our authors. I required the students to keep journals, since this is how all of our texts were first conceived, and, after the trip, they had to put these notes into standard English, type them up, and make enough photocopies for the whole class.

Organizing the trip presented a few logistical problems. To avoid liability, I did not list the trip as an official requirement (two students decided not to go and turned in short papers instead of journals); no school funds were used for the trip, and we all shared the costs of food, fees, and rented cars. To distribute the work of planning, I split the class into groups of four, each with an experienced student to coordinate food, equipment, and safety. In the woods, each group hiked alone so as not to crowd the trail, and I kept in the background as much as possible. Hence, the students felt more like adventurers and less like tourists than is usual on field trips where everything is planned for them.

We set out on the first weekend of October, when the weather is warm and the schoolwork light. Baxter State Park is 450 miles from New Haven, so we spent most of Thursday driving up. As might be expected, the students reacted to the Maine woods with a mixture of fear, fascination, and awe. Several had never backpacked before, let alone climbed a mountain, and for some even a simple stream crossing seemed like a rite of passage. Others, more experienced, felt as if they were coming home; they welcomed the cold, clear nights, the strenuous climbing, and the heady exposure along the famous Knife-Edge that leads down from the summit. A few had been to the area before and wanted to strike out on their own; I had to remind them forcibly that they were part of a class. But generally a spirit of friendly cooperation prevailed, with the stronger mountaineers encouraging and guiding the weaker.

Even though most students found it difficult to write during the climb, there was much discussion of Thoreau around campfires and along the trails. I frequently reminded them to write in their journals so that these ideas would not be lost, and to set an example I kept one of my own. Generally, my role shifted from instructor to participant; the land became the teacher.

Needless to say, things were quite different in class after the trip. Discussions were crisp and lively, and the air felt charged with energy. Why the change? First, I think, because the students had now become personally involved with the issues raised by our authors, through the encounter with a powerful wild place. Katahdin had touched them deeply, as it had touched Thoreau: now they became partners with him in an intellectual and emotional search. Moreover, they could now appreciate the intensity with which Muir had responded to the Sierra or Abbey to the high desert, and, as they struggled to capture the flavor and meaning of their experiences in words, they came to respect the literary achievements of such writers.

Second, the trip created a strong sense of community in the class. I noticed a marked drop in competition and stress: comments were more constructive and less self-serving, and students tended to address each other instead of merely speaking to me. Many said later that they looked forward to the class as a refreshing change from the normal regimen. I suspect that this spirit stemmed not only from the cooperation and intimacy forced on the class by the field trip but also from the fact that Katahdin meant something different to each person, varying with background, self-image, aspirations, and interests. Thus, although it was a group trip, each person came away with something special that had not been gained at another's expense, something that could be shared with others but never taken away.

Without the field trip this seminar would have been no more engaging than any other course in which the material is approached in a primarily cerebral manner, through readings and discussions. The visceral, personal encounter with wilderness made it memorable, much as a laboratory dissection gives one a firsthand knowledge of anatomy. Katahdin was our emotional, intellectual, and spiritual laboratory.

My next opportunity to teach wilderness literature came during a three-year stint as visiting assistant professor of English at the University of Utah. Like most large public universities, Utah differs vastly in curriculum, sociology, and clientele from private schools like Yale, so new strategies were required for presenting the same material. Since I had been working closely with the Liberal Education Program, I proposed to offer a section of their humanities core course "Problems in Human Values" to be called "The American Wilderness Conscience and the Ethics of Land Use."

At Utah, the Liberal Education Program requires each student to take one core course and several distribution courses in each division outside the major. The distribution courses are selected from normal departmental offerings, while the core courses, designed to exemplify the materials and methods of each division, are broader in scope and generally interdisciplinary. Humanities has two core courses, "The Intellectual Tradition of the West" (a three-quarter survey of philosophical and literary classics) and "Problems in Human Values," which focuses on a single issue of particular concern to the instructor, demonstrating how college training could be applied to important social, ethical, or personal choices.

The first day about sixty people came to class, ranging in age from nineteen to thirty-eight and majoring in everything from advertising to mining engineering. Some were fluent and articulate, while others seemed really slow. Most did not know the subject of my particular section; they needed a core course and this one fit their schedules. As for wilderness, most had only a casual interest in it, rather remarkable in a state that boasts five national parks, seven national forests, and hundreds of square miles of primitive BLM (Bureau of Land Management) land.

Even after lopping the class to the standard size (forty), there were still too many for a seminar. Besides, any sort of field trip was out of the question: Utah students tend to marry young, and most hold jobs that take up their out-of-class time. So I had to find another way to engage them personally with the material.

It was simple to alter the syllabus: I merely trimmed it to seven books and introduced more background material in lectures, providing study incentives with weekly quizzes and a final exam. There were also three written assignments: a letter to a member of the Utah congressional delegation (expressing an informed opinion about some land-use issue in the state), a three-page paper on the meaning of wilderness (these were graded to emphasize verbal and intellectual clichés), and a five-page paper analyzing some particular land-use issue in depth, based on research prepared for an in-class debate.

This debate was my strategy for getting students involved with the issues. I wanted them to have a feel for how land-use decisions are made, and, because such decisions are always political, the class as a whole had to grade the debates. Students were given ballots and asked to indicate their stand on the issue before each debate, the team they felt had won, and the grade they felt each team deserved. Only one team could win— no ties allowed—and the losers could get no higher than B-plus. Since they were being graded by their peers, the students worked very hard preparing their presentations (I suppose they felt they could not "psych out" the class as well as they could me), and several told me afterward they had spent more time on this class than on most but had had more fun doing it.

The debate topics reflected current land-use controversies in Utah that involved wilderness in some way or other. They had to be broad enough to draw upon the philosophical issues raised by our weekly readings but specific enough to address pending decisions. They were stated as resolutions to be argued pro and con: (1) control of federal lands in the West should be turned over to the states (the so-called Sagebrush Rebellion); (2) large-scale energy projects should be given priority over wilderness in southern Utah; (3) energy and mineral use should be given priority over wilderness in the Overthrust Belt; (4) species other than *Homo sapiens* have a right to a pristine habitat; (5) the MX missile should be built in the Great Basin; (6) real estate and ski development should take priority over wilderness in the Wasatch canyons.

Early in the quarter students had to sign up for a first- and second-choice topic so that, when making up teams, I could give everyone a chance to research his or her area of interest. Pro and con sides were assigned by a toss of the coin, a move that disturbed the students initially since they rightly perceived an environmentalist tilt in the class. But I argued that since half the class would have to defend an unpopular position, it was in everyone's interest to be as fair as possible; moreover, the research paper, which did not have to take the same side as the student took in the debate, would count much more heavily in determining the course grade. In practice, the class did try to be objective: the wilderness side did not always win, and the vote was often quite close. It appears that having the class grade the debate gave them an incentive to pay closer attention than they might have under ordinary circumstances.

To help students prepare their cases, I made up a three-page handout that included debate rules, lists of resource materials, and names of organizations to which they might go for information (mining companies, utilities, environmental groups, and federal agencies). I also gave some hints for conducting a research program and presenting an effective case, and I urged them to start early and divide up the work. Finally, I met with each team at least once prior to the debate to resolve any last-minute problems.

We had one debate a week for most of the quarter, and the format was rigidly adhered to. Each side had five minutes to deliver an opening statement, then five minutes to rebut what their opponents had said. Then came ten minutes of "open debate" followed by ten minutes of questions from the class (much like a press conference). Finally, each side had two minutes to present closing statements. This left eight minutes for the class to decide on the winner and fill out their ballots. The arrangement seemed to work, though students complained that they were not able to present all of their material; I often sensed that the debate could have gone on for another hour.

Needless to say, both teams came in very keyed up and, as the quarter progressed, the presentations became more and more imaginative. Students quickly realized that the opening and closing statements offered the best opportunities for making a strong impression, so they began to use posters, charts, drawings, photographs, handouts, and other visual aids to emphasize and clarify their positions. One team, arguing for the protection of endangered species, presented a beautiful slide show synchronized to folk music; their opponents countered by bringing out a papier-mâché tombstone with the inscription "*Homo sapiens* R.I.P." On another occasion, a team opposed to dams on the Colorado climaxed their statement by flourishing a silt-choked fish in front of their astonished opponents (they lost, but the vote was close). These sorts of gestures helped make the debates interesting and fun without lapsing into mere silliness. The students all knew they had to convince the class, so they could not afford to leave themselves open to ridicule; nor could they risk trivializing their position by assuming the class would agree with it. They soon learned that it would be fatal to treat the audience with easy familiarity or implicit condescension. Thus, the debates maintained a fairly uniform level of seriousness leavened from time to time by genuine wit.

After their class presentations, students had a week to prepare their research papers, which were supposed to weigh all the evidence and reach the most reasonable conclusion, stated in the form of a recommendation. Here they could present the full fruits of their work, and the paper was therefore given four times the weight of the debate in determining the final grade. It was supposed to be not a polemic but an objective analysis, and I stressed that the students should not feel compelled to argue the position they had defended in class.

Like the Katahdin trip, the debate proved the most memorable part of the course. It tapped unsuspected reserves of initiative and creativity, and it proved very informative to all. I am sure I could not have got as much work out of the class if I had merely assigned research papers on these issues. Because they had to stand up and present a position before their peers, they put their best efforts into it, becoming local experts on their subjects (as the letters to congresspeople showed). Some even continued their political activity after the end of the term.

These experiences suggest that wilderness literature is an appropriate subject to introduce at both private and public schools. It is timely, readable, and intellectually stimulating, and it speaks to students of experiences with which they can readily identify, providing concepts and imagery for interpreting activities in which they frequently engage. In these respects it fulfills the function of all worthy literature, but it has the added advantage of contributing in a small way to solving a major dilemma facing human society. Finally, it responds well to the customary forms of literary and historical analysis and thus can readily be fitted to traditional curricula. Where special programs like college seminars do not exist, it should be possible to teach it in freshman seminars, American studies programs, environmental studies programs, or general education programs such as Utah's.

In the end, such courses must contribute to the search for a viable relation between human society and the rest of the living world. Just as a journey of a thousand miles begins with a single step, so great social changes begin with individual choices. The literature of the American wilderness contains not merely facts and poetry but wisdom that has helped many people form their relations to the wild and the human worlds. For a teacher who is personally involved in such issues, communicating this sort of lived truth is always more satisfying than reciting traditional catechisms. In fostering the encounter between students, literature, and land, one can take a small but firm step in the direction of planetary survival.

The Literature and Experience of Nature*

Charles A. Bergman

How can we translate the life of the mind into the pragmatics of living? In his life and his art, H. D. Thoreau confronted the question directly, intensely. He was both a philosopher and a woodsman—a man who tried to live his ideas. Though he frequently explored the tension between thought and action, it was the simultaneity of these two parts of life that Thoreau emphasized. He stressed the pedagogical implications of his concern with the conduct of life. The student, he wrote, should know both chemistry and "How his bread is made" (*Walden* 59). In the 1980s, with vocational pragmatism increasing among students, the great challenge facing teachers of humanities remains integrating the theoretical and the practical, the art of living, the head and the hands.

I have designed a course, "The Literature and Experience of Nature," around the issue Thoreau identifies. The course is an experiment in addressing the problems of life both theoretically and practically. For two years now, during the January interim session, I have taken students to the woods of Minnesota and Arizona to study environmental literature because I do not want us "to *play* life, or study it merely . . . but earnestly [to] live it from beginning to end" (*Walden* 59).

In the course I wanted to exploit the complicated interplay and interdependence of both the active life and the contemplative life. The on-site class was a means of examining the importance and limitations of each and, if a sense of reconciliation was possible only for brief moments, at least of trying to accommodate them one to the other. In "The Bean Field," Thoreau says that working his beans "attached me to the earth, so I got strength like Antaeus" (*Walden* 137). I wanted my students to feel some of the connective power of praxis—between subject and object, person and idea, individual and environment.

Yet doing or acting was by no means an end in itself. I also wanted students to recognize the ambiguities and complications in the nexus between thinking and doing. For Thoreau, in many respects the mind *is* practice. He writes, "My head is my hands and feet" (*Walden* 95). His sense of irony, his humor, and his playfulness acknowledge the limits of the bean field, for example, and qualify his complete integration with the soil, and of mind and action. He was, he admits, playing at roles, "a very *agricola laboriousus*" (*Walden* 138).

The courses I taught were themselves forms of "playing life," and yet they transcended the limits of the typical classroom. While maintaining a sense of irony about, say, using freezing outhouses for almost a month in

*Parts of this essay were published in a different form as "Teaching Environmental Literature, on Location," *Journal of English Teaching* 11 (1981): 57–66.

Minnesota's winters, we were still able to take our experiment seriously. That we would and did leave after a month indicates that the courses were in fact a kind of play—but play in Johan Huizinga's sense: we achieved in the woods a new consciousness that we carried back with us when we left.

In January 1979, ten of us ranging in age from eighteen to forty-seven lived in the North Woods of Minnesota, in pine cabins near the Canadian border. In January 1980, twenty of us lived in the Sonoran Desert, near the Chiricahua Mountains of southeastern Arizona. We read environmental authors, held classes, and studied our place in nature. Although these sites were at opposite ends of the country, offering completely different eco-systems and personal challenges, we found that, as Thoreau says, "All climates agree with brave Chanticleer" (*Walden* 117).

The Gunflint Trail in northern Minnesota winds for sixty miles into the back country, west of Grand Marais and Lake Superior, among deep glacial lakes and marshy swamps. This is canoe country, the Boundary Waters Canoe Area, the home of the Chippewa Indians and the French Canadian voyageurs who traded with them, heading toward Lake Athabaska. Recently, much of the area has been given federal wilderness protection, banning motorized vehicles and exacerbating local antagonisms. At the remote end of the Gunflint Trail, located on islands in Seagull Lake, is Wilderness Canoe Base, where my students and I lived for over three weeks.

On the entrance doors of the main lodge, where we took our meals, hung an unavoidable twelve-inch Fahrenheit thermometer; it confronted us every morning on our way to breakfast. In our journals, we each kept a record of the daily high and low temperatures, as well as the times of sunrise and sunset. On cold, clear days, the thermometer needle would stay below zero. The average low temperature was about twenty below; the average high, about twenty above. To live in this climate, we learned to pay close attention to our bodies and to each other. Not only did we learn to recognize signs of fatigue, hypothermia, and overheating, but we also learned to control the heat our bodies manufactured on hikes by, say, taking a glove off. As important, we learned to watch for reactions to the cold in each other and got skilled at detecting symptoms for each other. Our physical environment threw us more closely upon each other.

In *A Sand County Almanac*, Aldo Leopold writes that there are two main dangers in living in the city (6). One is thinking that heat comes from a thermostat; the other is thinking that breakfast comes from the grocery store. Our cabins were small and rough-hewn, made from trees on the island and heated only by small wood-burning Fisher stoves. When we first saw our cabins, they were unheated and uninviting; at minus fifteen degrees, the windows were covered with two inches of ice—on the inside—and the stoves, unlit, looked far too small to keep us warm. Although we had electric lights (to which one purist objected), we had no running water for showers or toilets. Even in the coldest weather we used an outhouse: styrofoam seats proved excellent insulation against the cold wood. Our living cabins were on a small island, about half a mile from the main island of the camp; for the most part, we were self-reliant.

We chopped our own wood, and some of us got skilled enough to split quarters in two strokes. While chopping our wood, we learned where the heat we rely on comes from. Chopping wood became a simple but vital activity in our lives, our own "small Herculean labor," akin to Thoreau hoeing his beans, a way of becoming cousin to the pine. As with Thoreau's French Canadian woodchopper, in whom "the animal man was chiefly developed" (*Walden* 131), our wood chopping made us part of the country we were living in, and more and more our characters became, as it were, expressions of the land and the snow and the trees.

Approximately twice a week, we had large wood-chopping and ice-chopping "festivals." We chopped not to store wood for our cabins but to pile wood for our saunas. Developing a sense of place in my students was a major goal in both Minnesota and Arizona. But I could not have foreseen how the sauna would transform and define our experience for us. It became a central ritual.

We took our saunas together. Built of Norway pine, the sauna sat on a hill; a long window high in the sauna room overlooked a bay of Seagull Lake. We would sit in the sauna, at about 115 degrees, gazing out on the frozen lake. After chopping about half a cord of wood, we chopped a hole in the twelve-inch ice, about five feet by five feet, over a few feet of water. We used water from the lake to pour over rocks in the sauna, for steam and for our "showers" in the sauna. André, a Chippewa Indian, taught us to gather cedar boughs to help clean and excite the skin. No one really believed that we would actually jump through the ice, into the freezing lake water. But the dip, as it turns out, is the essential part of the experience. Though all were reluctant, we watched through the window, fascinated and cheering, while the first person jumped in. We all followed, one after another, in an uproar of enthusiasm. In socks and swimsuits we ran across the ice and into the water, head and all.

It was not easy during all this to relinquish my educated self-consciousness—which Annie Dillard calls "the curse of the city and all that sophistication implies" (82)—and I found myself laughing at myself frequently. But finally the experience was fully engaging. We had accepted nature on its terms, had surrendered in trust, had let go.

After our first sauna, we discussed its significance in class. We had been reading Sigurd Olson and Aldo Leopold, focusing on the themes of developing a sense of place and of becoming a part of the complex interrelations in nature. Our experience clearly illustrated the literature, giving both the readings and the discussions a relevance to the lives we were leading.

There is, however, another dimension to this question as well. Through our experience, our reading, and our discussions, students I think learned how pure experience is metamorphosed by intellect into meaningful form. The literature helped supply terms for us to interpret our experience. The sauna, for example, came to symbolize for us our whole experience in Minnesota. The problem of student motivation was also transcended. Feeling more sure of themselves and having a sense of the importance of discussions, students expressed themselves more openly. If on the one hand experience affirmed literature, on the other hand students discovered the ways in which intellectual questions are implicit in and emerge from experience. Blood came to flow in our words.

Jerome Bruner describes three ways of learning, partially translatable one into the other. One is through action: we learn by doing. A second is through imagery, "a representing ikon." The image stops and summarizes the action. The third is by symbol, the preeminent example of which is restatement in words (7–8). In Minnesota and Arizona, I tried to place academics in the broader context of life and to deploy all these strategies of learning. The students were engaged and active and explored ideas in various ways: living, doing, reading, talking, thinking, writing. As with the sauna, a reinforcing cycle of perception, experience, struggle, and vision was reenacted countless times in different undertakings with the students. The result was an integrated educational experience, an education for the whole person, for all of us.

Each student was required to undertake a project: each was to observe closely, over time, a clearly defined natural phenomenon. Together, the students and I worked out the phenomena to be observed. Their observations were to be supplemented with secondary research—such information as could be discovered through readings and interviews—and records of their investigations were to be maintained. Thoreau's study of the freezing dates of Walden Pond is a good model for the methods and purposes of this project. In Minnesota, one student made trees his project: he identified and described the trees of the region, the communities and ecosystems they form, the conditions they prefer, and the values different human societies have attached to them. In Arizona, using Joseph Wood Krutch's *The Voice of the Desert* as a model for intelligent investigation of natural phenomena, one student made roadrunners her project. One objective she never accomplished: to hear its call, which Krutch describes as a "modified Bronx cheer."

In both classes students grew in confidence. Partly this was the result of living in conditions that were, if not hostile, at least primitive and foreign. Partly it was attempting new and challenging experiences. In both Minnesota and Arizona, we camped out. In Minnesota we spent one full night camped under the stars and a big orange moon, sleeping on the ice of a small and remote lake. We lit a large fire on the ice—since heat rises, the fire burned only a couple of inches into the ice. Huddling around the fire, we ate high-calorie, starchy foods and recited Robert Service poems. Each of us had two down sleeping bags, one stuffed inside the other, and we spent the night deep within the bags, like larvae. Although the air was cold and the night was clear, we had no idea how cold it got overnight. Not until the next day did we learn. That night had been the coldest of the year: minus thirty-seven.

In Arizona the next January, I focused even more explicitly on two themes: making connections with the earth and cultivating a higher consciousness that can be integrated into the lives we lead. In both our living and our learning, my goal was to combine participating and reflecting.

The Price Canyon Ranch is eighteen thousand acres at the end of a seven-mile dirt road winding through the high Sonoran Desert into the

Chiricahua Mountains. From some high cliffs back in the mountains, we could see New Mexico, about ten miles to the east, and old Mexico, forty miles to the south. Within a five-mile radius of the ranch headquarters we had access to several different ecosystems: from mesquite desert through live-oak transition to live oak and juniper fields, through oak and pine mountain slopes to ponderosa pine forest at the mountaintops, at 8,000 feet. The headquarters, at 5,600 feet, sat among live oaks and open fields.

In "The Land Ethic," Aldo Leopold argues for an extension of human ethics to include the land, which he defines as the inclusive community of soil, plants, and animals. Humans are a part of the land community, and the land ethic is the result of a love, a feeling, for the land we are a part of. The reason, Leopold argues, that conservation has been ineffective, that education has failed, is that the feeling of relationship to the land is missing. The individual must feel a personal engagement with the land he or she lives on (201–26). This concept has pedagogical implications. As Michael Polanyi writes in his theory of personal knowledge, knowledge must be informed by passion and a personal commitment. There is a kind of "tacit knowledge" in which the knower participates in the shaping of knowledge; the result is an intimacy between the person knowing and what is known (12–13). This is an integrative vision of education; intellectual maturity is measured by the ability to form and discover relationships. To be complete, knowledge must become personal, internal. Discovering linkages with the earth, then, not only creates a kind of ethic, a state of being, but it also serves as a pedagogical strategy, enabling humans to translate a theme into personal terms. The themes of environmental literature dovetailed with the pedagogical theory of the on-location courses. One paradigm applied to both living and knowing. In *Pilgrim at Tinker Creek*, Annie Dillard says she may not know why she is in the world, but she can at least know where in the world she is. She can sit up and look around; she can explore the neighborhood. Intuitive, personal meaning coalesces in particular places.

Although I wanted students to feel close to the earth, I wanted them also to be able to reflect on and rise above the tangible. They were to learn to move from inarticulate knowledge to articulate knowledge in a continuing cycle of experience and concept. I used several means to this end. Each student had to tell a story to the class. The stories were highly successful: they developed a better sense of rapport and community in the group, and they demonstrated at a basic level how we make meaning out of experience.

In addition, we cultivated our powers of observation. Through an exact perception of details, we simultaneously cultivated a detached awareness. Our reading helped vastly in teaching us what to look for and how to look. For example, Joseph Wood Krutch describes the mating procedures of the pronuba moth on the yucca tree, and his description revolutionized our view of the common yucca. Charles V. Riley made the classic observation a hundred years ago. The moth lays her eggs on the yucca flower. She then goes through a series of purposeful actions "which have no other function except to fertilize a flower which could be fertilized in no other way. If we naively interpreted its actions, we should find ourselves compelled to say that it 'knows what it is doing' " (*Voice* 82). The pronuba larvae feed on the seeds, but the female derives no immediate benefit from her actions. To become moths, the larvae must bore their way out of the pods formed by the flowers, and, as a result, all yucca pods must have small holes in them. The yucca will not form seed pods unless it has been fertilized by the moth. Discovering this interaction of yuccas and moths led to intense debate about the role of consciousness in evolution, broadly Darwinian versus Lamarckian. We also saw yuccas in a new way and were unable to find a pod without a hole, though we searched the desert. As Krutch says, "It is not ignorance, but knowledge which is the mother of awe" (149).

To develop our powers of informed observation more fully, we all undertook carefully defined projects. The projects combined secondary research, using the libraries available, and personal observation. We focused, each of us, on one plant or animal and tried to learn as much about it as we could, identifying also important questions that still needed to be answered about the species.

Our discussions were attempts for us as a class to come to terms with both our readings and our experiences. Each student began and led at least one class discussion, based on a question we worked out together from the readings. Class sessions averaged about two hours per day, five days per week. Some classes were only an hour, and at least one ran for five hours. With no bell to signal the end of the discussion, we kept going until the topic was exhausted. Some discussions were precisely defined and focused: what, for example, is Leopold's land ethic, and what are its implications for our behavior? We also read Keats and Thoreau out loud, discussing each paragraph; these were highly successful classes, revealing a great deal about some students' reading comprehension and what they needed to learn. Some discussions were more abstract and grew wide-ranging: what is Krutch's concept of evolution, and how does it differ from Cartesian mechanism? Or, how successful has humanity's domination of the world been? Students also maintained journals; I provided suggestions on the types of entries that make for good journals.

The logistics and organization of off-campus wilderness courses are crucial to the success of the courses, but they are not as difficult to work out as people always imagine they are. How does one find and select the places to go? I wrote the local tourist bureaus and church headquarters in Minnesota and Arizona. I also consulted travel agents. From these sources, I compiled a list of camps and ranches in each state. For Arizona, I found a booklet listing ranches, with descriptions and prices—an extremely useful source. From the list of prospective locations, I immediately wrote the ones that interested me most, asking for additional information—photographs, activities available, philosophy behind their operation, kinds of meals, types of accommodations. For Minnesota, I did my own correspondence. For Arizona, I engaged a travel agent. Not only does this save considerable time and bother, but the travel agent knows more about logistics and prices and can in fact become a bargaining agent for you. For the Minnesota trip, students were responsible for their own travel arrangements to Grand Marais, on Lake Superior; we met at the bus depot at a designated time. I had thought having students plan their travel would save me trouble; however, it was more complicated for me to keep the various arrangements straight than to have a travel agent arrange group transportation. I became a travel agent, willy-nilly. For Arizona, an agent made all travel arrangements. All connections—and there were several crucial ones, between plane and chartered bus, bus and truck, or bus and limousine—came off with precision. Students were, of course, able to make their own arrangements for travel if the group itinerary did not correspond to their needs.

Expense is a major factor. Students had to pay tuition over and above expenses incurred for the traveling. Wilderness Canoe Base charged $240 for three full weeks, cabins and three meals per day. The food was whole grain, for the most part—tasteful and nutritious. For one lunch, we had bear. I have not been able to match their price since. Students then supplied their own transportation. Not including tuition and spending money, the Minnesota interim cost each student about $500. Room and board in Arizona, cabins and three meals per day, was $21 per day. Transportation was more complicated and more expensive. We traveled by air, bus, and limousine. Each student's travel expense for eighteen days was about $640. To this were added my expenses. Minnesota offered free lodging to me; not so Arizona. Finally, I was not sure how much travel expenses would actually be for the Arizona trip, and I wanted a small contingency fund. A reserve for unanticipated expenses was a wise provision—I used it. I therefore had each student deposit $705 in an account. After the course, I gave them each a refund.

For the sake of planning, it is useful to devise a method of sign-up and reservation for such a course. I did not have one for the Minnesota trip and did not know until the last minute how many for sure intended to go. For the Arizona trip, I required a $75 nonrefundable deposit, which reserved them a place in the course. First come, first reserved. I asked that the balance be paid two months before the class began; with that money I was able to buy airline tickets early, to beat the almost monthly fare increases. With a reservation system, fewer students backed out in the final weeks, and I spent the two months before the class under less pressure concerning enrollment figures and logistical planning.

If possible, visit the location. I did in Minnesota and did not in Arizona. At least, have an extensive discussion with the owners or managers over the telephone. Try to anticipate and prevent any misunderstandings, some of which are inevitable. Explain to them the course, its goals, and the type of group you will be bringing. You do not want to lead an invasion into their territory. For your part, learn how the camp or ranch is run, its schedule, what rules they enforce, how you and your group will fit into their operation. Learn the kinds of groups they are used to and what activities are available. Find out what kinds of meals will be served. The food will be very important; the ranch in Arizona served bologna for every lunch, which was unpopular. Learn precisely what to expect of climate and terrain: you want no misconceptions among students on this. Perhaps most important, try to get a feeling for the kind of people you will be living with—how rigid or accommodating they are.

I hold interest and organizational meetings for the students during the semester preceding our trip. Make sure they understand what they are in for. I show slides of the area. The first few days in the actual location are traumatic and require adjustments, and accurate preconceptions will ease transitions, especially with regard to physical environment. Explain how you will be living. I also explain class goals and the syllabus and lay down the ground rules for personal behavior and group dynamics.

In choosing the bibliography for the courses, I include one or two titles by indigenous or local authors and one or two whose value does not depend on time or place. In Minnesota, we read Sigurd Olson's *The Listening Point*; he lived in Ely, a famous canoe-country town. We also read Aldo Leopold's *A Sand County Almanac*, about his farm in Sand County, Wisconsin. The two other readings were H. D. Thoreau's *Walden* and selected poems by John Keats, most notably "Ode to a Nightingale." In Arizona, we read Edward Abbey's *Desert Solitaire*; he has worked and lived in parks throughout Arizona and Utah. Joseph Wood Krutch's *Voice of the Desert*, written from his home outside Tucson, was particularly informative and stimulating. We read several of Leopold's essays, concentrating on "The Land Ethic," which generated excellent discussions. Leopold worked in Arizona and New Mexico. We culminated with *Walden*, which contains most of modern environmentalism. Students were assigned in both classes to read one of the titles before they arrived at location.

I did everything that was required of the students: project, journal, dishes. Whatever authority I was to maintain in the class I had to earn. It did not come with a classroom, blackboard, and lectern—all the accoutrements of the professorial role. I tried to develop an honest and human interaction with the students so that we all developed different roles. My roles were complex, much more so than for a teacher under normal circumstances. I had to balance various guises as a teacher, an authority figure, a leader, a hiking partner, a guide, a friend, a confidant, a roommate, an intellectual, a birdwatcher.

I am convinced of the value of these courses. They provide an excellent way to study environmental literature and its relation to the environment itself. Further, they offer a model for ways the ideals of a humanistic education can be related to the lives our students actually lead. The tradition of a humanistic education is rooted in training students for a life of action. Both More and Erasmus were men of learning and action. Our teaching should demonstrate that learning is not adventitious but integral to the conduct of life. Elizabeth Wooten Cowan says that teachers of humanities need to get off their *ars poetica*. Through living in nature, Thoreau grew intellectually and practically. He sought to perfect not merely the parts but the whole person. We should teach our students how to think, certainly, and how to act. We should teach them how they can produce their blossoms and fruits in season.

Winter Term: Teaching Environmental Literature in the Snow

Vernon Owen Grumbling

A likely place in the academic calendar to initiate a field-integrated environmental literature course is the short term of a four-four-one schedule, which is usually the winter term. Student travel is not limited by conflicts with other courses, and the short term itself is often viewed as a time for attempting innovative courses. Consequently, teachers may find it relatively easy during the winter term—or during the January hiatus, if the institution closes for the month—to institute a course that combines outdoor experience with analysis of nature literature.

Nor is winter an unpromising time for nature study. On the basis of the "Nature in Midwinter" courses I have taught at the University of New England, I am convinced that the distinctive features of the northern winter can enhance college students' understanding and appreciation of both literature and the natural environment.

It is difficult to exaggerate the energy directed by students toward the problems of winter survival and carried over to their reading and composing. When engaged with "To Build a Fire," for example, while attempting conditions that approximate the frozen world faced by Jack London's protagonist, students read the text with surprising acuity: they note subtle connotations and intuit slight turns of plot almost as if their lives depended upon it.

A second argument for teaching an integrated course in the winter lies in the value of understanding the natural world in its less typically celebrated forms, since these provide analogues to the harsher themes of literature. To feel "one with nature" only during the harvest season while lying "on a half-reap'd furrow . . . / Drows'd with the fume of poppies" does not necessarily lead one to understand the revolutions of nature or the cycles of the literary mythoi derived by the human imagination. Furthermore, the winter landscapes provide students with the chance to observe the vitality of the human imagination as it molds the matter of experience, perhaps finding joyful beauty in a scene labeled cold and sterile by convention.

2

The general goal of "Nature in Midwinter" is to give students an opportunity to view the natural world from a position that enables them to better understand "both what they half-create and what perceive." Consequently, I selected literature that provided more than the predictable mythos of irony and that was written in a variety of genres during several different historical periods.

Readings

1. Jack London, "Lust for Life," "To Build a Fire," "To the Man on Trail"
2. Robert Service, *The Spell of the Yukon and Other Verses*
3. James Thomson, *Winter* (1746)
4. Alexander Pope, "Winter: The Fourth Pastoral, or Daphne" (1709)
5. Donald Stokes, *A Guide to Nature in Winter*
6. John Danielsen, *Winter Hiking and Camping*
7. Peter Matthiesson, *The Snow Leopard*
8. William Wordsworth, "Lines Composed . . . above Tintern Abbey," excerpts from *The Prelude*
9. John Clare, "The Badger," "Snow Storm," "Winter Walk"

Two of London's stories, "To Build a Fire" and "Love of Life," feature ironic and romantic mythoi in similar settings, while the treatments of winter in Pope, Thomson, and Service provide interesting contrasts in perception and attitude.

The imaginative literature interacted with the field component in an unpredictable but valuable way. It provided students with insights into the practical task of survival in cold weather, not by its technical information, but by its portrayal of human emotion. Students in the course have stated repeatedly that they profited in the field from the literary descriptions of emotional reactions to climatic and psychological stress. Two students, for example, hiking through thirty-mile-an-hour winds at five degrees below zero from our base camp into the foothills of Maine's White Mountains, found when they confronted an old logging road marked by a turned-around signpost that not only their jelly sandwiches but also their liquid compasses had "frozen up." After some initial bewilderment, they climbed trees in order to rough-orient their map to the contours of the landscape. That completed, they decided to contradict the sign and walked directly back to camp, arriving about an hour before sunset. There they reported that London's descriptions of cold and discomfort causing uncritical judgments had remained prominent in their minds, more so apparently than statements from the survival handbooks.

But this, according to my own pedagogical assumptions, is as it ought to be. The liberal arts should be not the "useless" knowledge of "refined" minds but rather the tools by which creative intelligence criticizes and molds experience in order to create truer and ultimately happier lives for ourselves and those we touch.

A second pedagogical assumption might be shared by potential teachers of a course like mine. My democratic bias led me to keep costs low so that less wealthy students could enter it. By scavenging for inexpensive winter clothing, by tapping the institution's food service (usually contracted to provide raw food materials for official outings at no extra cost), and by rotating gear such as skis and crampons, we kept the incidental cost down to about seventy dollars per student, including even one triumphant post-expeditionary visit to a pub. The cabin we used for a week was donated by a friend, but teachers elsewhere might find a hunting camp that can be rented with little cost, if a base camp is necessary.

3

The integration of classroom and field components in a course like this must be planned carefully in order to avoid a simple outing devoid of intellectual challenge, on the one hand, or an unsafe experience, on the other. In this section I will outline the integration of the three weeks' work and in the following section explain the special precautions necessary for safe field experiences under winter conditions.

During the first week mornings are devoted to lectures on the physiological demands of the course, including the proper use of equipment, clothing, and food. Afternoons are spent discussing literary theory and applying it to texts on the reading syllabus. Since most of my students pursue professional programs in health science, many are taking their first college-level course in literature. Consequently, the discussions include basic material on the demands of the short story, the journal, the descriptive essay, and a few poetic forms. Discussions also provide an introduction to tools of analysis such as plot, setting, characterization, diction, imagery, and point of view. Students are composing descriptive and interpretive essays from their own experiences on solo outings during this first week. Their attempts at composition combined with our initial analyses of stories and poems lead to questions about theme and tone, which in turn lead to formal discussions of the literary mythoi.

The second week, the heart of the course, we spend in a cabin on Twichell Pond, near Bethel, Maine, on the border of the White Mountain National Forest Preserve. Water is hauled from a nearby stream, and a small wood stove keeps indoor temperatures above freezing. During the week we instruct one another in a host of activities: hiking, orienteering, skating, snowshoeing, cross-country skiing, identifying deciduous trees and signs of animal life, rock climbing, and cutting firewood. Each night, after an early supper, the class discusses literature, often in terms of the day's experience. After class, the students make entries in their journals, often modeling the composition upon descriptions or stories discussed in class. Generally, by the second week our initial analyses of London's stories and the various poems on winter have prepared us for examination of more subtle themes, such as the tones coloring a writer's perception of natural phenomena. The *Guide to Nature in Winter*, which integrates graphic and verbal arts with scientific information, becomes popular with students at this time.

The activities of the second week culminate in a major field experience such as an extended snowshoe tour or an ascent of a peak in the White Mountains.

The final week of the course is devoted again to classroom work and punctuated by field experiences near the campus. In the classroom we read and criticize each other's journals and compositions and continue to evaluate the literature from the new perspectives attained in the field.

4

Any wintertime field experience set in the north requires careful preparation and cautious execution. Inevitably, the teacher must undergo some degree of self-education in order to render his or her personal expertise sound enough to take responsibility for relatively inexperienced students. The winter environment presents peculiar dangers often compounded by unpredicted changes in weather patterns. Hypothermia, the lowering of body temperature, and frostbite, the freezing of tissue, are the ultimate dangers. Often these arise out of confusion brought on by dehydration, disorientation, or fatigue. The body may actually require more water on a subzero day in January than on a cool day in June; the appearance of snow-covered terrain can be quite deceptive, especially on a windy day; and travel on ice or through deep snow can be extremely tiring. On a very cold day one's clothing may be adequate for action but inadequate for resting.

Getting wet from rain or even from perspiration can lead directly to hypothermia. Consequently, down clothing and sleeping bags must be well protected from moisture or, better, left home in favor of synthetics such as PolarGuard or Fiberfill. Keeping clothes dry is a special problem in New England, where a January rainstorm can give way in an hour to northwest winds and subzero temperatures.

The preceding paragraphs are but a brief outline of the major hazards involved in winter activities. A host of small problems, undreamed of in the summertime, may beset the winter camper. In subzero weather, for example, water bottles are carried not in a pack but beneath one's coat—to prevent freezing. On any ambitious excursion, one member of the party should pack a sleeping bag, since the only adequate first aid for hypothermia is to strip the patient and a buddy to the skin and place them in a sleeping bag together, a fact that seems to generate a lot of ribbing about the need for "hypothermia drills."

Well before beginning any outdoor activity every student should read and be quizzed on a good cold-weather survival handbook. An excellent, inexpensive text is John Danielsen, *Winter Hiking and Camping*. Its close-up photographs of frostbitten hands and feet provide an object lesson itself worth the price of the book.

An essential part of the course preparation is the screening of applicants, and this begins with the course description. It should, I think, carefully explain that close reading and thoughtful discussion are required, and it should describe the outdoor component as a serious activity requiring discipline and hard work. No matter how grim the language, applicants will be plentiful. I have found it extremely useful to enroll a senior student with substantial experience; he or she might even be remunerated as a student assistant.

It is good to meet with the final group before preregistration concludes in order to explain potential dangers and work requirements. My course last year actually began at this first meeting, because a regular series of meetings followed it: two before Thanksgiving, another early in December, and the last during finals week, which at UNE takes place before Christmas. At the first meeting after preregistration, we discussed objectives and the bibliography. Just before Thanksgiving vacation I gave a long, required lecture on cold-weather dangers and equipment, including a checklist of essentials. At this time I advised students to visit friends during vacation and speak for gear that might be borrowed. I also suggested that they begin to make their own: secondhand clothing stores, for example, often provide a wealth of good woolens (to replace useless cottons) that may be altered easily to make underwear, knickers, shirts, and pants. When, soon after Thanksgiving, we met to evaluate personal gear, I suggested that those lacking essentials might place them on a Christmas hint list. At the final preliminary meeting—during finals—I assigned the survival handbook as required reading over the long Christmas break, and this tactic I heartily recommend.

Meanwhile, material preparations were being made. From the earliest meetings I made it clear that all support for our field activities—food, cooking, travel, group equipment—must be worked out by students. I would advise and supervise but never take over primary responsibility: if we were not prepared for the field, we would remain in the classroom. This built a lot of goodwill among the students, for they began to delegate tasks to one another and to assume new tasks as each arose. Initially, I laid out general work areas and the students formed committees under each head: food, equipment, transportation, accounting, library, map making—and, in the mountains, cooking, cleanup (all but the cooks), and water carry. One biology major constructed a meal-by-meal menu, taking into consideration special needs for cold-weather activity, and another wrestled with the food service until a satisfactory list of raw materials was agreed on.

One extremely important preparation is the construction of laminated topographic maps for each student. By cutting and splicing, the mapmakers can assemble a compact, waterproof, detailed map of the particular areas to be visited—in our case the Presidential Range, on one side, and, on the other, the Maine foothills of the White Mountains.

5

Much of this essay has been devoted to discussing the field component of the course, since I assume that my readers possess substantial techniques in the teaching of poems, journals, and short stories. Nonetheless, I would like to pass on some of my experiences teaching the literature.

"Nature in Midwinter" is the most rewarding course I have taught, not so much for the obvious enjoyment it afforded in the out-of-doors but for the complex kinds of learning that seemed to take place among the members of the class. The literature we read enhanced our appreciation of the environments we visited, and our experiences there, in turn, illuminated the literature. Of the many kinds of education that have taken place in this course over the years, I will attempt to relate only two examples.

During the first week students exhibited some typical, frustrating literary habits, most notably a disinclination to perceive the order with which art gives structure to reality. Near the end of "To Build a Fire," for example, the protagonist, who has already committed a half-dozen stupid errors, experiences a "mystical" attraction to his own death. Many students easily perceived London's almost heavy-handed irony in the scene and judged that the character's imaginings were a sign of advanced hypothermia, consistent with his earlier errors in judgment. But others insisted that the scene revealed a "non-Western" view of death they wanted to defend.

Now, the question to be resolved was not the relative merits of Eastern versus Western eschatology but rather the reality that the author depicted in the text; after that was accomplished, the former question might prove very valuable. A problem existed: an inability to sympathize with the author's imagination, an inability to learn a new point of view before evaluating what one wished to hear.

Once during the second week of the course we attempted to hike to a hut atop Mount Adams, one of the northernmost Presidentials. What would have been a fairly easy walk in the summer or in good snow proved difficult because of icy trails. The trail grew more steep and more slick, but the entire group tacitly insisted on continuing until we reached timberline, where we encountered cliffs of ice impassable without the aid of technical climbing gear, which not all members of the party possessed that year.

Back at the cabin that night conversation changed radically from that of the previous evening. On into the night I heard a half dozen informal, articulate discussions about death and war, conflict and cooperation, perception and reality, all the topics grounded in the environmental challenges faced that day.

A week later our classroom discussion turned again to the death of London's ironic protagonist, but with a new perspective: we had all measured—from a distance—the possibility of death, worn it, as one student remarked, on the soles of our feet. Although none of our experiences had been any more foolhardy than driving on an icy road, the immediacy of the experience on the mountain led us to speak of what Henry Beston calls an "elemental presence," the reality of natural force that impinges upon our sensations and, though masked by the contrivances of technology, sets the bounds to our existence.

The high point of the entire course one year was a hike to the summit of Mount Washington, which holds records for the worst climatic conditions in the United States. Although no technical ice climbing was planned, members of the party were equipped with crampons and ice axes for walking on icy slopes. The night before the climb, just after we finished packing, I read to the group the words Henry David Thoreau wrote about Mount Katahdin, the tallest peak in Maine and much like Mount Washington. I think it safe to say that the students who later experienced the mountain—

the wind and the cold and the color—became intimate with Thoreau's words and with his themes.

The students' understanding coalesced when they descended to sea level for the final week of the course and completed their essays and journals. Their writings contained none of the easy clichés; they made intense attempts to find words that would represent the elemental presence of the wind and the cold. One freshman last year made this journal entry: "To stand in the open and let Nature batter me is where the real excitement lies—not in a bottle or on a roller coaster, but here, confronting Nature, feeling her tremendous power. I wasn't supposed to be here, she was telling me, but somehow I had to be."

Courses in environmental literature offered in the field during the winter will draw students to unique appreciations of both the cold white natural world and the literary works that describe and interpret it. With proper preparation the course need not involve inordinate danger, but the excitement it generates will certainly inspire students to hard work and thoughtful analysis.

The National Audubon Society Expedition Institute: Environmental Reeducation

Frank Trocco

What makes education environmental? This question makes the implicit assumption that some education is not environmental (see McInnis and Albrecht). There is, however, a questionable boundary between education and environmental education. When we think of environmental education we automatically assume a positive, environmentally supportive learning experience. A traditional definition of environmental education would describe it as "aimed at producing a citizenry that is *knowledgeable* concerning the total environment and its associated problems, aware and skilled at *how* to become involved in helping to solve these problems, and motivated to work toward their solution" (Stapp 49). This definition unknowingly excludes cultural influences that significantly determine our interests, motivations, and needs, adjust our attitudes and behavior, and directly educate us as to how to react and respond to the natural world.

If the importance of this point was recognized, premeditated environmental education course work would be labeled environmental *ree*ducation. This is the actual process that occurs in the Audubon Expedition Institute (AEI) programs. Previously learned biases are conceptually confronted, and space is made for environmentally sensitive perspectives and behaviors. The depth of this outlook in the individual student constitutes the measure of an environmentally effective program.

There are many ways to teach an environmental education course, just as there are many ways to teach any grouping of material. However, is environmental education merely the study of a "grouping of material"? Can an individual learn about the natural environment in the same defined manner in which someone would approach French or calculus? The obvious answer is that there is no subject, belief system, or gathering of data that places as many demands on the learning individual as does an understanding of nature. We do not live in geometry or history, but we do live as functioning intercommitted parts of the planet, although most of our civilization is directed toward denying this connection. Even more crucial, we are not "part of" chemistry or Spanish, but we are part of the environment. Traditional subjects are based on cultural criteria and definitions, whereas the environment exists as a living complex entity. In our pursuit of knowledge of the parts, we have fragmented and thereby avoided comprehending the whole. If the environment becomes just "subject matter," its vitality and breadth become words, books, and photographs.

When students study statistics, the life sciences, and taxonomy they are not being reeducated. In fact much of this course work contributes to

our basically structured, orderly, clean viewpoint, which is far from nature's continuous fluctuation. Students who master the biological relations
within a pond are in the same position. Many techniques of environmental
education, although seemingly beneficial, merely reinforce in the student
previously memorized misconceptions and fears about the planet and his
or her relationship with it. At best, these techniques may produce negligible
damage to a preexisting and powerful environmentally destructive life
stance.

Environmental education is everywhere. When we walk into the first
day of a calculus, German, or zoology class, we probably have very little
prior life experience creating a foundation for the subject. There may be
some general feeling that calculus is complicated or that German is more
difficult than French, but a beginning student usually has few concrete
perceptions of class content. Look at how differently we are educated in
terms of the environment. Anyone growing up in any culture develops
reams of unquestioned assumptions, proclivities, attitudes, and ideas about
the natural world, all collated and neatly filed away. Our culture may not
teach us much calculus before the eleventh grade, but by the time we're
ten years old, we have imbibed enough environmental information to en-
title us to a graduate degree! We know intimately how we feel about the
dark, spiders, dirt, the woods, and living outdoors. We know what kind
of life-style we require and the level of our needs. We have been taught
indirectly, through thousands of hours of intimate contact, to think as an
extension of our culture. Our information, regardless of its accuracy, forms
the basis for value decisions and judgments of personal behavior regarding
nature. Herein lies the difficulty: (1) most of this information is incorrect
and based on unquestioned assimilation; and (2) reeducation aimed at
modifying this information is much more difficult than education, because
you are not merely filling a receptive space but first pushing out (often
painfully) previously learned and accepted data.

From the moment of perceptible cognition a human is saturated with
knowledge. Our cultural environment encourages, promotes, and insists
on distance from nature. How can you evaluate students in an environmental education program in a traditional research style, when it is quite
possible that the behaviors and attitudes you are searching for are culturally
counterproductive if not downright subversive (see Willauer)? How can
you be an environmental reeducator when you are just as saturated in
cultural answers as are your students?

I have a huge stake in the wilderness, since I am part of it by virtue
of descent. Every bit of me, everything I touch, is a chip of the planet. I
have spent the last ten years attempting to teach this seemingly simple
and obvious relation to young people. It is a difficult task. At every turn
their reliance on culturally initiated media attitudes obliterates the recognition of their own environmental dependence. The places where they live
are so full of distracting stimuli that it is difficult to get them to listen to
the imperceptible murmur of the forest. The wilderness offers only its
mundane self. It cannot be made to offer the thrill and risk of speeding
down a highway at fifty-five miles per hour or flying in a jet at 35,000 feet.

Or can it? The director of one outdoor challenge school states, ". . . there is no denying that there are always greater risks encountered in [our program] than those normally found in one's everyday life. This is the nature of the sea and wilderness" (Outward Bound 2).

Is all "outdoor" or "experiential" education environmental reeducation? Does it alter the ingrained attitudes that avoid recognition of our mutually dependent relationship with a living planet? It seems evident that many adventure programs or experiential education programs merely readjust some typically human attitudes and locate them in an outdoor setting. Unsurprisingly, the routine of wilderness sports does little to replace deeply imbedded environmental phobias and preconceptions. The thrill, challenge, or amusement of rock climbing, white-water canoeing, spelunking, and river rafting often fits our wilderness stereotype while precluding notice of the real out-of-doors. Numerous students have described their one- to three-day "nature contemplative" solos as being spent "half the time in sleeping and half the time in contemplating food." When you think about it, you see that there is little difference between white-water canoeing and snowmobiling in terms of their inability to sensitize an individual to nature. Both distract the participant from the natural environment. Both are people-created, people-centered, people-oriented.

The Audubon Expedition Institute is a workable approach to creating harmony between people and nature. It is in design and practice an expeditionary bridge between the imaginative needs of people and the predicament of a voiceless universe. Twenty students and three to four guides set out on a year-long trek across the continental United States. Travel is in a school bus that contains all our camping, cooking, and personal gear. Since 24 people and their total possessions for a year are jammed onto one bus, the vehicle (at 175 people-miles per gallon) is a close equivalent to using public or mass transportation. The amount of energy (water, oil, gasoline, buildings, electricity, propane) that is not utilized by the students because they did not remain at home for a year easily surpasses the total low-budget energy consumption of our Spartan existence.

The expedition is goal-oriented and real. Its purpose is to expose the participants to as many varying habitats, cultures, biomes, and ecosystems as possible in an attempt to reveal an individual's nature and integrate it with the nature of a living planet. The curriculum is the expedition. All daily life activities have survival value while on an expedition and therefore are inherently educational. For each day, three meals have to be planned, bought, prepared, and eaten; decisions have to be made as to itinerary and scheduling; appointments, administrative duties, public relations, and correspondence have to be worked on; personal problem areas have to be resolved; entertainment has to be designed; the bus has to be maintained; appropriate shelter and sleeping arrangements have to be provided. Each of these responsibilities unavoidably falls on each expedition member. There is no escaping this responsibility because there is no invisible authority to smooth out the rough edges. Our schedule for a particular day may also include farm labor with an Old Order Mennonite, hiking six miles to study a glacier, work on a southwestern archaeological dig, fossil collecting and identification, library or museum visits, slide talks, lectures or seminars with one of the hundred resource people we encounter in the field, a visit to an astronomical observatory, cross-country skiing on the Mogollon Rim, canoeing into the Okefenokee Swamp to study bird life, collecting old-time fiddle tunes and tales for the Library of Congress, confronting a senator or congressperson, cave exploration, folk dancing, or writing workshops.

On the Mennonite farm we might trade a few hours of our labor for seminars, discussions, and field trips with the farmer, covering life-style, agricultural methods, religion, politics, social life, worldview, and one-room-schoolhouse education. Perhaps it is obvious from this rather lean description that a random day might cover the disciplines of business administration, American history, citizenship, physical education, home economics, anthropology, sociology, religion, philosophy of education, and government. There is no attempt on the expedition to separate the fields in this way, because there is no need to. The experiences are all integral parts of the daily life process—of survival in a learning climate. Scholastics come naturally, partially because they are not labeled as such. In our daily lives outside of formal education we seldom label our responsibilities, work, interests, hobbies, and recreation as "course work," although it is difficult to doubt their ability to educate us.

Our environmental reeducation course is the expedition itself. The AEI attempts to counteract the conditioning that tends to insulate the individual from the natural world. The method is simple in design, although rather complex in practice. It consists of giving the participants the choice of conceptually returning to nature while stripping them of as much outward cultural support as possible. By choice, the participants lose all orientation in a world where the necessities of life, previously thought of as indispensable, are missing. A choice is made to reject the causes of our ecological dilemma in favor of gaining exposure to visible alternatives. Electricity and its gadgetry are nowhere to be found. Human authority, with its ready-made solutions to unasked questions, is a rarity. No one wants to play the authority role—it's too exhausting. People become sensitized and resistant to its use. Permanent living quarters and sources of food, with the security they provide, are not depended upon. Self-reliance is not merely encouraged—it is a necessity.

One of the most fascinating encounters with reeducation we experienced one school year was our visit to the Leaky prehistoric site in Calico, California. There we found the remains of stone implements purportedly chipped and formed by human hands more than fifty thousand years ago. The resident archaeologist showed us how to make stone axes, using rocks as hammers to chip the stone. The students spent the entire morning making axes with rock hammers. Inferences as to Stone Age people's direct dependence on the environment were discussed. We then proceeded to Death Valley, California, arriving in the face of a blinding, choking dust storm. Immediately we began to set up our tents to provide ourselves with some respite from the wind and tearing sand. Surprisingly, most of the students could be found at the rear of the bus, standing in line, coughing with eyes tearing, waiting to use the single hammer in the tool kit to drive in their tent stakes! One or two students were not in line. They had already hammered in their stakes, using one of the numerous rocks strewn around the campsite. The inconceivable had happened. Students who had been taught to use rocks for hammers just three hours before had somehow forgotten that rocks could be used for hammers. Choking and with stinging faces, they waited in line for their turn to use the metal hammer to which they had been culturally conditioned. Only one or two out of a group of twenty had turned directly to the rocks in their environment in this time of need. Most were busily complaining that the school had not provided enough hammers for emergencies. I could see that the authority was being labeled and duly chastized. During our evening meeting, someone suggested that the school had escaped near disaster that afternoon, and we should be sure to remember to purchase adequate hammers the next time we went shopping. That statement initiated the forum to discuss the day's curious sequence of events.

The next four hours and parts of the following two weeks were spent in introspective searching. Why did a store-bought hammer assume such compulsive importance? What was it in our backgrounds that allowed the lessons of the previous morning to dissipate or at least be ignored? What is a hardware-store hammer linked to in the form of electricity, smelters, trees, oil, air, and water? How often do we react automatically to stimuli that we do not consciously perceive, with responses that damage the environment?

On the expedition, there is no electricity and therefore no modern method of entertainment. Other resources have to be investigated, such as learning to play instruments, traditional dancing, singing, story telling, and perhaps collecting songs, stories, dances, and tales along the way from those who remember them. Without social lubricants in our community, participants must turn to each other to figure out problems, resolve disagreements, make sense, and discover personal relevance. There is no human authority, so participants must be self-governing and responsive to the needs of the community.

It is interesting to note that the Audubon expedition's unique formula for environmental reeducation has been recognized by colleges, universities, and high schools nationwide. The academic significance and relevance of its direct, forceful contact with the environment is affirmed in a B.S.-M.S. degree program with Lesley College, Massachusetts. Institute undergraduate and graduate students are presently enrolled in degree programs in environmental education while actively involved on the expedition. Interns are completing two- to four-year programs to become professional guides and directors. Institute course work is also recognized for over 140 semester hours of undergraduate credit by the University of the State of New York Regents External Degree Program.

The basic recipe for the program is unashamed confrontation with a huge, perplexing, and essential planet. The basic assumption is that people are already environmentally educated and will probably be resistant on some level to reeducation wherever nature-sensitive values touch their ingrained cultural behavior. Students can sit around a pond and analyze its contents for a week's worth of class time, but they will not necessarily be reeducated. They may be accumulating knowledge, but if this knowledge is merely attached to previous cultural dispositions, the awareness of the relationship between a frog and its pond becomes—on a global survival level—as useless as theoretical awareness of grammar without the ability to write a grammatical sentence. The nature of people and their congruency with the nature of the pond and that frog must be orchestrated into the curriculum. The voice of nature through environmental reeducation must be made louder than the roar of humanity.

PART 5:

Regional Studies

Introduction

The sequence of essays in this text has emphasized a growing inclusiveness of pedagogy. This inclusiveness has involved the subject matter, the pedagogical method, and the teaching environment itself. The essays in this final part, "Regional Studies," represent the greatest inclusiveness and integration. They are, of course, very different. Thomas Tanner's course on the Glen Canyon dam uses a great diversity of learning resources and "The Mississippi River" a diversity of teachers, discipline approaches, and site visits, but both retain the classroom as the primary learning environment. The New England Literature Program as discussed by Walter Clark uses a field campus and New England itself as its learning environment but focuses on literary concerns as its main subject matter, whereas the other two courses, more limited in their teaching environment, more overtly integrate literature as one among several subject matters. What all these courses definitely have in common is the use of a particular American region, defined geographically and/or culturally, as their object of study. Their discipline is their region. The region can be thoroughly known only when known by means of a diversity of traditional disciplines and the unifying discipline of experience outside the classroom.

Unlike the other two, Thomas Tanner's "Glen Canyon Dam" course is issue-defined as well as place-defined. Glen Canyon Dam, completed in 1963, flooded the Colorado River and created Lake Powell. Tanner's concern is to trace the conflict over the building of the dam and its environmental effects once built, through an understanding of the river's ecology, history, and role in human culture, past and present. To this end he employs, in a classroom setting, resources ranging from legal texts to documentary films on the Colorado and Lake Powell to classics of environmental literature describing the river, such as Edward Abbey's *Desert Solitaire* and John McPhee's *Encounters with the Archdruid*. Tanner emphasizes the diversity of learning objectives that may be set and met in such a case-history structured, multimedia-informed course. Literature is an essential element in creating different individual views of the river's nature as dammed and free, views through which students can define their own responses to the more "objective" political, legal, and historical material in the course.

Like Tanner, Christensen and Vonalt, authors of the subsequent essay, "A First-Year Interdisciplinary Course—'The Mississippi River: Humanities and Civil Engineering,'" are not literature teachers yet recognize the complementarity of environmental literature and other disciplinary approaches to regional studies. Their situation suggests that one fruitful activity of English and literature teachers who might not be able to institute interdisciplinary environmental courses under the rubric of their own departments would be to encourage and assist the inclusion of literature in such offerings of other departments.

The New England Literature Program, as described by Walter Clark, is the most comprehensive and integrative program represented in this volume. As such, it cannot necessarily be used in toto as a model by many institutions, yet much can be drawn from it for use in more limited programs—particularly its strategies for encouraging students to think about the goals of liberal education and of learning in general. As a (roughly) six-week, eight-credit program, on its own rural New England "campus," the NELP has the advantages of intensity, duration, and autonomy not available to most teachers and students in the busy schedule of a traditional academic year.

Precisely because the program becomes a temporary college on its own campus, with some duration and permanency, it can retain the most valuable elements of traditional education's format—directed study, discussion, writing. It also provides a fundamental element of humanistic learning, what Clark calls "an unstrained atmosphere of intellectual life," which most pressured, credit-oriented academic curricula abandon. Clark emphasizes and discusses four pedagogical models that this protean program presents: "We teach literature in its environment; we run a small liberal arts college; we engage in a pastoral exercise; we are an offshoot of the university." Being both close to and distanced from the parent university, students in the program have the unique opportunity to evaluate its learning environment from outside, as one of many possible ones, without separating from it. They are also able, as Clark repeatedly emphasizes, to study the "representation" of things in the written modes of various disciplines while also experiencing that which is represented—the nature and human culture of the area itself.

Glen Canyon Dam

Thomas Tanner

Introduction

In this article I shall describe a case history of an environmental issue; recommend essays, a novel, other writings, and several films of artistic merit that relate to the case; suggest a few teaching techniques for the use of these; and present information for obtaining them at low cost. My object is to provide the reader with the information necessary to teach the case of Glen Canyon Dam. The learning objectives of this case study may vary according to the preferences of the instructor and the time available. They might include the analysis of theme and character development in the novel, a comparison of Edward Abbey the essayist with Edward Abbey the novelist, a study of films as opposed communications on a controversial issue, a consideration of aesthetics as a criterion in that issue or of the existential responsibility for citizen action on such an issue.

The Films and Their Use

The historic roots of the case can be traced back indefinitely, and its consequences are with us today. However, the most telling events may be regarded as having occurred between 1955 and 1974. An effective introduction to the case incorporates three films showing events of the period. These are beautiful thirty-minute color films that may be rented or purchased.

The first, *Operation Glen Canyon,* was produced by the U.S. Bureau of Reclamation. It depicts the building of Glen Canyon Dam on the Colorado River, approximately on the Arizona-Utah border, in the early 1960s. The second film, *Glen Canyon,* is from the Sierra Club and shows the spectacularly narrow, deep, tortuously winding desert canyons that were inundated when the waters of the reservoir, called Lake Powell, rose behind the dam. Some of these canyons were hundreds of feet deep, yet only a few feet across at top or bottom. As the film notes and shows, "they glowed with a light of their own." The canyons as they once were are contrasted visually with the "insignificant bays of Lake Powell" that they became. "Your son may pass close by, but neither he nor any man to follow will know what a magnificent gesture of nature was lost here."

Many ideas may be discussed at this juncture. The first film more or less revels in humankind's supposed mastery over nature; the second definitely does not. Relation of technique to message is clear: the first film has martial band music, lusty narration, and the sunbright hues of the red-rock desert; the second is muted in all respects—the shaded colors of the canyons, the quiet narration, the subtle strains of Debussy, Holst, and Shostakovich. I sometimes employ small discussion groups at this point, considering such questions as: Do the films represent two different world-views? If so, will these come into conflict more or less often in future? What sort of standard or measure should be used to resolve such conflicts? (After some discussion, I offer as a possible standard the maintenance of a maximally varied environment; see Tanner).

The third film, *Lake Powell: Jewel of the Colorado*, is the bureau's response to that of the Sierra Club. Its thesis is that Glen Canyon Dam has created beauty, not destroyed it. It follows a family as they boat into the side canyons, with much time for camping, hiking, fishing, and swimming.

Once again, there is considerable opportunity for written or spoken discourse after this film, especially on aesthetics. For instance, in the second film we saw a few people floating in rubber boats down a lonely stretch of river. The next showed one out of many families who were motorboating on Lake Powell. Did the people in the two films probably have different types of experience?

One may not have the opportunity to visit an unspoiled wilderness. But can one derive value from that wilderness just by knowing it is there?

Is the concept of good taste, as in art, music, and books, a valid one? In environment or outdoor recreation? If so, in which film(s) was good taste best represented?

Because of Lake Powell, people can now motorboat almost to the foot of Rainbow Bridge. Once the journey was a long float followed by a rugged six-mile hike up a side canyon. Of this change, Edward Abbey wrote, "Half the beauty of Rainbow Bridge lay in its remoteness. . . . All things excellent are as difficult as they are rare, said a wise man" (*Desert Solitaire* 217). What did Abbey mean?

The use and misuse of tools of persuasion (films, books, speeches) sometimes becomes a lively topic of concerned discussion when the instructor provides one final piece of information about the last film. It was made when Lake Powell was filled to only half its capacity, with two hundred vertical feet still to go. The film neglected to mention this. Many of the canyons in which the family was boating were still to be filled over their brims with water. Rainbow Bridge was shown high and dry, rather than with water at its base to a depth of forty-seven feet, as it is today!

The Case History

These few brief paragraphs provide a minimum outline of the events. More information is to be found in sources cited below, and a greater depth of human emotion and drama is added by the books discussed in the next section.

Carrying only one fifteenth as much water as the Columbia, the Colorado must provide for a large and growing population in a perilously dry land. A function of the Bureau of Reclamation has long been the building of dams on the river and its major tributaries, in order to conserve water as well as to produce electricity. In the mid-1950s the proposed Echo Park

Dam would have raised water high into the Dinosaur National Monument in northeast Utah, but the action was blocked by a coalition of conservation groups in what has been described as the most significant conservation battle in the four decades since the controversy that led to the formation of the National Park Service in 1916. The conservationists succeeded in having protective clauses added to the Colorado River Storage Project Act stating that no dam or reservoir authorized by the act could be within any national park or monument. With the amended law passed in 1956, construction began immediately on Glen Canyon Dam, which was to be of sufficient height to raise water illegally into Rainbow Bridge Monument, located in a tributary canyon upriver from the dam! But in order to comply with the law, the bureau proposed in 1956 to build a small barrier dam in the side canyon to keep the waters of Lake Powell from reaching the monument. That is, the bureau would build a "dam in reverse" to prevent upstream flow, rather than the usual restriction of downstream flow.

However, when the floodgates of Glen were closed in 1963, work on the barrier dam had still not begun. In fact, around 1960 the bureau had begun actively lobbying against the barrier dam (see Alderson). It now wished to fill Lake Powell, flood Rainbow Bridge Monument, and thus, presumably, establish a precedent for noncompliance with the law at other proposed dam sites; that is, it was allegedly quite happy to trade away one small dam so that it might gain the opportunity to build several large ones (see Moorman).

The waters of the reservoir slowly rose into the monument, and the case stood more or less in limbo until 1970, when citizen conservationists gained legal standing in federal courts. They brought suit against the bureau, and in 1973 a district judge ruled in their favor, ordering the bureau to lower the reservoir to its legal level below the monument. The bureau immediately appealed and won before an appeals court later that same year. In a five-to-two ruling, the court held that since Congress had never appropriated money for the barrier dam, it no longer wished to spare the monument. The dissenting judges wrote that Congress had also on six occasions refused to repeal the protective language of the Colorado River Storage Project Act, so the reservoir at full level would clearly be unlawful.

Next it was the conservationists' turn to appeal, to the Supreme Court. They were joined now by a coalition of another thirteen regional and national conservation groups, plus the attorneys general of sixteen states, who saw in this case a threat to federal parklands everywhere. But in early 1974, by a six-to-three vote, the court declined to hear the case. The vote was along the usual ideological lines, with five Republican appointees among the majority of six and two Democratic appointees among the minority of three.

Today Lake Powell is at full capacity. Each year, many thousands of recreationists use its marinas and campgrounds, drawn by advertising that promotes it as the "Jewel of the Colorado." And Edward Abbey writes of a relatively remote lakeside campsite on one of the drowned side canyons:

> Others have been here before, as the human dung and toilet paper, the tinfoil, plastic plates, abandoned underwear, fishhooks, tangled

lines, discarded socks, empty Coors cans, and broken glass clearly attest. But on the shores of Lake Powell, Jewel of the Colorado and National Recreational Slum, you have no choice. All possible campsites look like this one.   (*Abbey's Road* 118)

A few cogent facts may be noted briefly. Glen Canyon Dam has been criticized as being uneconomic as well as unaesthetic. When developing this case study several years ago, I was unable to obtain a clear economic justification of the dam from the bureau. There is no doubt that the agency and its personnel have a sincere desire to do necessary and productive work. On the other hand, it is a well-known fact that self-preservation becomes a major goal of any agency or institution, and this goal may lead to an unspoken organizational ethos of keeping busy, however unnecessary or even detrimental the work may be. Critics argue that bureau policy has for decades been overly guided by this credo. They claim, for instance, that the water storage and power production of Glen Canyon Dam could have been achieved downstream at Hoover Dam, which has been used at only sixty-six percent of capacity since it was built in 1935 (see Thompson).

The Sierra Club film states that the National Park Service capitulated to the bureau in this case because of the latter agency's greater power within the Department of the Interior. Other instances of this alleged bureau domination over the service and other interior agencies have been reported (see Baldwin).

The Literature of Glen Canyon

Edward Abbey is a confirmed desert rat whose haunts are the stark red canyonlands of eastern Utah. His *Desert Solitaire* is an angry, funny, audacious collection of what might be called adventure essays. Alone or in the company of a few scruffy friends, he rounds up wild horses, searches for dead hikers, becomes stranded on precipitous overhangs, consumes prodigious amounts of beer, and furtively removes survey markers planted by the Enemy—Industrial Tourism. He contemplates Baudelaire, Mencken, Rilke; his mind performs Bach, Schoenberg, Vivaldi. He fantasizes the demolition of Glen Canyon Dam and the abolition of the Bureaus of Reclamation and Indian Affairs. He loves and loathes lustily, sans inhibition. I like him.

His longest chapter, "Down the River," is about a predam float on the Glen Canyon section of the Colorado. Just he and one friend, alone on the river, adventuring. But always in the shadow of their knowledge of That Which Is to Be. I like it; so will the reader's students.

To say that one prefers Abbey the essayist to Abbey the novelist can still leave considerable latitude for enjoyment of his novel *The Monkey Wrench Gang*. The gang is a small band of highly individual, diverse, well-sketched Abbeyan *characters*. They live Abbey's fantasies for him—driving gargantuan earth movers into Lake Powell, sanding the crankcases of bulldozers, blowing a railroad bridge into the depths of a canyon. The author's debt to Romain Gary's *The Roots of Heaven* is clear; given Abbey's erudition, we may assume that the gang's kinship to Gary's corps of idealistic elephant defenders is not just coincidental. At the story's conclusion, Abbey's saboteurs have not yet fulfilled his ultimate dream—the conversion of Glen Canyon Dam into a major rapids. But they will.

Encounters with the Archdruid is the brilliant work of the arch-reporter, John McPhee. The subtitle, *Narratives about a Conservationist and Three of His Natural Enemies*, tells much. In "An Island," McPhee and David Brower go camping on a wilderness island with the man who is about to develop it. In "A Mountain," McPhee and Brower backpack in a wilderness area with a mining engineer who covets its rich veins of copper. In "A River," Brower and McPhee motorboat on Lake Powell with Floyd Dominy, U.S. commissioner of reclamation. And they float a wild portion of the Colorado which Dominy means to dam.

It was David Brower who led the successful battle against Echo Park Dam. And, in the wake of the conservationists' defeat at Glen Canyon, it was David Brower who stopped the next two dams scheduled for the Colorado, dams that would have invaded no less a sanctuary than the Grand Canyon itself. The dams that Dominy meant to build.

McPhee, once a radio Quiz Kid, is now the perfect mouse in the corner. He records the adventures and the conversations without intruding on them. His writing is lean and clear, his juxtapositions surprising but logical, his transitions powerful by their seeming absence. He examines the lives of his four protagonists, picks out with the deftness of a surgeon the key formative influences in those lives, and holds them up for our scrutiny. We come to understand, to admire, and even to *like* each man. The same relation grows between Brower and his adversaries. McPhee does not tell us it is happening; instead he allows us to watch it happen. In each case the two men part as good friends—and still as adversaries. For all its deceptive simplicity, the book is a moving testimony to that which Kenneth Clark has called the greatest contribution of civilization: that is, *civility*.

Other Resources

This section comprises brief references to course materials other than those already described or cited.

Film, *The River*, 1937, black and white, thirty-two minutes. Produced by Pare Lorentz for the Farm Security Administration. A classic, with superb cinematography, editing, narrative, and musical score. A promotion of federal dam building and its genuinely positive effects in the Tennessee Valley, this suggests reasons for our pre-1955 love affair with dams. The opening scenes and narrative of the first Glen Canyon film owe an obvious debt to this one. Available at many university film libraries.

Film, *Where Did the Colorado Go?* 1976, color, sixty minutes. One of the excellent NOVA films from PBS, produced by station WGBH, Boston, it examines some of the problems of Glen Canyon Dam and related issues of Colorado River water use. (Time-Life Multimedia, 100 Eisenhower Drive, Box 644, Paramus, NJ 07652.)

Besides those already cited, articles that give additional information on the legal history of the case include "Castles Made of Sand Fall in the Sea Eventually," by Hugh Nash (*Not Man Apart*, Jan. 1971); "Lake Powell: Suppose We Simply Didn't Fill It?" by David Brower (*Not Man Apart*, May 1973); and "River of Controversy," by Robert Coats (*Environment*, March 1984). Short and usually anonymous items in several conservation magazines provided running coverage of the court case during 1973 and early 1974, with *Not Man Apart* carrying articles in most issues.

Downstream ecological effects of Glen Canyon Dam are the subject of "Dam Changes on the Colorado River," by Steven Carothers and Robert Dolan (*Natural History*, Jan. 1982). These effects include the scouring away of beaches and a change of fish populations—perhaps not totally undesirable—in response to the clear, cold water that now issues from the dam.

Neil M. Judd's "Rainbow Trail to Nonnezoshe" (*National Parks and Conservation*, Nov. 1973) describes the first journey by white men to Rainbow Bridge, in 1909. A member of the expedition, Judd first published this account in 1927. Also see J. Y. Bryan's "Rainbow Bridge: 1973," in the same issue, and, in *National Geographic*, "Lake Powell, Waterway to Desert Wonders," by Walter M. Edwards (July 1967), and "Shooting Rapids in Dinosaur Country," by Jack Breed (March 1954). Breed's article alerted the public to the damage that would be done to Dinosaur National Monument by the proposed Echo Park Dam.

Mention should be made of two large, beautiful photo-essay books that are out of print but in many libraries: *The Place No One Knew: Glen Canyon on the Colorado*, by Eliot Porter (Sierra Club, 1963), and *Down the Colorado*, by John Wesley Powell and Eliot Porter (Promontory Press, 1969). Porter is a contemporary photographer; Powell was the courageous one-armed professor who led the first expedition through Glen and Grand Canyons in 1869. His 1878 *Report on the Lands of the Arid Region* was republished in 1983 by Harvard Common Press. Powell's warnings about overambitious irrigation projects went unheeded, bringing us back to the Glen Canyon Dam controversy a century later, and to three articles in a superb issue of *The Living Wilderness* (Summer 1982). In "Sumerian Implications," historian Frederick Turner describes how overirrigation of the Fertile Crescent contributed to the fall of an empire. "The Colorado Complex," by Dennis Hanson, is a case study of today's similarly excessive demands on the Colorado River. In "The Desert shall rejoice, and be made to blossom as the rose," James Degnan presents a history of federal reclamation laws and shows how their application in the western United States benefited large corporate farms instead of the small settlers who were the intended beneficiaries.

Finally, the alleged make-work philosophy of the Bureau of Reclamation has been the topic of numerous articles in conservation magazines and, to a lesser degree, in the popular press. The Garrison Diversion Project in North Dakota has attracted much of this criticism for years. Alvin M. Josephy's "Dr. Strangelove Builds a Canal" (*Audubon*, March 1975) is a moving account of lives that have been torn by the project and by the callousness of the bureau. The article won the National Magazine Award for reporting.

A First-Year Interdisciplinary Course— "The Mississippi River: Humanities and Civil Engineering"

Lawrence O. Christensen and Larry Vonalt

The interdisciplinary approach to courses that combine the disciplines of humanities and engineering is now commonplace. The University of Missouri–Rolla's course "The Mississippi River: Humanities and Civil Engineering" has some significant features, however, that distinguish it from other interdisciplinary courses and make it worthy of discussion as a possible model for other such courses. Our course admits freshman engineering students only, focuses on one subject, and brings together three previously separate courses in history, English composition, and engineering.

There are sound pedagogical reasons, we think, for the course to be at the first-year level. Required freshman courses are usually taught as separate entities in which the students can see no correlation of intellectual problems or solutions. Engineering is simply engineering, and history merely history. If these required courses are outside the students' major interests, they are often seen as obstacles to be hurdled before the students can get to the lifeblood of their studies. In the Mississippi River course we wanted to demonstrate that many engineering problems and solutions have aesthetic, historical, and technological implications and consequences. We thought that if engineering students could perceive, early in their careers, the integration of these problems and solutions, their attitudes toward both humanities and engineering would be altered constructively. They would recognize the value of effective writing, realize that the knowledge of the history of their own discipline could help them avoid the failures and repeat the successes of the past, and, most important, understand that there is seldom a problem or a solution in engineering that is solely technological.

A thematic course seemed better to us than a general interdisciplinary one because it allows for an easier correlation of the different disciplines and provides for in-depth study. For us, the Mississippi River seemed especially appropriate as a theme. It is relatively near the campus, and many of our students have had personal experience of it. In addition, the Mississippi is, historically, what Ralph Ellison has described as "that great highway around which the integration of values and styles was taking place" in nineteenth-century America (qtd. in Anderson 104). Artistically, the river has been the subject of paintings by such artists as George Caleb Bingham and Thomas Hart Benton and the focus for the writings of such novelists as Mark Twain and William Faulkner. From a technological perspective, the river in the nineteenth century was the workplace of such creative engineers as James B. Eads, Charles Ellet, and Henry Shreve, and in the twentieth century it has been the object of concerted effort by the U.S. Army Corps of Engineers.

A course such as ours has problems the traditional course does not have. A major problem is the integration of the course's different elements. Significant time must be allowed for planning and preparation. Our course was two years in the planning. We were fortunate to be awarded both a consultancy grant and a pilot-program grant from the National Endowment for the Humanities that gave us both the expertise of exceptionally well-informed consultants and the released time to fully develop the course. The released time and the availability of consultants were the main differences in doing the course with foundation aid. (Probably, too, the administration's interest in such a course would have been diminished without outside assistance.)

Even without outside aid, such a course as ours can still be successfully constructed. Success, with or without outside funding, depends in part on the faculty being open to new ideas and willing to spend more time than usual on planning. The faculty interested in such a course must freely exchange ideas about what the objectives of their separate courses are and how these goals can be attained and perhaps enhanced by the integrated course.

The heart of the integrated course is its teaching faculty. They should be experienced teachers who have an enthusiasm for the project that is always tempered by a realistic criticism of its methods and goals. Yet no matter how enthusiastic and experienced the teachers, their efforts can be in vain without the support of the administration. Probably there is no surefire way of convincing the administration of the value of trying a new approach to teaching, especially if that approach is going to cost more money. One idea that might help in the design of interdisciplinary courses is to plan the teaching load so that the administrator is not paying two or more teachers full-time to teach one three-credit-hour course each.

We took this approach in designing our course. As its base we used three courses required of all freshman civil-engineering majors. There were two three-credit-hour courses—"English Composition" and "American History"—and one two-credit-hour course, "Introduction to Civil Engineering." To these courses we added one seventy-five-minute meeting that we called a seminar. Each course was taught by its appropriate instructor, and all the instructors were present at the seminars. We reduced the teaching time of the history and English courses by twenty-five minutes. Each of these courses met twice a week, once for fifty minutes and once for seventy-five minutes, instead of meeting the normal three fifty-minute periods per week. The engineering course was reduced by fifteen minutes, so that each teacher added only about one hour of time in teaching the integrated course.

Such a method of integration puts a heavy burden on the seminars because they are the only times the students see all the instructors in action together. We hoped to reinforce the students' sense of integration by having the seminars focus on subjects that would be discussed that week in each of the individual classes. Probably the closest parallel we achieved was the seminar on the 1927 flood when the engineering class discussed flood control, the history class read Pete Daniels' history of the 1927 flood, *Deep'n as It Come*, and the English class read Faulkner's short novel *Old Man*. In the seminars we showed the films *Mark Twain* (prod. David Wolper) and *Planning for Floods* (Earth Defense League), and we began the course with the showing of Pare Lorentz's film *The River*. We had slide lectures on the images of the river, on bridge construction—especially Eads Bridge in St. Louis—on river exploration, and on river transportation. We had one seminar devoted to the students' analyses of problems in engineering ethics, and one of the last seminars was a general discussion among faculty and students about the conditions of the river today.

We hoped to expand the students' awareness of the integration by confronting them with related ideas and materials outside the classroom. We had two public lectures by humanists from other campuses. John Seelye entitled his lecture "Beautiful Machine: The Mississippi as Millenial Mechanism in Nineteenth-Century Literature," and Fredrick Dobney examined the history of the controversy concerning the replacement of Lock and Dam No. 26 at Alton, Illinois. We also planned two field trips: one to the St. Louis Art Museum and the other a barge trip down the Mississippi from Alton to Jefferson Barracks, just south of St. Louis. We hoped that the participation of all the students in all the activities would give them a strong sense of unity, if not of integration.

In teaching the course the first time we found that the best-laid plans do sometimes go astray or just never quite take off. Selections of appropriate texts proved one source of difficulty. We were cautious not to overload the students with more reading in the interdisciplinary course than they would have been assigned in the three separate courses. Though we were able to make use of readings assigned in the various segments of the course, the history instructor soon realized the need for a concise and general American history text in addition to the specialized texts pertinent to the topics discussed. When we did the course the second time, we added Morison, Commager, and Leuchtenberg's *A Concise History of the American Republic*, vol. 2.

Another problem was the seminar. With thirty-six in class, we knew that the traditional seminar approach would not succeed. We felt, however, that exchanges among faculty and between faculty and students would provide the interdisciplinary dimension, the different perspectives, that would make the course unique. We designated a topic for each seminar period, assigned individual faculty members as chiefly responsible for each topic, and roughly correlated topics to the historical period. To present the topics, we decided to emphasize films and slides, supplementing these with lectures and student-led activities.

From our experience in the first year we learned the need to preview all the films long before they were scheduled to be shown. Too often the films we used the first year fell flat because they were pitched at too elementary a level, repeated topics already dealt with, or were of poor cinematic quality. All films had to be ordered from off campus; frequently they arrived too late to be previewed. If a film that we did see in advance proved to have little merit, we rejected it, but that might be the afternoon before the morning seminar, a short time to prepare alternative materials. So even if we had an opportunity to preview a film, we overlooked less-than-blatant deficiencies and ran it.

Films we were familiar with worked well, stimulating wide-ranging discussion. Pare Lorentz's *The River* provided an excellent vehicle for launching the course. The U.S. Army Corps of Engineers' film *The Great Flood of 1973* and the environmentalist film *Planning for Floods* gave two distinctly different approaches to the river that provoked thought and heated discussion. But some slide presentations and specialized lectures, despite detailed planning, bored the students. As the course developed, it became clear that we had scheduled too many films, that the seminars needed better focus, and that student presentations needed to be increased. When we did the course the second year we made students responsible for about a third of the seminars. This responsibility strengthened the students' participation in the other seminars as well.

Even though of mixed quality, the seminars did expose students to faculty members from three disciplines talking about the same questions, agreeing and disagreeing. Faculty discussions exposed the students to different perspectives; they also reinforced such concepts as the importance of writing, the general applicability of logical thought, and the necessity for all to think about the societal impact of governmental, individual, and technological decisions.

At first students hesitated to enter the fray, but as they became better acquainted with each other and with faculty members, they joined in with exuberance. Occasionally, exchanges lasted beyond the alloted time and discussion had to be continued during the next day's class. By the time we discussed "The River Today," late in the semester, the results achieved exceeded our most optimistic expectations, as students addressed engineering and societal problems with sophistication.

A third problem was the field trips. We had scheduled a trip to the St. Louis Art Museum to view the George Caleb Bingham pencil sketches and paintings by him and others depicting the river. Students generally thought that the trip took too long for its benefits. A ride on a Corps of Engineers boat fell through when floodwaters demanded the ship's attention. Instead, we toured Lock and Dam No. 27 and saw the Eads Bridge and the Museum of Western Expansion in the Gateway Arch. Students enjoyed the visit to the lock and dam much more than they did the museum visits.

While criticizing the first field trip, in particular, students recognized that it afforded an opportunity to get to know the faculty outside the formal classroom. Evaluations commented on the camaraderie that developed during the course, and a number of students understood that the informality of shared bus rides of two hundred miles broke down barriers. The rapport between students and faculty established the atmosphere for those animated seminar sessions discussed above.

Despite the problems, the course achieved most of its goals; without a dissenting voice, the students thought that their experiences had been unique and wrote that they would recommend the course to other students. The remark from the evaluations we liked the best is, "We would have had to take three required courses of this kind anyway, but this way they all make more sense."

They all made more sense because the students saw and heard their

English and history instructors talking intelligently about engineers and engineering history and their engineering instructors discussing cogently the arts, especially the importance of aesthetics and writing to engineering projects. They came to realize that the engineer's work does have significant technological, social, political, and aesthetic impact.

The possibilities for other first-year courses shaped on this model seem particularly good. The ideal foundation upon which to build such courses is freshman English because of the emphasis it places on coherent writing and intelligent reading. An American history course that covers the nineteenth and twentieth centuries can also work well, though, as we experienced, it is sometimes difficult to maintain close parallels with particular seminar subjects and continue to provide the general shape of the country's history. We can also see the possibilities of sociology, introduction to philosophy, or art history making interesting combinations with other courses.

There are themes aplenty for such courses to examine: the American city (a good one for civil engineering, American history, and English), Americans and the automobile (mechanical engineering, American history, and English), the human environment (biology, philosophy, and English), space (astronomy, philosophy, and English), and whatever other combinations creative and dedicated teachers might construct. Many of these themes, as well as a number of others, have already been taught, and lists of possible texts for such courses have been published.

Most of these other courses integrate only two courses, but our model combines three. Using three courses reduces the possibility that a class will side with only one instructor. Another instructor adds still another perspective on the theme and provides another stimulus for the other teachers. Integrating three courses also allows schools on a quarter system to devote a whole quarter to the integrated program, which could give the students an in-depth study of a theme they would not likely otherwise encounter in the course of their undergraduate careers.

In addition to the three-course combination, other elements that we think fundamental are the class schedule—that is, the seminar and the separate classes—and the field trips. The class schedule allows the faculty to cover material pertinent to the individual discipline and to prepare for and recall the seminars. The seminar brings everyone together to discuss not only the material for a particular subject but also all that has so far been encountered in the course. Field trips are important as tools for opening students to unfamiliar educational experiences. But, as we have indicated, the greatest value of the field trips is the development of rapport between students and faculty. This rapport is one of the main ways that the interdisciplinary course differs from the traditional one.

For the instructors, "The Mississippi River: Humanities and Civil Engineering" brought a freshness, a liveliness, to the teaching of required courses on the freshman level. Each of us gained deeper respect for each other's discipline and for each other's particular talents. We are all eager to work together next semester in further improving the course so that another batch of civil-engineering students can see that the humanities are surely a vital part of technological endeavors and that technology plays a crucial role in understanding the humanities.

The New England Literature Program

Walter H. Clark, Jr.

Getting Started

Each spring the English department of the University of Michigan sponsors a program in New England literature in Wolfeboro, New Hampshire. It runs forty-five days (1 May through 15 June) and enrolls thirty-six students, who pay normal tuition plus a fee to cover food, housing, books, and travel expenses. The campus is a summer camp and the living style communal, staff and students sharing in work and study.

When Alan Howes and I began the program in 1975 we wanted to read Frost, Thoreau, Robinson, Hawthorne, and others in a setting similar to that in (and about) which they wrote. We believed that landscape had something to communicate about literature. We expected that isolation and communal living would have a good influence on the quality of learning. Experience has confirmed these beliefs and expectations, though we now look back in some wonderment at how much lay ahead of us in those early days waiting to be discovered.

I doubt that either Alan Howes or I would answer questions about the philosophical rationale of our venture twice in exactly the same way. Still, I should like to offer a dozen responses to the question "Why take undergraduates into the field to read literature and write?" (1) To enable students to see what they are reading about. (2) So that land and culture can exert their influence on readers' and writers' sensibilities. (3) To intensify the mutual interaction between the representation and the thing represented in the reader's mind (a variant of 2). (4) To provide opportunities for the student to think about the nature of the interaction between representation and the thing represented. (5) To encourage the student to consider the goals of liberal education, both in the abstract and as they relate to him or her. (6) So that the student may learn something about learning, both in a general sense and in a particular sense ("How do I learn things? What is the best way of learning for me? How can I be sure that I have really learned what I wish to learn?"). (7) To show that knowledge has physical and emotional aspects. (8) To incite students to think about some ordinary concepts, such as "ownership" and "work," in a more than casual way. To encourage them to examine abstract concepts and to make connections between the concrete and abstract. (9) To raise questions about as-ifness and its role in human knowledge. (10) To make opportunities for students to think about some of the perennial human problems (the nature of freedom, the existence of God) in a supportive context, free from the usual constraints of the classroom. (11) To consider some of the problems that our culture faces today. (12) To confront targets of educational opportunity consonant with the purposes of liberal education.

Listed so baldly, any catalog of reasons must seem rather remote from the classroom. I hope they may be kept in mind as the reader follows a more circumstantial account of the program.

Academics

New England Literature Program students receive eight credits for three courses, two literary and one in creative writing.

Each morning we meet for two hours (one hour if on the trail) to discuss either prose or poetry. Increasingly we have begun with a brief writing exercise on the central question of the day. This meeting of the whole breaks down as soon as possible into discussion groups of eight or ten. In style these are freer flowing, less directed, and more intense than similar ones in Ann Arbor. Teachers cede control, place more trust in the validity of the topic and the vitality of student interest.

One of the things our students have taught us is that the journal, which we originally assigned in the belief that some writing "would be a good thing," is actually a keystone of the enterprise. Students not only discuss Frost and Thoreau, they parallel them in passages that arise naturally out of their observations of the world around them.

> A few minutes ago I spotted a raccoon on the rock wall which lines the north end of this field. Our gazes met and I felt a tremendous surge of adrenalin in my body. As soon as I began to get up to get a closer look, the coon disappeared. There were leaves near the rocks and I knew if he split I would have heard him, but I heard nothing. He's still there. His coat color is the same as the rocks, and when I was near the rocks he didn't look at me, but I caught one glimpse of his head staring out into the forest, as if intending to hear and follow my every move with his ears.   (student journal)

The journal is a natural place for feelings to express themselves. To approach someone like Thoreau as a fellow journal writer makes for an upright posture. We encourage students to make quick judgments and then hang them out for a critical hearing. A student once polarized and energized an entire discussion with the charge that Thoreau was "an arrogant son of a bitch." Responses, pro and con, filled the air that morning and journals afterward. The journal is the right place for this, we feel, as for recording events of the day and copying passages from reading.

Now that we know more about what makes the journal a good thing, we take pains to prepare and encourage, believing that there is a middle ground between mere busywork and overdefinition. We try to get writing started several weeks before the program begins and even dare make assignments during final exam time in Ann Arbor. We hand out lists of possible topics and advise on how to give and receive criticism. Once in New Hampshire, students get together twice a week in groups of five or six to read and discuss. Typically, these two-hour sessions meet around a fire. At midterm the leader reads the journals from the group and writes a note to each student, which may be supplemented by a conversation.

After the program each journal is read by another faculty member, who also writes a note to the student and makes selections for a journal anthology published in the fall. We feel that it is valuable for students to see their writing in print, and we also like the idea of breaking time barriers that hedge the typical course. Our students often form new journal groups after returning to Ann Arbor. We have even experimented in a small way with further readings and meetings during the fall and winter terms.

In addition to class and journal meetings, we have what are called "societies." These organize around an author or theme and meet once a week for two hours to discuss additional readings or engage in special activities. Each student is asked to join one or two of some six or eight that organize more or less spontaneously. Frost, Emerson, Thoreau, Hawthorne, and Robinson are regulars, as is creative writing. Melville, Henry James, E. E. Cummings, May Sarton, and Annie Dillard have met one or more years. These societies focus on primary reading and do as much as they have time for. Other societies have dealt with Winslow Homer, learning to draw and paint, women's studies, gravestone rubbing, Eastern religions, comparison of city and country, etc. Initiatives for such societies usually come from students. We try to be affirmative in our responses and to make connections between the purposes of an individual society and the overall aims of the program. In 1980 the women's society read Margaret Atwood's *Surfacing*, the setting of which is similar to ours. In 1978 the Eastern religion society read books on Zen Buddhism, spent a weekend at a monastery in Vermont, meditated daily, heard a guest lecturer speak on Zen and Thoreau. In 1977 the city and country society read Leo Marx's *The Machine in the Garden* and spent considerable time discussing the pastoral aspects of our life in New Hampshire. In 1976 members of the Thoreau society took a ten-day canoe trip down the Allagash River after the program, retracing part of Thoreau's third trip to the Maine woods.

Models

There is an entirely different way of approaching the question "What are we up to?" It consists of examining models implicit in briefest answers to the question. I have answered casual questions about the New England Literature Program in at least four different ways. We teach literature in its environment; we run a small liberal arts college; we engage in a pastoral exercise; we are an offshoot of the university. Each of these has some truth to it and can be used to justify some of what we do. I shall consider each, illustrating with particulars, but must warn the reader of the partial nature of any such model.

We teach literature in its environment. There are clear advantages to this, but do they justify moving an entire class across the country? Let me say a word or two about clear advantages and then address some less obvious ones. College students today aren't asked to look carefully at the world around them nearly as much as they are asked to deal carefully with abstraction. Seldom are they asked to make connections between abstractions and specific observations that underlie them. Nevertheless, the lesson that there are such connections is itself worth learning, and there is also something to be said for the quality of learning that takes more time and explores such connections more deeply. A Dickinson poem about a hummingbird may make demands on a student's ability to deal with a text, but an actual hummingbird demands observation.

> What caught my attention was a small animal buzzing amid the purple flowers covering the plots. At first I thought it was a yellow jacket because of its black body and yellow markings. After closer examination I realized that the yellow markings were in fact the bands. The body was not the puffy or furry one of a bee. Instead of the blunt head of a yellow jacket, it had an elongated beak with which it was probing the centers and insides of each flower. The wings were much too small and solid for any bee. Since it was past eight and dusk had set in, this could not be the yellow jacket I had never seen after four or five at the latest, collecting pollen on her legs. This, I surmised, must have been a hummingbird. It is hard to comprehend an animal (bird) of these dimensions. Its nest must be phenomenally infinitesimal. It did not buzz as it levitated out of sight.   (student journal)

It is a matter of learning that the natural world is as worthy of careful consideration as the symbol system that represents it; learning, in Frost's phrase, that there are texts "done in plant."

Frost is to the purpose because his poems often call for a composition of scene that sends one to the natural world. A good example is "The Vantage Point," which we ask students to memorize and frequently use as our introduction to poetry reading. The poet goes to an upland pasture where he regards homes and graveyards (symbolizing human endeavor) from a distance. When he has enough of this he turns over to "look into the crater of the ant." He describes himself in the field as "amid lolling juniper reclined" and observes, on rolling over, "My breathing shakes the bluet like a breeze." We read the poem in a pasture so as to be able to point out juniper or suggest, "Roll over. Those are bluets under your nose." More is involved than identification, however. The characteristic shape of juniper gives a clue as to the disposition of the poet's body, his attitude toward what he is seeing. One might give quite a lecture on this in the classroom, but only in the field can students make the observation for themselves. Similarly, when students compare the stance of pine and bluet some may infer that the overt difference in scale between ants and humans is paralleled by a covert one between men and some being who looks on the forest as if it were a field of bluets. It is important to see how a bluet stands up in the grass, how a pine stands up in its grove. This is not to argue against traditional literary training. It is merely to add a dimension to what can be done in the classroom.

Let me now say something about less obvious advantages of our environment. One is that it is beautiful; another is that it is different. The beauties of nature are quiet and unassuming. They do not clamor for attention but have their due effect on the growth of the mind. They provide the journal writer with a focus, the reader with illustrations; most important, they furnish the mind with the material of metaphor and the substance from which abstraction is fashioned.

The environment does away with much that ordinarily preempts attention. What things are different in our environment? Sound, smell, touch, architecture, the quality of movement between destinations, the quality of social contact. What things are less controlled? Weather, specificity of educational events.

We run a small liberal arts college. The first thing to say is that we run a *small* liberal arts college—thirty-six students, to be exact, or three van loads. We tried four van loads one year. It was too many. As far as possible, we encourage interest in the natural and social sciences. We have always had a naturalist on our staff. We have microscopes, telescopes, field manuals, and books on geology, the atmosphere, ecology, and history of technology. We are always on the lookout for writing exercises that focus on nature. We have histories of Maine, New Hampshire, Vermont, New England, the logging industry, argiculture. Our students attend the monthly meetings of the town's historical society, meet local people, exchange visits with students from nearby schools.

Our approach to knowledge is active, placing greater emphasis on knowing how than knowing that. A rich, even extravagant, educational context allows for mental flights and returns that a more economical curriculum cannot accommodate. This is how one of our students put it:

> Startling the mind is not the way to arouse it—rather, it needs to be fed enormous plates of all sorts of food—followed by only the darkest red and strong wine—glass after glass in warmth and splendor. Then one may proceed to coax it out from under the tremendous loads of mundane life—feed it. Gently holding the exposed edge, one may tease and pull it further toward exposure. This is the sole purpose of warmth and splendor. This dark hermit molds its own world of metaphor. (student journal)

We engage in a pastoral exercise. This is at once our richest and most difficult model. The pastoral impulse, which is as old as the city, seeks relief from complexity in flight. The promise of life in a garden, where all aspects of the personality may grow and spread as they please, is illusory, as is the notion that nature (reality) will not encroach upon the ego. But the illusion is generative. It is the fact that this promise can never fully be redeemed that makes the pastoral literary form so capacious, allows for the expression of so many different attitudes. In educational terms, "reservations" justify themselves by the degree to which they foster intellectual growth. We do not require that our educational gardens offer more than a transitory habitation. The questions one asks of them, like the questions the therapist asks of a fantasy, have to do with intrinsic form and real-world function.

Pastoral takes place in some happy spot, at once beautiful and conducive to harmonious activity. It calls forth the best that is in us, for only by becoming poets can we do it justice. Thoreau found such a spot at Walden Pond. For our students it is located at Camp Kehonka on Lake Winnipesaukee.

Ideally considered, pastoral combines work and leisure, solitude and society in such proportions as to make an aesthetic unity. Work, for our students, means doing one's portion of the necessary chores shared by all, a tacit recognition of Thoreau's remark that "the student who secures his coveted leisure and retirement by systematically shirking any labor necessary to man obtains but an ignoble and unprofitable leisure, defrauding himself of the experience which alone can make leisure fruitful" (*Walden* 143). More than that, it means doing the reading and writing that together constitute three academic courses—the central reason for our presence in New Hampshire. Insofar as the subject matter includes pastoral (Thoreau, Frost, Hawthorne), examination of the way one is living and consideration of its significance become part of work.

The convention of a harmonious merging of work and leisure fits our educational beliefs. Leisure and an unstrained atmosphere of intellectual life make the best context in which to think about values, religious belief, growth—matters of concern to our students but not included in the official curriculum.

The pastoral world is one in which humans live at ease together and strife is subdued by ritual. A basic reason for our encouragement of community lies in what students can teach each other. On the first sunny day after arrival we drop students off in fours and fives to find their way back to camp through woods with map and compass. Later there are overnight hikes. These provide grist for journals, as well as a sense of shared adventure. In-class and out-of-class communities merge easily together. Discussion of reading takes place as naturally at the dinner table as in class. In such a tight-knit group students look more carefully at themselves and at others.

Naturally, close living brings strains, but the need for privacy can be met in several ways. Those who heed Thoreau's example and rise early find plenty of time and space. The camp itself is large, and there are numerous unfrequented roads nearby. We encourage students to spend a day alone at some point, and about two thirds of them do. This accomplishes in miniature one thing that the program provides on a larger scale— withdrawal in space, time out, a chance to consider what one is doing. Often students find that a short absence from society clarifies what it means to them.

The pastoral experience is, of course, constructed. The very artificiality of our situation provides a vantage point from which to observe nature, society, and pastoral itself. Students who arrive with thoughts of plunging themselves into an actual wilderness are soon disabused. The discovery that one is not in the wilderness leads, in the most natural way, to an examination of the ties that bind one to the city. Some refuse to concede anything to nature. Others intellectualize it. Our hope is that students will pause to think about the relation between the country and the city and from this move to a consideration of the artificial nature of the pastoral, the artificial nature of teaching university courses in a garden—not that we apologize for artifice. Nor do we wish to turn their eyes from a world that is right in front of them. We read Hawthorne's *Blithedale Romance* to encourage consideration of the kind of life we live for six weeks. We read Oscar Wilde's "The Decay of Lying" as a way of sharpening the distinction between artifice and nature and to suggest that there may be some interpenetration of the two.

We are an offshoot of the university. The temptation is strong among some of our students to think of being in New England as an escape. This, of course, is no more possible than it is for inhabitants of the garden to escape the civilization that supports both the idea of the garden and its actuality. Our students earn university credit. The New England Literature Program exists at the pleasure of the university, with its support and oversight.

It is not in the university's interest to have students who are passive consumers. We believe that learning requires an active role and that any attempt on the part of either teacher or student to turn the student into a mere receptor is corrupting to both. The modern university is in a way like some very complicated tool that can be put to many different uses. The challenge for the undergraduate is to learn what can and cannot be done with it and to use it in accordance with his or her best notions of what an education should be. Those who do not adopt an active attitude toward the university run a very real risk that it will simply process them and run them through like so many Charlie Chaplins going through the machine in *Modern Times*. It is of no value, either to the university or to the society that surrounds it, to turn out such graduates.

If I may return one final time to the pastoral, we can distinguish between those that have a purely decorative function, in which the theme of escape is paramount, and those more serious ones ("Lycidas" and "The Scholar Gypsy" would be examples) that circle back to confront the real world. The idea behind the New England Literature Program is not so much to effect an escape from the university as it is to gain perspective through distance and to struggle against a kind of educational anomie brought on in part by university conditions, in part by the culture at large, and in part through the complicity of the students themselves. Our aims conform to the purposes of the university, historically considered. If our methods are "different" or "exciting" we will take a bow, but that should not disguise the fact that our purposes are fundamentally conservative, and what we hope to conserve is not so much social or economic conditions as a certain spark in the mind.

Works Cited

Abbey, Edward. *Abbey's Road*. New York: Dutton, 1979.

———. *Desert Solitaire: A Season in the Wilderness*. New York: McGraw, 1968.

———. *The Monkey Wrench Gang*. Philadelphia: Lippincott, 1975.

Adato, Perry Miller, dir. *Georgia O'Keeffe*. The Originals: Women in Art. Films Inc., 1977.

Alderson, George. "Rainbow Bridge Is Being Drowned, Being Drowned. . . ." *Environmental Action*, 23 June 1973, 3–5.

Alexander, Stanley. "Cannery Row: Steinbeck's Pastoral Poem." In *Steinbeck: A Collection of Critical Essays*. Ed. Robert Murray Davis. Englewood Cliffs: Prentice, 1972, 135–48.

Allen, Francis. *A Bibliography of Henry David Thoreau*. Boston: Houghton, 1908.

Allen, Gay Wilson. *The New Walt Whitman Handbook*. New York: New York UP, 1962.

Altieri, Charles. "A Report to the Provinces: Reflections on the Fate of Reading among Behavioral Scientists." *Profession 82*, 27–31.

Anderson, Jervis. Profile of Ralph Ellison. *New Yorker* 22 Nov. 1976, 55–104.

Asselineau, Roger. *The Evolution of Walt Whitman*. Cambridge: Harvard UP, 1962.

Atwood, Margaret. *Surfacing*. New York: Simon, 1972.

Audubon, John James. *Ornithological Biography*. 5 vols. Edinburgh: Black, 1831–39.

———. *The Quadrupeds of North America*. 3 vols. 1845–53. Salem: Ayer, 1972.

Austin, Mary. *The American Rhythm: Studies and Reexpressions of Amerindian Songs*. 2nd ed. Boston: Houghton, 1930.

———. *The Arrow Maker*. 2nd ed. 1915. New York: AMS, 1969.

———. *Earth Horizon*. Boston: Houghton, 1932.

———. *The Flock*. Boston: Houghton, 1906.

———. *The Ford*. Boston: Houghton, 1917.

———. *Isidro*. 1905. Upper Saddle River: Literature House, 1970.

———. *The Land of Journey's Ending*. 1924. New York: AMS, 1969.

———. *Land of Little Rain*. Boston: Houghton, 1903.

———. *Lost Borders*. New York: Harper, 1909.

———. *One-Smoke Stories*. Boston: Houghton, 1934.

———. *Outland*. London: John Murray, 1910.

Bailey, Liberty Hyde. *The Country-Life Movement in the United States*. New York: Macmillan, 1911.

———. *The Garden of Gourds*. New York: Macmillan, 1937.

———. *The Holy Earth*. 1915. Ithaca: New York State Univ. College of Agriculture, 1980.

———. *The Outlook to Nature*. 2nd ed. New York: Macmillan, 1911.

———. *Wind and Weather*. New York: Scribner's, 1916.

Bakker, Elna. *An Island Called California*. Berkeley: U of California P, 1971.

Baldwin, Malcolm F. *The Southwest Energy Complex: A Policy Evaluation*. Washington: Conservation Foundation, 1973.

Bannister, Robert C. *Social Darwinism: Science and Myth in Anglo-American Social Thought*. Philadelphia: Temple UP, 1979.

Barrus, Clara, ed. *The Life and Letters of John Burroughs*. Boston: Houghton, 1925.

Bates, Henry W. *The Naturalist on the River Amazon*. 2nd ed. London: Murray, 1864.

Beebe, William. *Half-Mile Down*. New York: Harcourt, 1934.

Bell, Barbara Currier. "Humanity in Nature: Toward a Fresh Approach." *Environmental Ethics* (Fall 1981): 245–57.

Bergquist, William H., et al. *Designing Undergraduate Education*. San Francisco: Jossey, 1981.

Bernstein, Jeremy. "Science Education for the Non-Scientist." *American Scholar* 52 (1982–83): 7–12.

Beston, Henry. *Northern Farm: A Chronicle of Maine*. 1948. New York: Ballantine, 1972.

———. *The Outermost House: A Year of Life on the Great Beach of Cape Cod*. New York: Doubleday, 1928.

Bodsworth, Fred. *The Last Curlew*. New York: Dodd, 1955.

Bolles, Frank. *Land of the Lingering Snow*. Boston: Houghton, 1891.

———. *At the North of Bearcamp Water*. Boston: Houghton, 1893.

Borland, Hal. *Beyond Your Doorstep*. New York: Knopf, 1962.

———. *Countryman: A Summary of Belief*. Philadelphia: Lippincott, 1965.

Botstein, Leon. "Beyond Great-Books Programs and Fads in the Curriculum." *Chronicle of Higher Education* 1 Dec. 1982.

Bouwisma, William J. "Models of the Educated Man." *American Scholar* 44 (1975): 195–212.

Brewster, William. *Concord River: Selections from the Journals of William Brewster*. Ed. Smith O. Dexter. Cambridge: Harvard UP, 1937.

———. *October Farm: From the Concord Journals and Diaries of William Brewster*. Cambridge: Harvard UP, 1936.

Brisbane, Albert. *The Social Destiny of Man; or, Association and Reorganization of Industry*. 1840. Reprints of Economic Classics. New York: Augustus M. Kelley, 1969.

Brooks, Paul. *The House of Life: Rachel Carson at Work*. Boston: Houghton, 1972.

———. *Speaking for Nature: How Literary Naturalists from Henry Thoreau to Rachel Carson Have Shaped America*. Boston: Houghton, 1980.

Brower, Kenneth. *The Starship and the Canoe*. New York: Bantam, 1979.

Brown, Janet W. "Native American Contributions to Science, Engineering, and Medicine." *Science* 189 (1975): 38–40.

Bruner, Jerome. *The Relevance of Education*. Ed. Anita Gil. New York: Norton, 1973.

Brush, Stephen G. *The Temperature of History: Phases of Science and Culture in the Nineteenth Century*. New York: Burt Franklin, 1978.

Bryant, William Cullen. *Picturesque America; or, The Land We Live In*. New York: Appleton, 1872.

Buckle, Henry Thomas. *History of Civilization in England*. London: J. W. Parker, 1857–61.

Burroughs, John. *The Heart of Burroughs's Journals*. Ed. Clara Barrus. 1928. Port Washington: Kennikat, 1967.

———. *Works*. New Riverside Edition. 1895–96. Boston: Houghton, 1920.

———. *The Writings of John Burroughs*. Riverby Edition. 23 vols. Boston: Houghton, 1904–23.

Callenbach, Ernest. *Ecotopia*. Berkeley: Banyan Tree, 1975.

Campbell, Sheldon. *Lifeboats to Ararat*. New York: Times Books, 1979.

Camus, Albert. *Exile and the Kingdom*. New York: Random, 1965.

Capra, Fritjof. *The Tao of Physics: An Exploration of the Parallels between Modern Physics and Eastern Mysticism*. New York: Random, 1975.

Carr, Archie. *Ulendo*. New York: Knopf, 1964.

Carrighar, Sally. *Home to the Wilderness*. Baltimore: Penguin, 1974.

———. *One Day on Beetle Rock*. New York: Knopf, 1944.

———. *One Day on Teton Marsh*. New York: Knopf, 1947.

Carson, Rachel. *Silent Spring*. Boston: Houghton, 1962.

Catlin, George. *Letters and Notes on the Manners, Customs, and Conditions of the North American Indians*. 2 vols. 1844. New York: Dover, 1973.

Cavagnaro, David. *This Living Earth*. New York: American West, 1972.

Chambers, Robert. *Vestiges of the Natural History of Creation*. 1844. New York: Humanities, 1969.

Channing, William Ellery, II. *Thoreau: The Poet-Naturalist*. Ed. Frederick Sanborn. 1902. New York: Biblo and Tannen, 1966.

Chapman, Frank M. *Bird Life*. New York: Appleton, 1900.

Coatsworth, Elizabeth. *Personal Geography*. Brattleboro: Stephen Greene, 1976.

Commission on the Humanities. *The Humanities in American Life*. Berkeley: U of California P, 1980.

Conron, John, ed. *The American Landscape*. New York: Oxford UP, 1974.

Cooper, Susan Fenimore. *Rural Hours*. 1850. Syracuse: Syracuse UP, 1968.

Costello, David F. *The Desert World: Plant and Animal Life of the American Desert*. New York: Crowell, 1972.

Coues, Elliot. *Birds of the Northwest*. 1874. New York: Arno, 1974.

Craighead, Frank, Jr. *Track of the Grizzly*. San Francisco: Sierra Club, 1979.

Curtis, Edward S. *The North American Indian: Being a Series of Volumes Picturing and Describing the Indians of the United States and Alaska*. Ed. Frederick W. Hodges. 20 vols. Cambridge: Harvard UP, 1907–30.

Cutright, Paul R. *Theodore Roosevelt: Naturalist*. New York: Harper, 1956.

Czinner, Paul, dir. *As You Like It*. Audio Brandon, 1936.

Dana, D. D. *The Geological Story Briefly Told: An Introduction to Geology for the General Reader and for All Beginners in Science*. 1879.

Daniels, George H. *American Science in the Age of Jackson*. New York: Columbia UP, 1968.

Daniels, Pete. *Deep'n as It Come: The 1927 Mississippi River Flood*. New York: Oxford UP, 1977.

Danielsen, John. *Winter Hiking and Camping*. Glens Falls: Adirondack Mountain Club, 1978.

Darwin, Charles. *The Descent of Man*. 2 vols. London, 1871.

———. *On the Origin of Species*. London, 1859.

Dillard, Annie. *Pilgrim at Tinker Creek*. New York: Bantam, 1974.

Dobie, J. Frank. *The Voice of the Coyote*. Boston: Little, 1949.

Douglas, Marjory Stoneman. *The Everglades: River of Grass*. 1947. Atlanta: Mockingbird, 1981.

Douglas, William O. *A Farewell to Texas*. New York: McGraw, 1967.

———. *My Wilderness: East to Katahdin*. Garden City: Doubleday, 1961.

Drinnon, Richard. *Facing West: The Metaphysics of Indian-Hating and Empire Building.* Minneapolis: U of Minnesota P, 1980.

Dubos, René. *A God Within.* New York: Scribner's, 1973.

Dutton, Clarence. *The Tertiary History of the Grand Canyon District.* 1882. Santa Barbara; Peregrine Smith, 1977.

Earl, John. *John Muir's Longest Walk.* Garden City: Doubleday, 1975.

Earth Defense League, prod. *Planning for Floods.* Environmental Defense Fund, 1974.

Eastman, Charles. *From the Deep Woods to Civilization: Chapters in the Autobiography of an Indian.* Boston: Little, 1916.

Easton, Robert. *Black Tide: The Santa Barbara Oil Spill and Its Consequences.* New York: Delacorte, 1972.

Eckert, Allan W. *Wild Season.* Boston: Little, 1967.

Edwards, Ernest P. *A Field Guide to the Birds of Mexico.* Sweet Briar: Ernest P. Edwards, 1972.

Eiseley, Loren. *The Immense Journey.* New York: Random, 1957.

———. *The Night Country.* New York: Scribner's, 1971.

Emerson, Ralph Waldo. *Nature.* 1836. In vol. 1 of *Collected Works of Ralph Waldo Emerson.* Ed. Ralph Ferguson et al. Cambridge: Harvard UP, 1979.

Emig, Janet. "Writing as a Mode of Learning." *College Composition and Communication* 28 (1977): 122–28.

Empson, William. *Some Versions of Pastoral.* London: Chatto, 1950.

Fabre, Jean Henri. *Souvenirs entomologiques . . . études sur l'instinct et les moeurs des insects.* 10 vols. Paris: Delagrave, 1912–14.

Farb, Peter. *Living Earth.* New York: Harper, 1959.

Faulkner, William. "Old Man." In *Three Famous Short Novels.* New York: Random, 1958.

Fishbough, William. *The Macrocosm and Microcosm.* New York: Harper, 1852.

Fletcher, Colin. *The Man Who Walked through Time.* New York: Vintage-Random, 1972.

Foerster, Norman. *Nature in American Literature.* 1923. New York: Russell, 1958.

Forbes, Bryan, dir. *The Mad Woman of Chaillot.* With Katharine Hepburn, Danny Kaye, and Yul Brynner. Audio Brandon, 1969.

Fox, Stephen. *John Muir and His Legacy.* Boston: Little, 1981.

Frye, Northrop. *Anatomy of Criticism: Four Essays.* Princeton: Princeton UP, 1957.

Gangewere, Robert J., ed. *The Exploited Eden: Literature on the American Environment.* New York: Harper, 1972.

Gary, Romain. *The Roots of Heaven.* Trans. Jonathan Griffin. New York: Simon, 1958.

Gemming, Elizabeth and Klaus Gemming. *Block Island Summer.* Old Greenwich: Chatham, 1971.

Gillispie, Charles Coulston. *Genesis and Geology: The Impact of Scientific Discoveries upon Religious Beliefs in the Decades before Darwin.* New York: Harper, 1959.

Gilpin, William. *The Mission of the North American People.* 1874. New York: Da Capo, 1974.

Goode, Merlin. *Winter Outdoor Living.* Salt Lake City: Brighton, 1978.

Grayson, David [Ray Stannard Baker]. *Adventures in Contentment.* New York: Doubleday, 1907.

Greene, John C. *The Death of Adam: Evolution and Its Impact on Western Thought*. Ames: Iowa State UP, 1959.

Grinnell, George Bird. *American Big Game and Its Haunts*. New York: Forest and Stream, 1904.

———. *Blackfoot Lodge Tales: The Story of a Prairie People*. 1926. Lincoln: U of Nebraska P, 1961.

———. *When Buffalo Ran*. 1920. Norman: U of Oklahoma P, 1966.

Grinnell, George Bird, Caspar Whitney, and Owen Wister. *Musk Ox, Bison, Sheep, and Goat*. New York: Macmillan, 1904.

Grinnell, George Bird, and Charles Sheldon, eds. *Hunting and Conservation: The Book of the Boone and Crockett Club*. 1925. New York: Arno, 1970.

Gunter, A. Y. *The Big Thicket: A Challenge for Conservation*. Austin: Jenkins, 1971.

Guyot, Arnold. *The Earth and Man*. Trans. C. C. Felton. Boston: Gould, 1849. New York: Arno, 1970.

Halle, Louis. *Spring in Washington*. New York: Sloane, 1947.

Hanley, Wayne, *Natural History in America: From Mark Catesby to Rachel Carson*. New York: Quadrangle–New York Times, 1977.

Hawthorne, Nathaniel. *The Blithedale Romance*. 1852. New York: Norton, 1978.

Hay, John, and Peter Farb. *The Atlantic Shore*. New York: Harper, 1966.

Hays, Samuel P. *Conservation and the Gospel of Efficiency: The Progressive Conservation Movement, 1890–1920*. Cambridge: Harvard UP, 1959.

Heckman, Hazel. *Island Year*. Seattle: U of Washington P, 1972.

Heinlein, Robert. *Stranger in a Strange Land*. New York: Berkeley, 1968.

Hellman, Lillian. *Pentimento: A Book of Portraits*. Boston: Little, 1973.

Henze, Hans Werner. *Muzen Siziliens*. With Cornelius Schwarze, Dieter Lefsler, and Andreas Scheibner. Cond. Henze. Leipzig Gewandhaus Orchestra. Deutsche Grammophon, 1966.

Herbert, Frank. *Children of Dune*. New York: Putnam, 1976.

———. *Dune*. New York: Putnam, 1967.

———. *Dune Messiah*. New York: Putnam, 1976.

———. *The Eyes of Heisenberg*. New York: Berkeley, 1981.

Herschel, J. F. *A Preliminary Discourse on the Study of Natural Philosophy*. London: Longman, 1830.

Hicks, Philip. *The Development of the Natural History Essay in American Literature*. Philadelphia: U of Pennsylvania P, 1924.

Hillocks, George, Jr., ed. *The English Curriculum under Fire: What Are the Real Basics?* Urbana: National Council of Teachers of English, 1982.

Hofstadter, Douglas R., and Daniel C. Dennett. *The Mind's I*. New York: Bantam, 1982.

Hogins, James Burl, ed. *Literature*. 2nd ed. Chicago: SRA, 1977.

Holton, Gerald, ed. *Science and Culture: A Study of Cohesive and Disjunctive Forces*. Boston: Houghton, 1965.

Hoover, Helen. *A Place in the Woods*. New York: Knopf, 1969.

Hopi Tribe. "The Meaning of Corn." *Arizona Highways* 54 (Jan. 1978): 14.

Hornaday, William T. *Thirty Years War for Wild Life: Gains and Losses in the Thankless Task*. 1931. New York: Arno, 1970.

Hudson, William H. *The Naturalist in La Plata*. London: Chapman, 1892.

Huizinga, Johan. *Homo Ludens: A Study of the Play Element in Culture.* 2nd ed. 1950. Boston: Beacon, 1955.

Humboldt, Alexander von. *Aspects of Nature: In Different Lands and Different Climates; with Scientific Elucidations.* Trans. "Mrs. Sabine." Philadelphia: Lea and Blanchard, 1849.

———. *Cosmos: A Sketch of a Physical Description of the Universe.* Trans. E. C. Otté. New York: Harper, 1850.

———. *A Geognostical Essay on the Superposition of Rocks in Both Hemispheres.* London: Longman, 1823.

———. *Letters of Humboldt.* Trans. Friedrich Kapp. New York: Rudd, 1860.

———. *Views of Nature; or, Contemplations of the Sublime Phenomena of Creation.* Trans. E. C. Otté and Henry G. Bohn. London: Bohn, 1850.

Hutchins, Ross E. *Hidden Valley of the Smokies.* New York: Dodd, 1971.

Huth, Hans. *Nature and the American.* 1957. Lincoln: U of Nebraska P, 1972.

Huxley, Thomas H. *Evidence as to Man's Place in Nature.* London: Williams, 1863. Ann Arbor: U of Michigan P, 1959.

Jackson, Helen Hunt. *A Century of Dishonor: A Sketch of the United States Government's Dealings with Some of the Indian Tribes.* 1881. St. Clair Shores: Scholarly, 1972.

Jaeger, Edmund C. *Denizens of the Desert: A Book of Southwest Mammals, Birds, and Reptiles.* Boston: Houghton, 1922.

———. *Our Desert Neighbors.* Stanford: Stanford UP, 1950.

Japp, Alexander Hay [H. A. Page]. *Thoreau: His Life and Aims.* 1901. Folcroft: Folcroft, 1969.

Johnson, Josephine W. *The Inland Island.* New York: Simon, 1969.

Jones, Samuel Arthur. *Pertaining to Thoreau.* 1901. Folcroft: Folcroft, 1969.

Kapp, Friedrich, trans. *Letters of Humboldt.* New York: Rudd, 1860.

Kastner, Joseph. *A Species of Eternity.* New York: Knopf, 1977.

Kavaloski, Vincent C. "Interdisciplinary Education and Humanistic Aspiration: A Critical Reflection." In *Interdisciplinarity and Higher Education.* Ed. Joseph J. Kockelmans. University Park: Pennsylvania State UP, 1979. 224–43.

Keats, John. *Keats: Poems and Selected Letters.* Ed. Carlos Baker. New York: Scribner's, 1962.

Kieran, John. *A Natural History of New York City.* Boston: Houghton, 1959.

King, Clarence. *Mountaineering in the Sierra Nevada.* Boston: Osgood, 1872.

———. *Systematic Geology.* Washington: GPO, 1878.

King, Thomas Starr. *A Vacation among the Sierras: Yosemite in 1860.* Ed. John A. Hussey. San Francisco: Book Club of California, 1962.

———. *The White Hills: Their Legends, Landscape, and Poetry.* Boston: Crosby, 1860.

Kligerman, Jack. "A Seminar on Nature and the Nature Essay in American Literature." *Exercise Exchange* 20 (Spring 1976): 2–5.

Kockelmans, Joseph J., ed. *Interdisciplinarity and Higher Education.* University Park: Pennsylvania State UP, 1979.

Kornbluth, C. M. *Marching Morons and Other Famous Stories.* New York: Ballantine, 1959.

———, and F. Pohl. *The Space Merchants.* New York: Ballantine, 1953.

Krutch, Joseph Wood. *The Best Nature Writing of Joseph Wood Krutch.* New York: Pocket, 1971.

———. *The Desert Year.* 1946. New York: Vintage-Random, 1957.

———. *Great American Nature Writing*. New York: Sloane, 1950.

———. *Henry David Thoreau*. New York: Sloane, 1948.

———. *The Twelve Seasons*. New York: Sloane, 1949.

———. *The Voice of the Desert: A Naturalist's Interpretation*. New York: Morrow, 1954.

Lambert, Darwin. *Timberline Ancients*. Portland: Graphic Arts, 1972.

Lanman, Charles. *Letters from the Allegheny Mountains*. New York: Putnam, 1849.

———. *A Summer in the Wilderness*. Philadelphia: Appleton, 1847.

Le Guin, Ursula K. *The Lathe of Heaven*. New York: Avon, 1980.

———. *The Left Hand of Darkness*. New York: Ace, 1973.

Leiss, William. *The Domination of Nature*. New York: Oxford UP, 1949. Boston: Beacon, 1974.

Leopold, Aldo. *A Sand County Almanac and Sketches Here and There*. New York: Oxford UP, 1949.

Leveson, David. *A Sense of the Earth*. Garden City: Doubleday, 1972.

Lewis, C. S. *That Hideous Strength*. New York: Macmillan, 1975.

Lewis, Thomas. "Hubris in Science?" *Science* 200 (1978): 1459–62.

Leydet, François. *The Coyote: Defiant Song Dog of the West*. San Francisco: Chronicle, 1977.

Lillard, Richard G. "The Nature Book in Action." *English Journal* 62 (1973): 537–48.

London, Jack. *The Call of the Wild and Selected Stories*. New York: Signet, 1960.

Long, William J. *School of the Woods: Some Life Studies of Animal Instincts and Animal Training*. Boston: Ginn, 1903.

Lorentz, Pare, prod. *The River*. U.S. Dept. of Agriculture, 1937.

Lunt, Dudley Cammet. *Taylors Gut: In the Delaware State*. New York: Knopf, 1968.

Lutts, Ralph H. "The Nature Fakers: Conflicting Perspectives of Nature." In *Ecological Consciousness: Essays from the Earthday X Colloquium*. Proc. of a conference on the humanities and ecological consciousness. April 1980. Ed. Robert C. Schultz and J. Donald Hughes. Washington: UP of America, 1981.

Lyell, Charles. *Geological Evidences of the Antiquity of Man*. Philadelphia: Childs, 1863.

———. *Lectures on Geology*. New York: Greeley, 1843.

———. *Principles of Geology*. Boston: Hilliard, 1842.

———. *A Second Visit to the United States of North America*. New York: Harper, 1849.

———. *Travels in North America*. New York: Wiley, 1845.

McInnis, Neal, and Don Albrecht. *What Makes Education Environmental?* Washington: Environmental Education, 1975.

McPhee, John. *Encounters with the Archdruid: Narratives about a Conservationist and Three of His Natural Enemies*. New York: Farrar, 1971.

———. *The Pine Barrens*. New York: Farrar, 1968.

Marsh, George Perkins. *Man and Nature; or, Physical Geography as Modified by Human Action*. 1864. Ed. and introd. David Lowenthal. Cambridge: Harvard UP, 1965.

Marshall, A. J., ed. *The Great Extermination: A Guide to Anglo-Australian Cupidity, Wickedness, and Waste*. London: Heinemann, 1966.

Marshall, Robert. *Alaska Wilderness*. Berkeley: U of California P, 1970.

———. "The Problem of the Wilderness." *Scientific Monthly* 30 (1930): 141–49.

Marx, Leo. *The Machine in the Garden*. New York: Oxford UP, 1964.

Matthiesson, Peter. *The Snow Leopard*. New York: Viking, 1978.

Maxwell, Gavin. *Ring of Bright Water.* New York: Dutton, 1960.

Mill, John Stuart. *Principles of Political Economy, with Some of Their Applications to Social Philosophy.* London: Parker, 1848. In *The Norton Anthology of English Literature,* vol. 1. New York: Norton, 1980.

Millar, Margaret. *The Birds and the Beasts Were There.* New York: Random, 1968.

Miller, Olive Thorne [Harriet Mann Miller]. *A Bird-Lover in the West.* 1894. New York: Arno, 1970.

Mills, Enos. *The Story of a Thousand-Year Pine: And Other Tales of Wild Life.* Boston: Houghton, 1913.

————. *The Story of Estes Park and a Guidebook.* Denver: Outdoor Life, 1905.

————. *Your National Parks.* Boston: Houghton, 1917.

Mitchell, Lee Clark. *Witnesses to a Vanishing America: The Nineteenth-Century Response.* Princeton: Princeton UP, 1981.

Momaday, N. Scott. *House Made of Dawn.* New York: Harper, 1968.

Moorman, James W. "Bureaucracy vs. the Law." *Sierra Club Bulletin,* October 1974, 7–10, 39.

Morison, Samuel Eliot, Henry Steele Commager, and William E. Leuchtenberg. *A Concise History of the American Republic.* 2 vols. New York: Oxford UP, 1983.

Muir, John. *The Mountains of California.* New York: Century, 1894.

————. *My First Summer in the Sierra.* Boston: Houghton, 1911.

————. *Our National Parks.* Boston: Houghton, 1901.

————. *The Story of My Boyhood and Youth.* 1913. Madison: U of Wisconsin P, 1965.

————. *A Thousand-Mile Walk to the Gulf.* Ed. William F. Badé. Boston: Houghton, 1916.

————. *Travels in Alaska.* Boston: Houghton, 1915.

————, ed. *West of the Rocky Mountains.* 1888. Philadelphia: Running, 1976.

————. *Wilderness Essays.* Ed. Frank E. Buske. Salt Lake City: Peregrine Smith, 1980.

————. *The Yosemite.* 1912. Garden City: Doubleday, 1962.

Murie, Adolf. *A Naturalist in Alaska.* New York: Devin-Adair, 1961.

Murray, William H. H. *Adventures in the Wilderness; or, Camp-Life in the Adirondacks.* 1869. Ed. William K. Verner. Syracuse: Adirondack Museum, 1970.

Nash, Roderick. *Wilderness and the American Mind.* New Haven: Yale UP, 1973.

Nature Conservancy. *The Nature Conservancy Annual Report 1983.* Arlington: Nature Conservancy, 1984.

National Commission on Excellence in Education. *A Nation at Risk.* Washington: GPO, 1983.

Neruda, Pablo. *Memoirs.* New York: Farrar, 1977.

Nicholson, Marjorie Hope. *Mountain Gloom and Mountain Glory: The Development of the Aesthetics of the Infinite.* Ithaca: Cornell UP, 1959.

Odell, Rice. *The Environmental Awakening: The New Revolution to Protect the Earth.* New York: Ballinger, 1980.

Odum, Eugene P., et al. *Fundamentals of Ecology.* 3rd ed. New York: Holt, 1971.

Olmsted, Frederick Law. *Civilizing American Cities: A Selection of Frederick Law Olmsted's Writings on City Landscapes.* Ed. S. B. Sutton. Cambridge: MIT P, 1971.

————. *A Journey in the Back Country.* New York: Mason, 1860.

————. *A Journey in the Seaboard Slave States in the Years 1853–1854.* New York: Dixe Edwards, 1856.

———. *A Journey through Texas; or, A Saddle-Trip on the Southwestern Frontier.* New York: Dixe Edwards, 1857.

———. *Walks and Talks of an American Farmer in England.* 1859. Introd. Alex L. Murray. Ann Arbor: U of Michigan P, n.d.

Olsen, Jack. *Slaughter the Animals, Poison the Earth.* Simon, 1971.

Olson, Sigurd. *Listening Point.* New York: Knopf, 1958.

———. *The Lonely Land.* New York: Knopf, 1961.

Outward Bound. *The Paradox of Safety and Risk.* Denver: Outward Bound West, 1980.

Parkman, Francis. *The Oregon Trail: Sketches of Prairie and Rocky Mountain Life.* 1872. Philadelphia: Century Bookbinders, 1980.

Pearce, T. M. *Mary Austin.* New York: Twayne, 1965.

Playfair, John. *Illustration of the Huttonian Theory of the Earth.* 1802; facsim. rpt. New York: Dover, 1956.

Polanyi, Michael. *The Study of Man.* Chicago: U of Chicago P, 1959.

Porter, Eliot. *"In Wildness Is the Preservation of the World."* San Francisco: Sierra Club, 1962.

Powell, John Wesley. *The Exploration of the Colorado River of the West and Its Tributaries.* 1875. Chicago: U of Chicago P, 1957.

———. *Report on the Lands of the Arid Region of the United States.* Washington: GPO, 1878. Harvard: Harvard Common, 1983.

Prichard, James Cowles. *The Natural History of Man.* London: Baillière, 1843.

Pursell, Carroll, ed. *From Conservation to Ecology: The Development of Environmental Concern.* New York: Crowell, 1973.

Radin, Paul. *The Trickster: A Study in American Indian Mythology.* 1956. New York: Schocken, 1972.

Raths, Louis E., Merril Harmin, and Sidney B. Simon. *Values and Teaching.* Columbus: Merrill, 1976.

Remington, Frederic. *Pony Tracks.* New York: Harper, 1895.

Ritter, Carl. *Comparative Geography.* Tr. William L. Gage. Philadelphia: Lippincott, 1865.

Roberts, Charles G. D. *The Watchers of the Trails.* Toronto: Copp Clark, 1904.

Roosevelt, Theodore. *History as Literature and Other Essays.* New York: Scribner's, 1913.

———. *The Works of Theodore Roosevelt.* National Edition. New York: Scribner's, 1926.

Rosenblatt, Louise. *The Reader, the Text, the Poem: The Transactional Theory of the Literary Work.* Carbondale: Southern Illinois UP, 1978.

Russell, Franklin. *Secret Islands.* New York: Norton, 1966.

Ryden, Hope. *God's Dog.* New York: Coward, 1975.

Samson, John G. *The Pond.* New York: Knopf, 1979.

Sanborn, Franklin B. *Henry D. Thoreau.* Boston: Houghton, 1982.

Schwartz, William, ed. *Voices for the Wilderness.* New York: Ballantine, 1969.

Service, Robert. *The Spell of the Yukon and Other Verses.* New York: Dodd, 1906.

Seton, Ernest Thompson. *Trail of an Artist-Naturalist.* New York: Scribner's, 1940.

Sharp, Dallas Lore. *A Watcher in the Woods.* New York: Century, 1903.

Shepard, Paul. *Man in the Landscape.* New York: Knopf, 1967.

Sierra Club. *Glen Canyon*. 1965. Association Films, Ridgefield, NJ 07657, or Dublin, CA 94556.

Simon, Sidney B., Leland W. Howe, and Howard Kirschenbaum. *Values Clarification*. New York: Hart, 1972.

Skinner, B. F. *Walden Two*. New York: Macmillan, 1948.

Slater, Philip. *Earthwalk*. Garden City: Doubleday, 1974.

Smith, Roswell Chamberlain. *Atlas of Modern and Ancient Geography*. New York: Burgess, 1855.

Spears, Monroe K. *The Poetry of W. H. Auden: The Disenchanted Island*. New York: Oxford UP, 1963.

Stapp, William B. "Historical Setting of Environmental Education." In *Environmental Education*. Ed. James Swan and William B. Stapp. New York: Halsted, 1974.

Steinbeck, John. *Cannery Row*. New York: Bantam, 1971.

————. *The Log from the Sea of Cortez*. New York: Bantam, 1971.

Stewart, George R. *Earth Abides*. Issaquah: Archive, 1974.

Stokes, Donald W. *A Guide to Nature in Winter*. Boston: Little, 1976.

Stovall, Floyd. *The Foreground of Leaves of Grass*. Charlottesville: UP of Virginia, 1974.

Stratton-Porter, Gene. *Freckles*. New York: Doubleday, 1921.

————. *The Song of the Cardinal*. 1903. Folcroft: Folcroft, 1977.

Stromberg, R. *Intellectual History since 1789*. Englewood Cliffs: Prentice, 1975.

Sullivan, Mark. *Our Times: The United States, 1900–1925*. New York: Scribner's, 1930.

Sutton, Ann, and Myron Sutton. *Yellowstone: A Century of the Wilderness Idea*. New York: Macmillan, 1972.

Swan, James E. "Environmental Education: A New Religion?" *Journal of Environmental Education* 10 (1978): 44–49.

Szarkowski, John, ed. *The Photographer and the American Landscape*. New York: Museum of Modern Art, 1963.

Tanner, Thomas. "Freedom and a Varied Environment." *Science Teacher* 36 (April 1969): 32–34.

Teale, Edwin Way, ed. *The Wilderness World of John Muir*. Boston: Houghton, 1954.

Thomas, Lewis. *The Lives of a Cell*. New York: Viking, 1974.

Thomas, William, ed. *Man's Role in Changing the Face of the Earth*. Chicago: U of Chicago P, 1956.

Thompson, Robert H. "Decision at Rainbow Bridge." *Sierra Club Bulletin* 58.5 (1973): 8–9, 30–31.

Thoreau, Henry David. *Familiar Letters of Henry David Thoreau*. Ed. F. B. Sanborn. Boston: Houghton, 1894.

————. *The Maine Woods*. 1864. New York: Crowell, 1961.

————. *The Variorum Walden*. Ed. Walter Harding. New York: Twayne, 1962.

————. *Walden and Other Writings by Henry David Thoreau*. Ed. Joseph Wood Krutch. New York: Bantam, 1971.

————. *Walking*. Cambridge: Riverside, 1914.

————. *A Week on the Concord and Merrimack Rivers*. Boston: Monroe, 1849.

Toomer, Jean. *Cane*. New York: Liveright, 1975.

Tournier, Michel. *Friday and Robinson: Life on Esperanza Island*. New York: Knopf, 1972.

Traubel, Horace. *With Walt Whitman at Camden*. 3 vols. 1905. New York: Rowman, 1961.

Truffaut, François, dir. *The Wild Child*. United Artists, 1970.

Turner, Frederick Jackson. *The Frontier in American History*. New York: Holt, 1920.

Twain, Mark. *The Adventures of Huckleberry Finn*. 1885. New York: Signet, 1971.

———. *Life on the Mississippi*. 1883. New York: Signet, 1980.

U.S. Army Corps of Engineers, prod. *The Great Flood of 1973*. Modern Talking Picture Service, 1978.

U.S. Bureau of Reclamation. *Lake Powell: Jewel of the Colorado*. 1970. Bureau of Reclamation, Box 25007, Denver, CO 80225.

———. *Operation Glen Canyon*. 1961. Bureau of Reclamation, Box 25007, Denver, CO 80225.

Van de Bogart, Doris. *Introduction to the Humanities*. New York: Barnes and Noble, 1968.

Vonnegut, Kurt. *Breakfast of Champions*. New York: Dell, 1973.

———. *Slapstick*. New York: Dell, 1976.

Waage, Frederick. "Medicine in Literature: A Commented Journal." In *The Humanities: Philosophical Designs and Practical Visions*. Ed. C. Edward Kaylor, Jr. Charleston: Medical U of South Carolina P, 1981.

Warren, Robert Penn. *Audubon: A Vision*. New York: Random, 1969.

Weatherly, Mary Joan. "The Dispossessed Shepherd in Hardy's Longer Fiction." Diss. U of Alabama, 1974.

Welty, Eudora. *The Wide Net and Other Stories*. New York: Harcourt, 1973.

Westbrook, Perry D. *John Burroughs*. New York: Twayne, 1974.

Wheeler, William Martin. *Social Life among the Insects*. New York: Harcourt, 1923.

White, E. B. "Walden." In *One Man's Meat*. 1954. New York: Harper, 1964.

White, Gilbert. *The Natural History and Antiquities of Selborne, in the County of Southampton*. London: White, 1789.

White, Lynn. "The Historical Roots of Our Ecological Crisis." *Science* 155 (1967): 1203–07.

Whitman, Walt. *The Collected Writings of Walt Whitman*. Ed. Gay Wilson Allen and Sculley Bradley. 4 vols. New York: New York UP, 1961.

———. *Comprehensive Reader's Edition of* Leaves of Grass. Ed. Harold W. Blodgett and Sculley Bradley. New York: New York UP, 1965.

———. *Prose Works*. Ed. Floyd Stovall. 2 vols. New York: New York UP, 1964.

———. *Specimen Days*. Vol. 1 of *The Complete Writings of Walt Whitman*. New York: Putnam's, 1902.

Wild, Peter. *Pioneer Conservationists of Western America*. Missoula: Mountain, 1979.

Wilhelm, Kate. *Where Late the Sweet Birds Sang*. New York: Pocket, 1977.

Wilkins, Thurman. *Clarence King: A Biography*. New York: Macmillan, 1958.

Willauer, Peter O. *Hurricane Island Outward Bound School Director's Report*. Greenwich, Conn.: Outward Bound, 1980.

Wilson, Colin. *The Mind Parasites*. Oakland: Oneiric, 1972.

———. *The New Existentialism*. Bridgeport: Merrimack, 1981.

———. *The Philosopher's Stone*. New York: Warner, 1969.

Winthrop, Theodore. *Life in the Open Air and Other Papers*. Boston: Houghton, 1863.

Wolfe, Humbert, ed. *A Winter Miscellany*. New York: Viking, 1930.

Wolper, David, prod. *Mark Twain*. Media Five Film Distributor, 1963.

Worster, Donald. *Nature's Economy: The Roots of Ecology*. San Francisco: Sierra Club, 1977.

Young, George Malcolm. *Victorian England: Portrait of an Age*. 2nd ed. London: Oxford UP, 1953.

Zwinger, Ann. *Beyond the Aspen Grove*. New York: Random, 1970.

———. *Run, River, Run: A Naturalist's Journey down One of the Great Rivers of the West*. New York: Harper, 1975.

———. *Wind in the Rock: A Naturalist Explores the Canyon Country of the Southwest*. New York: Harper, 1978.

Additional Significant Works

Abbey, Edward. *Black Sun*. Santa Barbara: Capra, 1981.

―――. *Down the River*. New York: Dutton, 1983.

―――. *Fire on the Mountain*. Albuquerque: U of New Mexico P, 1978.

―――. *The Journey Home: Some Words in Defense of the American West*. New York: Dutton, 1977.

Abrams, K. S. "Literature and Science: An Interdisciplinary Approach to Environmental Studies." *Curriculum Review* 18 (1979): 302–04.

Arbib, Robert S., Jr. *The Lord's Woods: The Passing of an American Woodland*. New York: Norton, 1971.

Barbour, Ian G. *Western Man and Environmental Ethics*. Reading: Addison, 1973.

Barrette, Roy. *A Countryman's Journal: Views of Life and Nature from a Maine Coastal Farm*. New York: Rand, 1981.

Bates, Marston. *The Forest and the Sea: A Look at the Economy of Nature and the Ecology of Man*. New York: Random, 1965.

―――. *Gluttons and Libertines: Human Problems of Being Natural*. New York: Random, 1971.

―――. *Man in Nature*. Englewood Cliffs: Prentice, 1964.

Bateson, Gregory. *Mind and Nature*. New York: Bantam, 1979.

―――. *Steps to an Ecology of Mind*. New York: Ballantine, 1975.

Berry, Wendell. *Clearing*. New York: Harcourt, 1977.

―――. *A Continuous Harmony: Essays Cultural and Agricultural*. New York: Harcourt, 1972.

―――. *The Country of Marriage*. New York: Harcourt, 1975.

―――. *Farming: A Hand Book*. New York: Harcourt, 1971.

―――. *The Gift of Good Land*. San Francisco: North Point, 1981.

―――. *The Long-Legged House*. New York: Ballantine, 1971.

―――. *The Memory of Old Jack*. New York: Harcourt, 1974.

―――. *Nathan Coulter*. Boston: Houghton, 1960.

―――. *Openings*. New York: Harcourt, 1978.

―――. *A Place on Earth: Revision*. San Francisco: North Point, 1983.

―――. *Standing by Words*. San Francisco: North Point, 1983.

―――. *The Unsettling of America: Culture and Agriculture*. New York: Avon, 1978.

―――. *The Wheel*. San Francisco: North Point, 1983.

Biese, Alfred. *The Development of the Feeling for Nature in the Middle Ages and Modern Time*. 1905. New York: Burt Franklin, 1964.

Blackstone, W. T. *Philosophy and the Environmental Crisis*. Athens: U of Georgia P, 1974.

Blau, Sheridan B., and John von B. Rodenbeck, eds. *The House We Live In: An Environment Reader*. New York: Macmillan, 1971.

Brooks, Charles E. *The Living River*. New York: Doubleday, 1980.

Brooks, Paul. *The Pursuit of Wilderness*. Boston: Houghton, 1971.

------. *Roadless Area*. New York: Ballantine, 1978.

------. *The View from Lincoln Hill: Men and the Land in a New England Town*. Boston: Houghton, 1976.

Brown, Bruce. *Mountain in the Clouds: A Search for the Wild Salmon*. New York: Simon, 1982.

Brubaker, Sterling. *To Live on Earth: Man and His Environment in Perspective*. Baltimore: John Hopkins UP, 1972.

Cahn, Robert. *Footprints on the Planet: A Search for an Environmental Ethic*. New York: Universe, 1978.

Callenbach, Ernest. *Ecotopia Emerging*. Berkeley: Banyan Tree, 1981.

Carrighar, Sally. *The Glass Dove*. New York: Avon, 1977.

------. *The Twilight Seas: A Blue Whale's Journey*. New York: Ballantine, 1976.

Carroll, Peter N. *Puritanism and the Wilderness: The Intellectual Significance of the New England Frontier*. New York: Columbia UP, 1969.

Carson, Rachel. *The Edge of the Sea*. Boston: Houghton, 1979.

------. *The Sense of Wonder*. New York: Harper, 1965.

------. *Under the Sea-Wind: A Naturalist's Picture of Ocean Life*. New York: Oxford UP, 1952.

Clough, Wilson. *The Necessary Earth: Nature and Solitude in American Literature*. Austin: U of Texas P, 1967.

Cobb, Edith. *The Ecology of Imagination in Childhood*. New York: Columbia UP, 1977.

Cobb, J. B., Jr. *Is It Too Late: A Theology of Ecology*. New York: Glencoe, 1971.

Cohen, Michael J. *Across the Running Tide*. Freeport: Cobblesmith, 1978.

------. *Our Classroom Is Wild America*. Freeport: Cobblesmith, 1978.

Cole, John N. *Striper: A Story of Fish and Man*. Boston: Little, 1978.

Colinvaux, Paul. *Why Big Fierce Animals Are Rare: An Ecologist's Perspective*. Princeton: Princeton UP, 1980.

Commoner, Barry. *The Closing Circle: Nature, Man, and Technology*. New York: Bantam, 1972.

------. *The Poverty of Power*. New York: Bantam, 1977.

------. *Science and Survival*. New York: Penguin, 1967.

Cowdrey, Albert E. *This Land, This South: An Environmental History*. Lexington: U of Kentucky P, 1983.

Cowles, Raymond B. *Desert Journal: Reflections of a Naturalist*. Berkeley: U of California P, 1978.

------. *Zulu Journal: Field Notes of a Naturalist in South Africa*. Berkeley: U of California P, 1959.

Cronon, William. *Changes in the Land: Indians, Colonists, and the Ecology of New England*. New York: Hill, 1983.

Dasmann, Raymond F. *The Conservation Alternative*. New York: Wiley, 1975.

------. *The Destruction of California*. New York: Macmillan, 1966.

------. *A Different Kind of Country*. New York: Macmillan, 1970.

------. *The Last Horizon*. New York: Macmillan, 1971.

------. *No Further Retreat: The Fight to Save Florida*. New York: Macmillan, 1971.

Dean, Barbara. *Wellspring: A Story from the Deep Country*. Covelo: Island, 1979.

Dethier, Vincent G. *The Ecology of a Summer House*. Amherst: U of Massachusetts P, 1984.

Dillard, Annie. *Holy the Firm*. New York: Harper, 1977.

————. *Teaching a Stone to Talk: Expeditions and Encounters*. New York: Harper, 1982.

Doig, Ivan. *Winter Brothers: A Season at the Edge of America*. New York: Harcourt, 1980.

Douglas, Mary, and Aaron Wildavsky. *Risk and Culture: An Essay on the Selection of Technical and Environmental Dangers*. Berkeley: U of California P, 1982.

Douglas, William O. *My Wilderness: The Pacific West*. New York: Doubleday, 1960.

————. *The Three-Hundred Year War: A Chronicle of Ecological Disease*. New York: Random, 1972.

————. *A Wilderness Bill of Rights*. Boston: Little, 1965.

Dubos, René. *So Human an Animal*. New York: Scribner's, 1968.

Du Shane, Judy. "Experiential Education, Environmental Education, General Education: Putting It All Together." *Journal of Environmental Education* 11 (1980): 24–29.

Ehrenfeld, David. *The Arrogance of Humanism*. New York: Oxford UP, 1978.

Eiseley, Loren. *All the Strange Hours: The Excavation of a Life*. New York: Scribner's, 1975.

————. *The Firmament of Time*. New York: Atheneum, 1960.

————. *The Innocent Assassins*. New York: Scribner's, 1975.

————. *The Invisible Pyramid*. New York: Scribner's, 1972.

————. *The Man Who Saw through Time*. New York: Scribner's, 1973.

————. *Notes of an Alchemist*. New York: Scribner's, 1974.

————. *The Unexpected Universe*. New York: Harcourt, 1972.

Ekirsch, Arthur. *Man and Nature in America*. Lincoln: U of Nebraska P, 1973.

Elgin, Don D. "What Is 'Literary Ecology'?" *Humanities in the South* 57 (Spring 1983): 7–9.

Engel, J. Ronald. *Sacred Sands: The Struggle for Community in the Indiana Dunes*. Middletown: Wesleyan UP, 1983.

Fabre, Jean Henri. *The Mason-Bees*. New York: Dodd, 1914.

Feroe, Paul, ed. *Silent Voices: Recent American Poems on Nature*. St. Paul: Ally, 1978.

Finch, Robert. *The Primal Place*. New York: Norton, 1983.

Fisk, Irma. *The Peacocks of Baboquivari*. New York: Norton, 1983.

Flader, Susan L. *Thinking Like a Mountain: Aldo Leopold and the Evolution of an Ecological Attitude Toward Deer, Wolves, and Forests*. Lincoln: U of Nebraska P, 1978.

Fletcher, Colin. *The Thousand-Mile Summer: Desert and the High Sierra*. San Diego: Howell-North, 1964.

Foster, Steven, with Meredith E. Little. *The Book of the Vision Quest: Personal Transformation in the Wilderness*. Covelo: Island, 1980.

Fowles, John. *The Tree*. Boston: Little, 1980.

Franklin, Kay, and Norma Schaeffer. *Duel for the Dunes: Land Use Conflict on the Shores of Lake Michigan*. Urbana: U of Illinois P, 1983.

Fritsch, Albert J., et al., eds. *Environmental Ethics: Choices for Concerned Citizens*. Garden City: Doubleday, 1981.

George, Uwe. *In the Deserts of This Earth*. New York: Harcourt, 1979.

Glacken, Clarence. *Traces on the Rhodian Shore: Nature and Culture in Western Thought from Ancient Times to the End of the Eighteenth Century*. Berkeley: U of California P, 1976.

Graham, Frank. *The Adirondack Park: A Political History*. New York: Knopf, 1980.

————. *Since Silent Spring*. New York: Fawcett, 1977.

Griffin, Susan. *Woman and Nature: The Roaring inside Her.* New York: Harper, 1980.

Gussow, Alan. *A Sense of Place: The Artist and the American Land.* 2nd ed. San Francisco: Friends of the Earth, 1974.

Hardin, Garrett. *Exploring New Ethics for Survival: The Voyage of the Spaceship Beagle.* New York: Penguin, 1973.

———. *The Limits of Altruism: An Ecologist's View of Survival.* Bloomington: Indiana UP, 1977.

———. *Managing the Commons.* San Francisco: Freeman, 1977.

———. *Nature and Man's Fate.* New York: New American Library, 1961.

———. *Stalking the Wild Taboo.* 2nd ed. Los Altos: Kaufmann, 1978.

Haslam, Gerald. "Who Speaks for the Earth: A Course on Literature of the Environment." *English Journal* 62 (1973): 42–48.

Hay, John, and Peter Farb. *The Great Beach.* New York: Norton, 1980.

———. *The Run.* New York: Norton, 1979.

Hildebidle, John. *Thoreau: A Naturalist's Liberty.* Cambridge: Harvard UP, 1983.

Hoagland, Edward. *African Calliope.* New York: Penguin, 1981.

———. *The Circle Home.* New York: Avon, 1977.

———. *The Courage of Turtles.* New York: Random, 1970.

———. *The Edward Hoagland Reader.* Ed. Geoffrey Wolff. New York: Random, 1979.

———. *Notes from the Century Before: A Journal of British Columbia.* New York: Random, 1979.

———. *Red Wolves and Black Bears.* New York: Random, 1976.

———. *The Tugman's Passage.* New York: Random, 1982.

———. *Walking the Dead Diamond River.* New York: Random, 1973.

Hunter, Robert. *Warriors of the Rainbow: A Chronicle of the Greenpeace Movement.* New York: Harper, 1980.

Huth, Hans. *Nature and the American: Three Centuries of Changing Attitudes.* Lincoln: U of Nebraska P, 1972.

Inge, M. Thomas, ed. *Agrarianism in American Literature.* Indianapolis: Odyssey, 1969.

Ise, John. *Our National Park Policy: A Critical History.* 1961. New York: Arno, 1979.

Janovy, John. *Keith County Journal.* New York: St. Martin's, 1978.

———. *Yellowlegs.* New York: St. Martin's, 1980.

Jeffers, Robinson. *Selected Poems.* New York: Random, 1965.

Jones, Holway R. *John Muir and the Sierra Club: The Battle for Yosemite.* San Francisco: Sierra Club, 1965.

Kent, Rockwell. *Wilderness: A Journal of a Quiet Adventure in Alaska.* New York: Putman, 1920.

Kline, M. B. *Beyond the Land Itself: Views of Nature in Canada and the United States.* Cambridge: Harvard UP, 1970.

Kolodny, Annette. *The Lay of the Land: Metaphor as Experience and History in American Life and Letters.* Chapel Hill: U of North Carolina P, 1975.

Krutch, Joseph Wood. *Grand Canyon.* New York: Morrow, 1968.

———. *The Great Chain of Life.* Boston: Houghton, 1978.

Kumin, Maxine. *To Make a Living: Essays on Poets, Poetry, and Country Living.* Ann Arbor: U of Michigan P, 1979.

———. *Up Country: Poems of New England.* New York: Harper, 1973.

LaBastille, Anne. *Assignment Wildlife*. New York: Dutton, 1980.

———. *Women and Wilderness: Women in Wilderness Professions and Lifestyles*. San Francisco: Sierra Club, 1980.

———. *Woodswoman*. New York: Dutton, 1976.

Lehmberg, Paul. *In the Strong Woods: A Season Alone in the North Country*. New York: St. Martin's, 1980.

Leopold, Aldo. *Round River: From the Journals of Aldo Leopold*. New York: Oxford UP, 1953.

Levine, Stephen. *Planet Steward: Journal of a Wildlife Sanctuary*. Santa Cruz: Unity, 1974.

Lillard, Richard. *Desert Challenge: An Interpretation of Nevada*. 1942. rpt. Greenwich: Greenwood, 1979.

———. *The Great Forest*. 1947. New York: Da Capo, 1973.

———. *My Urban Wilderness in the Hollywood Hills: A Year of Years on Quito Lane*. Lanham: UP of America, 1983.

Lopez, Barry. *Desert Notes: Reflections in the Eye of the Raven*. New York: Avon, 1981.

———. *Of Wolves and Men*. New York: Scribner's, 1979.

———. *River Notes: The Dance of the Herons*. New York: Avon, 1980.

McCombs, Judith. *Against Nature: Wilderness Poems*. Paradise: Dustbooks, 1979.

McHarg, Ian. *Design with Nature*. New York: Natural History, 1971.

McIntosh, James. *Thoreau as Romantic Naturalist: His Shifting Stance toward Nature*. Ithaca: Cornell UP, 1974.

McKain, David, ed. *The Whole Earth: Essays in Appreciation, Anger, and Hope*. New York: St. Martin's, 1972.

McPhee, John. *Basin and Range*. New York: Farrar, 1981.

———. *The Curve of Binding Energy: A Journey into the Awesome and Alarming World of Theodore Taylor*. New York: Ballantine, 1976.

———. *The John McPhee Reader*. New York: Farrar, 1976.

———. *The Pine Barrens*. New York: Farrar, 1968.

———. *Survival of the Bark Canoe*. New York: Warner, 1977.

Madson, John. *Where the Sky Began: Land of the Tall Grass Prairie*. Boston: Houghton, 1982.

Marshall, Mel. *Sierra Summer*. Reno: U of Nevada P, 1979.

Meeker, Joseph W. *The Comedy of Survival: In Search of an Environmental Ethic*. 1974. Silverton: Finn Hill Arts, 1980.

Merchant, Carolyn. *The Death of Nature: Women, Ecology, and the Scientific Revolution*. New York: Harper, 1982.

Miller, G. Tyler. *Living in the Environment: Concepts, Problems, and Alternatives*. Belmont: Wadsworth, 1975.

———. *Replenish the Earth: A Primer in Human Ecology*. Belmont: Wadsworth, 1972.

Mostert, Noel. *Supership*. New York: Warner, 1976.

Mowat, Farley. *The Great Betrayal*. Boston: Little, 1976.

———. *Never Cry Wolf*. New York: Bantam, 1980.

———. *A Whale for the Killing*. New York: Penguin, 1973.

Nash, Roderick. *American Environment: Readings in the History of Conservation*. 2nd ed. Reading: Addison, 1976.

———, ed. *Environment and Americans: The Problem of Priorities*. Melbourne: Krieger, 1979.

Nearing, Scott, and Helen Nearing. *Continuing the Good Life: Half a Century of Home-steading*. New York: Schocken, 1980.

———. *Living the Good Life: How to Live Safely and Simply in a Troubled World*. New York: Schocken, 1971.

Nichols, John. *A Ghost in the Music*. New York: Holt, 1979.

———. *The Magic Journey*. New York: Pocket, 1979.

———. *The Milagro Beanfield War*. New York: Ballantine, 1976.

———, and William Davis. *If Mountains Die: A New Mexico Memoir*. New York: Knopf, 1979.

Novak, Barbara. *American Painting of the Nineteenth Century: Realism, Idealism, and the American Experience*. New York: Harper, 1975.

Odum, Eugene P. *Ecology: The Link Between the Natural and the Social Sciences*. 2nd ed. New York: Holt, 1975.

Odum, Eugene P., et al. *The Crisis of Survival*. Glenview: Scott, 1970.

Odum, Howard. *Environment, Power, and Society*. New York: Wiley, 1971.

———, and Elizabeth C. Odum. *The Energy Basis for Man and Nature*. 2nd ed. New York: McGraw, 1981.

Ogburn, Charlton. *The Southern Appalachians: A Wilderness Quest*. New York: Morrow, 1975.

———. *The Winter Beach*. New York: Pocket, 1971.

Olson, Sigurd F. *The Hidden Forest*. New York: Penguin, 1979.

———. *The Lonely Land*. New York: Knopf, 1961.

———. *Open Horizons*. New York: Knopf, 1969.

———. *Reflections from the North Country*. New York: Knopf, 1976.

———. *Runes of the North*. New York: Knopf, 1963.

———. *Sigurd F. Olson's Wilderness Days*. New York: Knopf, 1975.

Passmore, John. *Man's Responsibility for Nature: Ecological Problems and Western Traditions*. New York: Scribner's, 1974.

Peattie, Donald Culross. *Flowering Earth*. New York: Viking, 1939.

Perrin, Noel. *First Person Rural: Essays of a Sometime Farmer*. New York: Penguin, 1980.

Petullo, Joseph M. *American Environmentalism: Values, Tactics, Priorities*. College Station: Texas A&M UP, 1980.

Potter, David M. *People of Plenty: Economic Abundance and the American Character*. Chicago: U of Chicago P, 1954.

Pyne, Stephen J. *Fire in America: A Cultural History of Wildland and Rural Fire*. Princeton: Princeton UP, 1982.

Regan, Tom. *All That Dwell Therein: Animal Rights and Environmental Ethics*. Berkeley: U of California P, 1982.

Reiger, George. *Wanderer on My Native Shore: A Personal Guide and Tribute to the Ecology of the Atlantic Coast*. New York: Simon, 1983.

Richardson, Elmo. *The Politics of Conservation: Crusades and Controversies, 1896–1913*. Berkeley: U of California P, 1962.

Sanford, Charles L. *The Quest for Paradise: Europe and the American Moral Imagination*. 1961. New York: AMS, 1977.

Sauer, Carl. *Land and Life: A Selection from the Writings of Carl Sauer*. Berkeley: U of California P, 1974.

———. *Man in Nature: America before the Days of the White Man*. Berkeley: Turtle Island Foundation, 1975.

————. *Sixteenth-Century North America: The Land and People as Seen by the Europeans.* Berkeley: U of California P, 1971.

Scheffer, Victor. *Adventures of a Zoologist.* New York: Scribner's, 1980.

————. *Messages from the Shore.* Seattle: Pacific Search, 1977.

————. *The Year of the Whale.* New York: Scribner's, 1969.

Schmitt, Peter J. *Back to Nature: The Arcadian Myth in Urban America.* New York: Oxford UP, 1969.

Sewell, Elizabeth. *The Orphic Voice: Poetry and Natural History.* 1960. New York: Harper, 1971.

Shepard, Paul. *Man in the Landscape: A Historic View of the Esthetics of Nature.* New York: Knopf, 1967.

————. *Nature and Madness.* San Francisco: Sierra Club, 1983.

————. *Thinking Animals: Animals and the Development of Human Intelligence.* New York: Viking, 1978.

————, and Daniel McKinley, eds. *Environ/Mental: Essays on the Planet as Home.* Boston: Houghton, 1970.

————, eds. *The Subversive Science: Essays toward an Ecology of Man.* Boston: Houghton, 1969.

Shrader-Frechette, K. S. *Environmental Ethics.* Pacific Grove: Boxwood, 1980.

Skolimowski, Henryk. *Eco-Philosophy.* Topsfield, Mass: Merrimack Book Service, 1981.

Smallwood, William Martin, and Mabel Smallwood. *Natural History and the American Mind.* 1941. New York: AMS, 1978.

Smith, Henry Nash. *Virgin Land: The American West as Symbol and Myth.* Cambridge: Harvard UP, 1970.

Snyder, Gary. *Back Country.* New York: New Directions, 1968.

————. *Earth House Hold.* New York: New Directions, 1969.

————. *Myths and Texts.* New York: New Directions, 1978.

————. *The Old Ways: Six Essays.* San Francisco: City Lights, 1977.

————. *The Real Work: Interviews and Talks.* New York: New Directions, 1980.

————. *Regarding Wave.* New York: New Directions, 1970.

————. *Turtle Island.* New York: New Directions, 1974.

Stewart, George R. *Fire.* New York: Random, 1948.

————. *Not So Rich As You Think.* Boston: Houghton, 1967.

————. *Ordeal by Hunger.* New York: Holt, 1936.

————. *Storm.* New York: Random, 1941.

Stilgoe, John R. *Common Landscape of America: 1580 to 1845.* New Haven: Yale UP, 1982.

————. *Metropolitan Corridor: Railroads and the American Scene.* New Haven: Yale UP, 1983.

Stone, Christopher. *Should Trees Have Standing: Toward Legal Rights for Natural Objects.* Los Altos: Kaufmann, 1974.

Storer, John. *Man in the Web of Life.* New York: Signet, 1968.

————. *The Web of Life.* New York: Signet, 1972.

Swanson, C. P. "The Role of the Humanities in Environmental Education." *American Biology Teacher* 37 (1975): 84–89.

Szarkowski, John. *The Photographer and the American Landscape.* New York: Museum of Modern Art, 1963.

Teal, John, and Mildred Teal. *Life and Death of the Salt Marsh.* New York: Ballantine, 1974.

Teale, Edwin W. *The American Seasons.* 4 vols. New York: Dodd, 1966.

Terry, Mark. *Teaching for Survival: A Handbook of Environmental Education.* New York: Ballantine, 1971.

Thomas, Keith. *Man and the Natural World: A History of the Modern Sensibility.* New York: Pantheon,1983.

Thomas, Lewis. *The Medusa and the Snail.* New York: Bantam, 1980.

———. *Night Thoughts while Listening to Mahler's Ninth Symphony.* New York: Viking, 1983.

Thoreau, Henry David. *Cape Cod.* New Haven: College and University Press, 1951.

———. *Henry David Thoreau: A Writer's Journal.* Ed. Laurence Stapleton. New York: Dover, 1960.

———. *The Portable Thoreau.* Ed. Carl Bode. New York: Penguin, 1977.

———. *The Writings of Henry David Thoreau.* Princeton: Princeton UP, 1971– .

Tichi, Cecilia. *New World, New Earth: Environmental Reform in American Literature from the Puritans through Whitman.* New Haven: Yale UP, 1979.

Tuan, Yi-Fu. *Landscapes of Fear.* New York: Pantheon, 1980.

———. *Space and Place: The Perspective of Experience.* St. Paul: U of Minnesota P, 1977.

———. *Topophilia: A Study of Environmental Perception, Attitudes, and Values.* Englewood Cliffs: Prentice, 1974.

Tucker, William J. *Progress and Privilege: America in the Age of Environmentalism.* Garden City: Doubleday, 1982.

Turner, Frederick. *Beyond Geography: The Western Spirit against the Wilderness.* New York: Viking, 1980.

Udall, Stewart. *The Quiet Crisis.* New York: Avon, 1964.

Wallace, David R. *Dark Range: A Naturalist's Night Notebook.* San Francisco: Sierra Club, 1978.

———. *Idle Weeds: The Life of a Sandstone Ridge.* San Francisco: Sierra Club, 1980.

———. *The Klamath Knot.* San Francisco: Sierra Club, 1983.

Warner, William W. *Beautiful Swimmers: Watermen, Crabs, and the Chesapeake Bay.* New York: Penguin, 1977.

———. *Distant Water: The Fate of the North Atlantic Fisherman.* Boston: Little, 1983.

Watson, J. Wreford, and Timothy O'Riordan, eds. *The American Environment: Perceptions and Policies.* New York: Wiley, 1976.

Watts, May T. *Reading the Landscape of America.* 2nd ed. New York: Macmillan, 1975.

Williams, George H. *Wilderness and Paradise in Christian Thought.* New York: Harper, 1962.

Wilson, David Scofield. *In the Presence of Nature.* Amherst: U of Massachusetts P, 1978.

Wolf, Peter. *Land in America: Its Value, Use, and Control.* New York: Pantheon, 1981.

Worster, Donald, ed. *American Environmentalism: The Formative Period, 1860–1915.* New York: Wiley, 1973.

Wyant, William K. *Westward in Eden: The Public Lands and the Conservation Movement.* Berkeley: U of California P, 1982.

Zwinger, Ann. *A Desert Country near the Sea: A Natural History of the Cape Region of Baja California.* New York: Harper, 1983.

Environmental Bibliographies and Information Centers

Anglemyer, Mary, et al., eds. *A Search for Environmental Ethics: An Initial Bibliography.* Washington: Smithsonian Inst., 1980.

Bureau of Land Management, Office of Public Affairs, U.S. Department of the Interior, Washington, DC 20240.

Conservation Foundation, 1717 Massachusetts Avenue, N.W., Washington, DC 20036.

Cresswell, Peter. *Environment: An Alphabetical Handbook.* London: Murray, 1971.

Dunlap, Riley E., and Kent D. Van Liere. *Environmental Concern: A Bibliography of Empirical Studies and Brief Appraisal of the Literature.* Vance Bibliographies 44 (Public Administration Series). Monticello: Vance, 1978. Address: P.O. Box 229, Monticello, IL 61856.

Environment Information Center, 292 Madison Avenue, New York, NY 10017 (phone: 212 949-9494).

Environmental Law Reporter. Washington: Environmental Law Inst., 1971–.

Environmental Periodicals Bibliography: Indexed Article Titles. Santa Barbara: International Academy Environmental Studies Inst., 1972–.

Environmental Protection Agency, Public Information Center (PM215), Washington, DC 20460.

Environmental Protection Careers Guidebook. Washington: GPO, 1980.

Fish and Wildlife Service, Office of Public Affairs, Room 3240, Interior Building, Washington, DC 20240.

Gold, Seymour N., ed. Man and the Environment Information Guide Series. Detroit: Gale, 1975–. This is a series of bibliographies in many areas of environmental studies. Particularly relevant to this volume is *Environmental Values, 1860–1972: A Guide to Information Sources,* ed. Loren C. Owings (1976).

Hodge, Guy R. *Careers Working with Animals: An Introduction to Occupational Opportunities in Animal Welfare, Conservation, Environmental Protection, and Allied Professions.* Washington: Humane Soc., 1980.

Institute of Ecology, Holcomb Research Building, Butler University, Indianapolis, IN 40208.

Kitazoni, Oki, ed. *Directory of Nature Centers and Related Environmental Education Facilities.* New York: National Audubon Soc., 1979.

The McGraw-Hill Encyclopedia of Environmental Sciences. 2nd ed. New York: McGraw, 1980.

National Park Service, Office of Communications, Room 3043, Interior Building, Washington, DC 20240.

Troost, Cornelius J., and H. Altman, eds. *Environmental Education: A Sourcebook.* New York: Wiley, 1972.

United States Directory of Environmental Sources. Washington: GPO, 1979.

U.S. Geological Survey, Information Office, National Center, Reston, VA 22092.

U.S. International Environmental Referral Center, Environmental Protection Agency, Room 2902, 401 M St., S.W., Washington, DC 20460.

Walters, LeRoy, ed. *Bibliography of Bioethics*. Detroit: Gale, 1973–.

World Directory of Environmental Organizations. San Francisco: Sierra Club and Center for California Public Affairs, 1973–.

World Environmental Directory. Silver Spring: Business Publishers, 1974–.

Periodicals

American Forests. Editor: Bill Rooney. Monthly. American Forestry Assn., 1319 18th St., N.W., Washington, DC 20036.

The Amicus Journal. Editor: Peter Borrelli. Quarterly. Natural Resources Defense Council, 122 E. 42nd St., New York, NY 10168.

Audubon. Editor: Les D. Line. Bimonthly. National Audubon Soc., 950 3rd Ave., New York, NY 10022.

Coevolution Quarterly. Editor: Stewart Brand. Quarterly. Point Foundation, Box 428, Sausalito, CA 94965.

Defenders. Editor: James G. Deane. Bimonthly. Defenders of Wildlife, 1244 19th St., N.W., Washington, DC 20036.

Ecology. Editor: Lee N. Miller. Bimonthly. Arizona State Univ., Tempe, AZ 85287.

Ecophilosophy. Editor: George Sessions. Philosophy Dept., Sierra College, Rocklin, CA 95677.

Environment. Editor: Jane Scully. 10 issues per year. Heldref Publications, 4000 Albemarle St., N.W., Suite 504, Washington, DC 20016.

Environmental Action. Editor: Gail Robinson. Environmental Action, Inc., 1346 Connecticut Ave., Washington, DC 20036.

Environmental Education Report. 10 issues per year. American Society of Environmental Educators. Durham, NH 03824.

Environmental Ethics. Editor: Eugene C. Hargrove. Quarterly. Dept. of Philosophy and Religion, Univ. of Georgia, Athens, GA 30602.

Environmental Review. Editor: John Opie. Triennial. Environmental History Soc. Periodical address: College Hall, Duquesne Univ., Pittsburgh, PA 15219.

Environmental Science and Technology. Editor: Russell Christman. Monthly. American Chemical Soc., 1155 16th St., N.W., Washington, DC 20036.

EPA Journal. Editor: Charles Pierce. 10 issues per year. U.S. Environmental Protection Agency, 401 M St., S.W., A-107, Washington, DC 20460.

Historic Preservation. Editor: T. J. Colin. Bimonthly. National Trust for Historic Preservation, 740–748 Jackson Place, N.W., Washington, DC 20006.

Journal for the Humanities and Technology. Editor: John S. Tumlin. Annual. Humanities and Technology Assn., English and History Dept., Southern Technical Inst., Marietta, GA 30060.

Journal of Environmental Education. Editor: Mary Singer. Quarterly. Heldref Publications, 4000 Albemarle St., N.W., Suite 504, Washington, DC 20016.

Journal of Forest History. Editor: Ronald J. Fahl. Quarterly. Forest History Soc., 109 Coral St., Santa Cruz, CA 95060.

Landscape. Editor: Blair Boyd. Triennial. P.O. Box 7107, Berkeley, CA 94707.

The Living Wilderness. Editor: James G. Deane. Quarterly. Wilderness Soc., 1901 Pennsylvania Ave., N.W., Washington, DC 20006.

National Parks. Editor: Eugenia H. Connally. Bimonthly. National Parks and Conservation Assn., 1701 18th St., N.W., Washington, DC 20009.

National Wildlife. Editor: John Strohm. Bimonthly. 8925 Leesburg Pike, Vienna, VA 22180.

Natural History. Editor: Alan Ternes. 10 issues per year. American Museum of Natural History, Central Park West at 79th St., New York, NY 10024.

The North American Review. Editor: Robley Wilson, Jr. Quarterly. Univ. of Northern Iowa, Cedar Rapids, IA 50613.

Not Man Apart. Editor: Tom Turner. Monthly. Friends of the Earth, 124 Spear St., San Francisco, CA 94105.

Orion Nature Quarterly. Editor: George K. Russell. Quarterly. Myrin Institute, 136 E. 34th St., New York, NY 10021.

Rain: Journal of Appropriate Technology. Editor: Lance de Moll. Monthly. The Rain Umbrella, 2270 N.W. Irving St., Portland, OR 97210.

Ranger Rick's Nature Magazine (children). Editor: Trudy Dye Ferrand. Monthly. National Wildlife Federation, 1412 16th St., N.W., Washington, DC 20036.

Science, Technology, and Human Values. Editor: Marcel C. La Follette. Quarterly. Massachusetts Inst. of Technology, Room 20B–125, 18 Vassar St., Cambridge, MA 02139.

Sierra. Editor: Frances Gendlin. Bimonthly. Sierra Club, 530 Bush St., San Francisco, CA 94108.

Snowy Egret. Editor: Humphrey A. Olsen. Biennial. 205 S. 9th St., Williamsburg, KY 40769.

Organizations

Alliance for Environmental Education, 1619 Massachusetts Ave., N.W., Washington, DC 20036.

Alliance for Historic Landscape Preservation, c/o Robert R. Harvey, Dept. of Landscape Architecture, College of Design, Iowa State Univ., Ames, IA 50010.

American Forestry Association, 1319 18th St., N.W., Washington, DC 20036.

American Littoral Society, Sandy Hook, Highlands, NJ 07732.

American Society for Environmental History, Dyson College of Pace Univ., Pleasantville, NY 10570.

Appalachian Mountain Club, 5 Joy St., Boston, MA 02108.

Center for Action on Endangered Species, 175 W. Main St., Ayer, MA 01432.

Center for Environmental Education, 1925 K St., N.W., Suite 206, Washington, DC 20006.

Defenders of Wildlife, 1244 19th St., N.W., Washington, DC 20036.

Ducks Unlimited, Inc., 3158 Des Plaines Ave., Des Plaines, IL 60018.

Environmental Action, 1346 Connecticut Ave., N.W., Suite 731, Washington, DC 20036.

Environmental Defense Fund, 475 Park Avenue S., New York, NY 10016.

Forest History Society, 109 Coral St., Santa Cruz, CA 95060.

Friends of the Earth, 124 Spear St., San Francisco, CA 94105.

The Fund for Animals, Inc., 140 W. 57th St., New York, NY 10019.

Greenpeace, U.S.A., Fort Mason, Building E, San Francisco, CA 94123.

Humanities and Technology Association, English and History Dept., Southern Technical Inst., Marietta, GA 30060.

Izaak Walton League of America, 1800 N. Kent St., Suite 806, Arlington, VA 22209.

National Association for Environmental Education, P.O. Box 400, Troy, OH 45373.

National Association of Conservation Districts, 1025 Vermont Ave., N.W., Washington, DC 20005.

National Audubon Society, 950 3rd Ave., New York, NY 10022.

National Trust for Historic Preservation, 740–748 Jackson Place, N.W., Washington, DC 20006.

National Wildlife Federation, 1412 16th St., N.W., Washington, DC 20036 (children's group: Ranger Rick's Nature Club, same address).

Nature Conservancy, 1800 N. Kent St., Arlington, VA 22209.

Resources for the Future, Inc., 1755 Massachusetts Ave., N.W., Washington, DC 20036.

Wilderness Society, 1901 Pennsylvania Ave., N.W., Washington, DC 20006.

Contributors

Barbara Currier Bell teaches in the English department at Wesleyan University. She is currently working on a book associated with the course material described in her essay for this anthology.

Charles A. Bergman teaches courses on the English Renaissance, writing, and environmental literature at Pacific Lutheran University. His articles on natural history have appeared in *Audubon Magazine*.

Paul T. Bryant is professor of English and associate dean of the Graduate School at Colorado State University. He has done seasonal work for the National Audubon Society, the National Park Service, and the U.S. Forest Service and worked for eight years as an engineering and science writer and editor for Washington State University, the University of Illinois, and the American Society for Engineering Education.

Felicia Florine Campbell specializes in interdisciplinary courses at the University of Nevada, Las Vegas. Best known for her humanistic studies of gambling behavior, she has served as a director of environmental studies at UNLV and chaired the Nevada Governor's Commission on the Status of People.

Lawrence O. Christensen teaches history at the University of Missouri–Rolla. In 1976 he won the Author's Award for the best article published in the *Missouri Historical Review*. In 1980 he published, with William E. Parrish and Charles T. Jones, *Missouri: The Heart of the Nation* (Forum Press).

Walter H. Clark, Jr., has a joint appointment in the University of Michigan's Residential College and Department of English. He is cofounder, with Alan Howes, of Michigan's New England Literature Program, which was ten years old in 1984. He has published two books of poetry and a number of articles on literary aesthetics.

Vernon Owen Grumbling teaches writing and environmental literature at the University of New England in Biddeford, Maine. He is a member of the Maine Audubon Society and serves the Maine Department of Environmental Protection as a volunteer monitor of water quality at El Pond, Maine. Currently, he is editing an anthology of environmental literature written in the English and American traditions.

Betsy Hilbert, professor of English at Miami-Dade Community College, Miami, has written extensively on higher education in such journals as *Educational Forum* and the *Chronicle of Higher Education*.

Jack Kligerman teaches English and American literature, photography, and composition at Herbert H. Lehman College, CUNY. His publications include *A Fancy for Pigeons, The Birds of John Burroughs: Keeping a Sharp Lookout*, and "Photography as a Celebration of Nature," in the *Structurist*.

Richard G. Lillard, once an ecologist with the U.S. Bureau of Entomology and Plant Quarantine and later a ranger naturalist with the Park Service, is professor emeritus of American studies and English from California State University, Los Angeles. He is author of books and articles on Nevada, the Southwest, Southern California, and American forests.

Ralph H. Lutts is director of the Blue Hills Interpretive Centers, Milton, Massachusetts. He is also an adjunct member of the faculty at Hampshire College, Amherst, Massachusetts, teaching courses in environmental ethics, nature literature, environmental education, and environmental history.

Margaret McFadden specializes in interdisciplinary studies at Appalachian State University in Boone, North Carolina. She is the author of entries on nature writers in Ungar's four-volume American Women Writers reference series and has coauthored the Loren Eiseley volume (with L. E. Gerber) for Ungar's Modern Literature Monographs.

Bruce Piasecki is an assistant professor at Clarkson University's Center for Liberal Studies. His articles on alternatives to dumping toxic wastes have appeared in *Science 83*, *Washington Monthly*, and *Technology Review*; and he was coordinating editor of *Beyond Dumping: New Strategies for Controlling Toxic Contamination* (Greenwood Press, 1984). He is currently writing a cultural history of America in the age of environmentalism and a book on European hazardous waste systems. In 1983 he founded the American Hazard Control Group, an advisory consulting group that provides legal, policy, and business development advice on the best available means to treat and destroy toxic substances.

John Tallmadge teaches English at Carleton College and has published on Darwin and John Muir.

Thomas Tanner is associate professor of environmental studies and education at Iowa State University. His articles on environmental education have appeared in a number of journals representing a variety of disciplines and have frequently been reprinted. A collection of his case studies was published by the National Audubon Society. His book *Ecology, Environment, and Education* is considered by many to be the standard introduction to and overview of environmental education at the precollege level.

Frank Trocco has spent the last nine years working in the field with students in expedition education programs. He is at present codirector of the Audubon Expedition Institute, 950 3rd Avenue, NY 10022, which provides high school, college, and graduate students with one to four years of direct contact with the environment.

Larry Vonalt teaches English at the University of Missouri–Rolla. He has published essays and reviews in *Sewanee Review*, *Parnassus*, *Christianity Today*, *Critique: Studies in Modern Fiction*, and the *Malahat Review*.

Joan Weatherly teaches courses in English and American literature and linguistics in the interdisciplinary University College at Memphis State University.